Development Problems in the Niger Delta Region

T0316964

European University Studies

Europäische Hochschulschriften
Publications Universitaires Européennes

Series XXIII
Theology

Reihe XXIII Série XXIII
Theologie
Théologie

Vol./Bd. 930

PETER LANG

Frankfurt am Main · Berlin · Bern · Bruxelles · New York · Oxford · Wien

Clement Oloruntusin Akinseloyin

Development Problems in the Niger Delta Region

A Study in Christian Development Ethics

PETER LANG
Internationaler Verlag der Wissenschaften

Bibliographic Information published by the Deutsche Nationalbibliothek
The Deutsche Nationalbibliothek lists this publication in the Deutsche Nationalbibliografie; detailed bibliographic data is available in the internet at http://dnb.d-nb.de.

Zugl.: Frankfurt (Main), Phil.-Theol. Hochschule Sankt Georgen, Univ., Diss., 2011

F 42
ISSN 0721-3409
ISBN 978-3-631-63364-9

© Peter Lang GmbH
Internationaler Verlag der Wissenschaften
Frankfurt am Main 2012
All rights reserved.

www.peterlang.de

Table of Contents

Foreword

The wealth from oil exploration, the poverty of the people and the ecological damages of oil industry form an explosive mixture in the Niger Delta. This has in recent years continually led to violent conflicts between youth groups on the one hand and with security forces of the state and those engaged by oil companies on the other hand. In his impressive study0, Clement Akinseloyin combines social scientific publications and development ethics reflections on the causes of these conflicts, in order to formulate on this basis, social ethical orientations that would aid a political reform in favour of the poor in the Niger Delta.

His description of the problem situation consists of an impressive introduction to the societal development of Nigeria in general and the Niger Delta in particular (Chapter 1) and a convincing examination of the development problems of the region (Chapter 3). In his in-depth analysis of the socio-economic causes of the problem he treats clearly the resource curse and the associated phenomenon of corruption. He unsparingly paints the picture of how the enormous oil revenues create loyalty to the oil industry at all political levels and allow corruption to proliferate, how they make all political measures, that would have negative effects on the profits of oil multinationals impossible, and at the end even divert opposition groups from their legitimate goal and draw their focus towards benefiting from the oil revenues.

In the search for a theoretic ethical foundation for social ethical orientation, Akinseloyin has made an appropriate find in Amartya Sen. Painstakingly, he develops Sen's well-read development ethics in line with the book, *Development as Freedom* (Chapter 6), adequately showing the connection to Catholic Social Teaching.

In his orientations for action, Akinseloyin convincingly names concrete steps towards a political reform, which would above all increase chances of development for the poor in the Niger Delta (Chapter 8). He solicits, among other things, the strengthening of the anti-corruption agencies, for a proper supervision of the Master Plan-activities of the Niger Delta Development through NGOs and reassessment of small development projects. Finally, he urges the Church to do more in taking political stance in favour of the poor in the Niger Delta.

In the engaging and richly interdisciplinary study, Akinseloyin convincingly analyzes the development problems of the Niger Delta, especially the acute poverty and the shocking ecological damages caused by the oil industry. On the basis of a solid development ethics, he proffers political counsels to the problems that have been presented. Many readers would be impressed by the book, especially those seeking new ways to advance the social and environmental development of the Niger Delta.

Prof. Dr. Bernhard Emunds

Acknowledgment

"If the lord does not build the house, in vain do its the builders labour" (Psalm 127, 1). That this book sees the light of the day it is the Lord's own doing. To God be the glory for ever and ever Amen. As the saying goes "success has many parents and relatives". I am indeed indebted to many people who assisted me in various ways in the course of writing this work. It is impossible to mention everybody in this short acknowledgement. Some are, however, deserving of mention. For granting me the permission to pursue the doctoral program at all and the moral support received, I would like to thank my Bishops – Most Rev. Francis Alonge (Bishop emeritus of Ondo Diocese) and his successor Most Rev. Jude Arogundade. My sincere appreciation goes to my Moderator, Professor Dr. Bernhard Emunds who with scholarly assistance and inspiring interest directed the development of the thesis from the beginning to the end. Many thanks too to my second Moderator, Professor Dr. Josef Schuster S.J for his insightful comments and suggestions that have enriched the work. Many thanks to the members of staff of Nell-Breunig Institute as well as those in the "Bibliothek" for their help in sourcing for literature. I am forever grateful to the **Sisters of Good Shepherd** in Hofheim am Taunus for the conducive accommodation and financial support they gave me all through the period of study. A special thanks goes to Sr. Gudula Busch for her motherly care for me. Immerse gratitude to the *Franz Fuger Gedächtnis Stiftung* for the scholarship granted me to pursue this dissertation. It would have been pretty difficult to acquire most literature for the research without the scholarship. I appreciate the kindness of the Ursuline Sisters in Königstein, particularly Sr. Angela Starker. My stay in Germany was made less stressful by the friendship and support I got from some good people, among whom are the Montag family in Küllstedt, Rev. Fr. Gerhard Hemker, Rev. Fr. Hans Hauk, Mrs. Bernadette Geppert, Mrs. Ute Stark, Mr. Hugo Edward, Mr. & Mrs. Hartman, Dr. Reske, Mrs. Elfi Braun, Late Mrs. E. Brandt and her Children (Andrea and Martina), Mr. & Mrs. Olbrich as well as Ms. Anneliese Gerhard. I am grateful to my fellow Nigerian priests for their support and encouragement. I would like to thank Rev. Fr. Dr. Tai Oludare for reading through the manuscript. Many thanks to Rev. Fr. Dr. Anthony Asoanya, Rev. Fr. Dr. Jude Asanbe, Bishops Emmanuel Badejo and Felix Femi Ajakaiye for their warm friendship and encouragement. For the camaraderie and technical assistance I got from Frs. Augustine Akhogha, Samuel Rapu, Pius Benson and Donatus Onuigbo I am very grateful.

Clement Akinseloyn, Frankfurt am Main 2010

Introduction

Statement of the Problem

"The joy and hope, the grief and anguish of the men of our time, especially of those who are poor or afflicted in any way, are the joy and hope, the grief and anguish of the followers of Christ as well."[1] This opening sentence of the Pastoral Constitution of the Church in the Modern World of the Second Vatican Council finds relevance in the situation of the majority of the people in the Niger Delta region of Nigeria. This is because the state of poverty and underdevelopment in the region depicts the grief and anguish of the people.

The Niger Delta is one of Nigeria's least developed regions. It is characterised by extreme poverty, serious dearth of serviceable infrastructure, environmental degradation caused by oil spillage, violence and youth restiveness. About 70% of the population are living below the poverty line[2], that is, less than $1 per day, and millions of youth are unemployed. Generally, the Niger Delta people have poor access to basic social services such as electricity, safe drinking water, roads and healthcare facilities that are taken for granted in some other parts of Nigeria.

It is a fact that the Niger Delta produces the oil wealth that accounts for the bulk of Nigeria's foreign earnings. It is on record that 90% of Nigeria's annual foreign earnings come from the oil sector. Paradoxically, these vast revenues from an international industry have barely touched the Niger Delta's own pervasive local poverty with percentage income at below $280 (GDP) despite its high population. Health indicators lag behind national average. The region's human development index (HDI) score, a measure of well-being encompassing the longevity of life, knowledge and a decent standard of living, remains at a low value of 0.564 (with 1 being the highest). This is far below countries or regions with similar oil and gas resources. For example, the HDI for Saudi Arabia in 2003 stood at 0.800, while in 2003 the United Arab Emirates, Kuwait, Libya, Venezuela and Indonesia achieved scores of 0.849, 0.844, 0.799, 0.772 and 0.697,

---

1 GS,1. This abbreviation refers to "Gaudium et Spes" of the Second Vatican Council (1963-1965). All such documents as well as Papal encyclicals are hereafter referred to by such abbreviations. See List of Abbreviation.

2 Cf. Niger Delta Regional Development Master Plan, p. 14.

15

respectively[3]. The society is socially dislocated and the environment, that is, ecological system that used to support agricultural engagement of the local people. Thus, their economy is seriously polluted with oil spillage and industrial wastes.

Beginning with the colonial regime in the late 1950s up to the present day democratic regime, there have been development interventions by the Nigerian government as well as from oil companies and other stakeholders. For example, more states and local government areas have been created in the region with the supposed aim of bringing government closer to the people. Agencies and commissions have been set up by the government to initiate development programmes, etc. such as the Niger Delta Development Board (NDDB), Presidential Task Force (PTF), Oil Mineral Producing Areas Development Commission (OMPADEC), the Niger Delta Development Commission (NDDC) and most recently the Ministry of Niger Delta Affairs. However, apart from the Ministry of Niger Delta Affairs whose performance is still too early to judge, each of the other attempts has made very little positive impact on the state of poverty and underdevelopment of the Niger Delta region. Reasons adduced for the failure of these attempts range from poor governance, financial misappropriation, lack of focus, shortage of funding from government and corruption, but above all lack of accountability.

To a large extent, these allegations are tenable because the political structure in Nigeria accommodates such practices, so too the social and economic structures of the country. Nigeria is currently operating a monoculture or rather a rentier economy. She depends mainly on the revenues from oil export. Agriculture, where majority of Nigerians are engaged and which used to be the major source of income to the Nigerian government before oil exploration began, is being neglected. Added to all these, is the fact that since the discovery and exploration of oil in the Niger Delta, several interest groups have emerged. These include, among others, the multi-national oil companies and their home governments, the Nigerian Government, the states and local government areas, local politicians in different political parties, traditional rulers, community leaders, youth leaders of various factions, league of contractors both local and foreign, armed militias, NGOs, various trade unions, etc. Each of these groups has its influence somehow in the region. Attempts by the various interest groups, perhaps apart from the NGOs, to exercise their influences and pursue their interests in the region, which is basically to have a share of the oil revenue, have contributed to the crises and underdevelopment of the region. The traditional social, political and economic structures that were built on the structure of solidarity within the various ethnic communities that constitute the Niger Delta have been virtually

---

3   UNDP Niger Delta Human Development Report 2006, pp. 56-57.

displaced or, where they still exist, are in conflict, with new interest groups that have accompanied the extractive industry to the region.

The Catholic Church in Nigeria is making concerted efforts aimed at addressing the social problems of the nation. However, the voice of the local Church in this region has not been loud enough to be heard or make tangible impact. On the national level, the Catholic Bishops' Conference of Nigeria, through the Justice Development and Peace Commission, has made a statement on the oil and gas wealth in Nigeria titled "**Nigeria – The Travesty of Oil and Gas Wealth**" in 2006. The various Dioceses in the region are engaged with the social problems of the poor and the needy through the charity work of the religious and lay apostolates and the Justice Development and Peace Commission/Caritas. But a systematic study of the development problems in the light of the social teachings of the Church is not yet a popular academic endeavour.

Aim and Relevance of the Study

This study aims at examining the state of development and the development problems (social, political and economic) of the Niger Delta region in Nigeria. It makes social and political analysis of the problems in the light of recent social philosophical findings by Amartya Sen, and presents a holistic development ethics based on *Populorum Progressio* and *Sollicitudo rei Socialis* as a plausible approach to the development of the Niger Delta region.

Methodology of the Study

The study follows the traditional method of social analysis which is the three-step approach of See, Judge and Act, that is, the descriptive, analytic and normative-practical approach. The work is made up four parts. Part one presents the development problems in the region. Part two treats the socio-economic and political analysis of the problems. Part three seeks to offer an ethical orientation and part four focuses on assessment of and suggestions for development agents based on the ethical orientation.

Part one is divided into three chapters. Chapter one gives a brief historical overview of Nigeria as a nation, localizes and discusses peculiarity of the Niger Delta region. Chapter two treats the theoretical framework of the development concept and chapter three focuses on the actual development problems, that is, the state of poverty and underdevelopment in the Niger Delta.

Part two presents the socio-economic and political analysis of the causes of the development problems in two separate chapters respectively. In chapter four, attention is given to resource curse which is the characteristics of oil-exporting countries that are not able to translate oil wealth into development of the people, as in the case of Nigeria. Corruption in Nigeria also features in this chapter. Chapter five treats the interests of national and international stakeholders as factors informing the policies and structures relating to the Niger Delta.

Part three concentrates on presenting an ethical orientation in three chapters. Chapter six treats the Capability Approach to development based on the socio-philosophical findings of Amartya Sen as presented in his book Development as Freedom. Chapter seven presents impulses from the rich tradition of Catholic social teaching, drawing on the social principles and the development model according to *Populorum Progressio* and *Sollicitudo rei Socialis*. And Chapter eight proffers an agenda of development for the Niger Delta region based on both Sen's Capability Approach and the Impulses from the Catholic social teaching.

Part four makes, in two chapters, an assessment of development agents' contributions and offers suggestions on the way forward based on the ethical orientation. Chapter nine considers development efforts being made by international stakeholders and the international community, including the Church in industrialized countries. Chapter ten addresses national stakeholders including the local Church of Nigeria.

Argument of the Thesis

The thesis seeks to state that the powerful and influential stakeholders in the extractive industry have not always considered the interests and concerns of the local inhabitants in the Niger Delta region in all their dealings. Corruption, financial misappropriation and lack of accountability to the citizenry by the governments and stakeholders in the oil and gas industry are responsible for the present state of poverty and development problems in the Niger Delta region. The situation is accommodated by the prevailing political structure which operates on rentier economic system / revenue allocation kind of system. The generality of the population does not participate in the oil income. To change the situation, there is the need for a development ethics that will address the current political and economic structures. This ethics can be found in the social teaching of the Church, precisely in *Populorun Progressio* and *Sollicitudo rei Socialis*. The local Church of Nigeria will make the "joy and hope, the grief and anguish" of the Niger Delta people fully her own when she engages the structures that are responsible for poverty and underdevelopment of the region.

18

Map of Nigeria

Map of Niger Delta

Part I
Development Problems in the Niger Delta Region

1. Nigeria since Independence in 1960 – A Historical Overview

1.1 Introduction

This chapter intends to achieve two things: firstly, to give the historical background and overview of Nigeria as a nation. This would enable us to understand the socio-cultural, economic and political scenario in the country. Secondly, it is to locate and ascertain the peculiarity of the Niger Delta region and its human development situation.

1.2 Political History of Nigeria

The Federal Republic of Nigeria has a landmass extending over 923,768 square kilometres, with the land covering 910,768 km^2 and water 13,000 km^2. Nigeria is located on the shores of the Gulf of Guinea, with the Republic of Benin to the west, Niger Republic to the north, Chad to the north-east, and Cameroon to the east and south-east. The population was enumerated at 140.003,542 according to the provisional results of the census of March 2006, with an average density of 157.2 per sq km.[4] however, recent estimations put it at an average of 150 million.[5]

Thus, with a population of about 150 million Nigeria is the most populous country in Africa. The population is a mixed one, making the country a pluralistic and multifaceted society, comprising over 250 ethnic groups and languages, of which the major ones are Hausa, Yoruba, and Ibo.[6] The landmass could be divided into three major parts: North, South-West and South-East, according to the pattern of the major rivers (Niger and Benue) that traverse the country.

---

4   Mabogunje, Akin L., Nigeria: Physical and social Geography. *In*: Africa South of the Sahara, London, Routledge Taylor and Francis Group [37]2008, p. 876.

5   See World Fact Book, https://www.cia.gov/library/publications/the-world-factbook/geos/ ni.html. Visited on 23 November 2010.

6   Uwechu, Raph et al(Eds.), Africa Today, London, Africa Books 1991, pp. 1441-1442.

In the light of democracy and to ensure fair representation of all tribes and tongues, Nigeria is governed under a three-tier federal structure, comprising 36 State Governments, 774 Local Governments Areas (Lgas), and the Federal Capital Territory, Abuja. The structure at the Federal level consists of the President, the Vice-President and the Ministers, who constitute the Executive, and the two chambers of the National Assembly, which form the Legislature and the Judiciary. At the State level, the structure takes a similar form whereby the Governor, Deputy Governor and the Commissioners serve as the Executive Council; but the Legislature is a single chamber. The Judiciary is also visible at both the Federal and State levels. The states are grouped into six geopolitical zones namely: North East (Adamawa, Bauchi, Bornu, Gombe, Taraba, and Yobe); North West (Kaduna, Kano, Katsina, Jigawa, Kebbi, Sokoto, and Zamfara); Middle Belt – North Central (Benue, Kogi, Kwara, Nassarawa, Niger, and Plateau); South East (Abia, Anambra, Ebonyi, Enugu, and Imo); South West (Lagos, Ekiti, Ogun, Ondo, Osun, and Oyo); and South South (Akwa-Ibon, Bayelsa, Cross River, Delta, Edo, and Rivers). The third tier is the Local Government Council (to which has been added a legislature).[7] At the Local government level, an elected Chairperson assisted by supervisory councilors administers the government. The elected members of the Local Government Council form the legislative organ at this level. The councils can make by-laws in the area of their jurisdiction. Area or customary courts form the judiciary at the local government level.[8]

1.2.1 Nigeria before Independence

The various peoples that constitute the Nigerian nation have their different and separate historical origins far back into the past. They existed as separate and distinct empires, kingdoms, principalities, and other types of social and political formations. These separate peoples were brought together, and though unified by the instrumentality of the superior British colonial force, were not united.[9] Although our focus is the political history of Nigeria since independence, we cannot but allude to the fact of colonial heritage. Suffice to state that the period of colonialism precipitated the foundation on which Nigeria was built at Indepen-

---

7 Ali-Akpajiak, Sofo C. A and Pyke Tony, Measuring Poverty in Nigeria, Oxfam working Papers, 2003, p. 21.
8 Niger Delta Regional Development Master Plan, p. 52.
9 The amalgamation took place during the government of Lord Lugard as the Governor General of the Northern and the Southern protectorate in 1914. The reason for amalgamation was to reduce the cost of administration. The name Nigeria comes from the River Niger that runs through the country from north to the south (Niger area).

dence in 1960. For example, the amalgamation of Northern and Southern Protectorates in 1914 and subsequent fashion of governance formed the foundation of the structure of the present-day Nigeria, especially the political and to some extent, the administrative structures. It was a union that many have described as 'marriage of convenience' brought about for the sole benefit of the colonial lords and their country.

According to Matthew H. Kukah, throughout the colonial period, "Nigeria was administered along largely divisive lines. The British were mainly interested in unifying those aspects of administration that would enhance their control and monopoly of the country. They did this through the unification of the railway system, the standardization of the currency and the unification of taxation, the judiciary and the bureaucracy"[10]. Nothing was done to encourage mutual interaction among the various tribes in Nigeria nor was there any program aimed at the developing the human persons particularly in the rural areas. In fact, Kukah points out that "migration and contacts between the north and the south were very limited as a result of the attitude of the different colonial administrators working in various regions and provinces"[11].

Through missionary enterprise, Southern Nigeria had earlier access to Western education than Northern Nigeria. Responsible for the dichotomy was the system of governance practiced by the colonialists. This Omeje describes thus:

After the 1914 amalgamation, which in law defined Nigeria as one united country, the British colonial government continued to rule the Northern and Southern Protectorates as two distinct entities with very minimal attempts at administrative, institutional and social coordination. At the time the British proclaimed a Protectorate over Northern Nigeria, the traditional rulers in the area, the Emirs, were promised that there would be no interference in matters of religion. Missionary activities were therefore disallowed. As a consequence, the Northern region was in the main excluded from European education, largely provided by the missionaries in Southern Nigeria[12].

Rather than viewing education as positive capacity building and achievement, the British soon began to see these newly educated southerners as a thorn in their flesh because, unlike their counterparts elsewhere, the conquest of the country did not make them easily influenced. On the contrary, access to Western education made them more confident and reluctant to submit to colonial rule. The British painted a negative picture of the southerners as belligerent, corrupt and

---

10   Kukah, Matthew, Human Rights in Nigeria. Hopes and Hindrances, Aachen, Missio 2003, pp. 5-6.
11   Kukah, Matthew, Human Rights in Nigeria, p. 6.
12   Omeje, Kenneth C., High Stakes and Stakeholders: Oil conflict and security in Nigeria, Ashgate, England 2006, p. 26. For the rest of this work this book will be referred to as Omeje Kenneth, High Stakes and Stakeholders.

audacious[13]. While the missionaries were evangelizing people in southern Nigeria through schools and hospitals, the non-interference pact which cordoned off the Northern emirates, shielded them from missionary activities. This permitted the powerful Muslim Emirs to conduct local administration and governance through existing centralized political structures as in the pre-colonial time. This was indirect rule. Contrary to what was obtaining in the North, the colonial authorities applied more direct and authoritarian methods of administration in the South that further weakened and, in some cases, obliterated a number of traditional institutions, because the anti-colonial struggle for independence was stronger and the traditional political systems were comparatively more diffused in the Southern Protectorate.

To further fan the embers of disunity, the colonial government divided the Southern Protectorate into Eastern and Western Regions in 1939, creating a geo-demographic imbalance that left the Northern region far larger than the Western and Eastern regions put together. Each region comprised one dominant ethnic group and a mosaic of minorities that lived under the perpetual fear and threats of domination by the majority groups. The three regions were still governed and operated separately until 1954 when a central government with a parliament was established, thus in legal terms or in theory making Nigeria a federation.[14]

1.2.2 Independence and Civil War (1960-1970)

By an act of the British Parliament, Nigeria was granted full independence on October 1, 1960, as a federation of three regions (Northern, Western and Eastern) under a constitution that provided for a parliamentary form of government. Under the constitution each of the three regions retained a substantial measure of self-government.[15] The federal government was given exclusive power in defense and security, foreign relations, and commercial and fiscal policies. In 1963, Nigeria became a republic within the Commonwealth. A fourth region (the Midwest) was established that year.

From the outset, Nigeria's ethnic, regional, and religious tensions were magnified by the significant disparities in economic and educational development between the South and the North[16]. The change in status called for no practical

---

13 Kukah, Matthew, Human Rights in Nigeria, p. 6.
14 Omeje, Kenneth C., High Stakes and Stakeholders, p. 26.
15 Dibie, Robert, Public Management and Sustainable Development in Nigeria: Military Bureaucracy Relationship, England, Ashgate Publishing Ltd 2003, pp. 4-5.
16 Obi , Cyril, The Changing Forms of Identity Politics in Nigeria under Economic Adjustment – The Case of the Oil Minorities Movement of the Niger Delta, Uppsala, Nordiska Afrikanstitutet, 2001, pp. 24-25.

alteration of the constitutional system. The President, elected to a five-year term by a joint session of the parliament, replaced the crown as the symbol of national sovereignty and the British monarch as Head of State. Nnamdi Azikwe became the Republic's first President[17].

On January 15, 1966 a group of army officers, mostly south-eastern Igbos, led by Major K. Nzeogwu overthrew the government and assassinated the federal Prime Minister and the premiers of the Northern and Western Regions. The federal military government headed by General Aguiyi Ironsi that assumed power was unable to quieten ethnic tensions or produce a constitution acceptable to all sections of the country. Its efforts to abolish the federal structure greatly raised tensions and led to another coup in 28/29 July 1966. The coup-related massacre of thousands of Igbos in the North prompted hundreds of thousands of them to return to the South-East, where increasingly strong Igbo secessionist sentiments emerged. This second coup brought Lt. Col. and later General Yakubu Gowon into power.

In a move that gave greater autonomy to minority ethnic groups, the military divided the four regions into 12 states. The Igbos rejected attempts at constitutional revisions and insisted on full autonomy for the East. Finally, on 30 May 1967 Lt. Col. Emeka Ojukwu, the military Governor of the Eastern Region, declared the independence of the Eastern Region as the "Republic of Biafra"[18], named after the Bight of Biafra. This led to a 30 months civil war that eventually ended on January 15, 1970.

1.2.3 Post Civil War Nigeria (1970 – 1979)

At the end of the war, the government of the federation declared: *no victor no vanquished.* It was to be expected that after the 30 months of civil war, a lot of families would be displaced, there would be casualties and loss of personal properties and dysfunctional public infrastructure, mutual mistrust among people, particularly among the various tribal groups. An estimated 1 to 3 million people died in the hostilities, from disease and starvation during the civil war, and more than 3 million Igbos became refugees.[19] This informed the Gowon's government policy of the three R's i.e. *rehabilitation, reconstruction* and *reconciliation.*[20]

---

17 LIBRARY OF CONGRESS – Federal Research Division Country Profile: Nigeria, June 2006, p. 4.
18 Bergstresser Heinrich, Nigeria, in; Handbuch der Dritten Welt, Bd 4, p. 357.
19 LIBRARY OF CONGRESS – Federal Research Division, Country profile: Nigeria, June 2006 p. 4.
20 Kukah, Matthew, Human Rights in Nigeria, p. 8. Cf. Maier, Karl, This House Has Fallen, New York, Public Affairs, 2000, p. 53.

Following the civil war, reconciliation was rapid and effective, and the country turned to the task of economic development. Foreign exchange earnings and government revenues increased spectacularly with the oil price rises of 1973-74.[21] In October 1970, Gowon announced his intention of staying in power until 1976, the target year for completion of the military's political program and return to an elected civilian government. In 1972 he partially lifted the ban on political activity that had been in force since 1966 in order to permit a discussion of a new constitution that would pave the way for civilian rule. The debate that followed became so chaotic that Gowon abruptly terminated the discussion.[22]

The Gowon regime came under fire because of widespread and obvious corruption at every level of national life. Inefficiencies compounded the effects of corruption. Crime also posed a threat to national security and had a seriously negative impact on efforts to bring about economic development. The political atmosphere deteriorated to the point where Gowon was deposed in a bloodless military coup in July 1975.[23] He was succeeded by General Murtala Ramat Muhammad, who was assassinated in an abortive coup on February 13, 1976. However his pro-people policies (like reducing the prices of food items) in his short time elevated him to the status of national hero. He set the agenda to hand over to a democratically elected government by October 1979. His next in command, Lt. General Olusegun Obasanjo was chosen as the successor.

1.2.4 Transition to Civilian Rule (1979-1983)

In 1979 under Obasanjo's leadership, Nigeria adopted a constitution based on the constitution of the United States that provided for separation of powers among the executive, legislative and judicial branches. Besides organizing successful elections that saw Alhaji Shehu Shagari become civilian president in 1979, Obasanjo initiated plans to move the federal capital from Lagos to a more central location in the interior at Abuja which later became the federal capital in December 1991.

On October 1, 1979 the civilian government of Shehu Shagari was sworn in. It should be noted that the presidential succession from Obasanjo to a civilian, President Shehu Shagari, was the first peaceful transfer of power since independence. Naturally, expectations were high, just as oil prices were high, and revenues were on the increase. The yearning for development in all ramifications by

---

21 NIGERIA, http://www.state.gov/r/pa/ei/bgn/2836.htm. Visited on 12.01.2008.
22 LIBRARY OF CONGRESS – Federal Research Division, Country Profile: Nigeria, June 2006, p. 4.
23 LIBRARY OF CONGRESS – Federal Research Division Country Profile: Nigeria, June 2006, p. 5.

28

Nigerians was palpable. Akinwumi puts it this way: "as optimism was expressed about the future of Nigeria when it became independent in 1960, so also was it expressed when Shagari took over"[24]. Unfortunately, the euphoria was short-lived. A number of weaknesses beset the second republic. First, the coalition that dominated federal politics was not strong, and in effect the victorious National Party of Nigeria (NPN) led by Shagari governed as a minority. Second, there was a lack of cooperation between the NPN-dominated federal government and the 12 states controlled by the opposition parties. Third, and perhaps most important-ly, the oil boom ended in mid-1981, precisely when expectations of continuous growth and prosperity were at a height. The recession that set in put severe strains on the Second Republic[25]. Hardly had Shagari begun his second term that the military struck on 31 December 1983 led by General Buhari because there was virtually, no confidence in the civilian regime.

1.2.5 The Return of the Military (1983-1999)

Allegations of fraud associated with Shagari's re-election in 1983 served as a pretext for the takeover. According to Buhari, the change became necessary in order to put an end to the serious economic predicament and the crisis of confi-dence that was afflicting the nation. While he acknowledged the then prevalent worldwide economic recession, he attributed the case of Nigeria, to the failure of the leadership to heed good advice.[26] The military regime under General Buhari tried to achieve two goals. First, it attempted to secure public support by reducing the level of corruption; second, it demonstrated its commitment to austerity by trimming the federal budget. In a further effort to mobilize the country, Buhari launched a "War Against Indiscipline" (WAI) campaign in 1984.[27] Perhaps it was well-intended, but the way and manner the program was executed was every-thing but discipline and human. For instance, he banned all political activities including public debate on the political future of Nigeria; university students

---

24 Akinwumi, Olayemi, Crises and Conflicts in Nigeria: A Political History since 1960, Münster, Lit Verlag 2005, p. 81.

25 LIBRARY OF CONGRESS – Federal Research Division Country Profile: Nigeria, June 2006 p. 5.

26 Kukah, Matthew, Human Rights in Nigeria, p. 8 Cf Major-General Muhammad Buhari, national broadcast, 1 January 1984.

27 LIBRARY OF CONGRESS – Federal Research Division Country Profile: Nigeria, June 2006 p. 6 WAI was a program aimed at inducing work ethics, patriotism, fighting corruption and promoting environmental sanitation in Nigeria. Good as the intention might have been, the brutal manner it was executed by the soldiers earned Buhari's regime public anger and international condemnation.

who protested against the cost of school fees were rusticated; medical doctors who protested against the appalling condition of medical hospitals and lack of drugs were sacked; pedestrians crossing the high way instead of using the overhead bridges were publicly flogged by soldiers, etc.

By 1985 General Babangida carried out his own coup premised on the rigidity and uncompromising attitude of General Buhari to issues of national significance. He accused Buhari of failure to recognise and appreciate the diverse polity and cultural differences in Nigeria, despite good counsel given him. For this reason, his government was alienated from the people.[28] The eight years of Babangida's regime was characterised and trailed by the agonising legacy of Structural Adjustment Program (SAP) and by a host of ephemeral populist ventures like the Directorate for Food Road and Rural Infrastructure (DFFRI), Mass Mobilization for Social and Economic Recovery (MAMSER), People's Bank, etc. Babangida addressed the worsening recession through the structural adjustment program of 1986. However, despite US\$4.2 billion of support from the World Bank and the rescheduling of foreign debt, the recession led to a series of currency devaluations, a decline in real income, and rising unemployment.[29]

1.2.6 The Crisis of June 12, 1993

President Babangida promised to return the country to civilian rule by 1990; this date was later extended to January 1993. In early 1989, a constituent assembly completed work on a constitution for the Third Republic. In the same year political activity was permitted. In October 1989 the government established two "grassroots" parties: the National Republican Convention (NRC), which was to be a "little to the right," and the Social Democratic Party (SDP), "a little to the left". Other parties were not allowed to register by Babangida's government.[30] In December 1990 the first stages of partisan elections were held at the local government level. Turnout was low and there was no violence. SDP won control of a majority of local government councils.

In December 1991, gubernatorial and state legislative elections were held throughout the country. Babangida decreed in December 1991 that previously banned politicians would be allowed to contest in primaries scheduled for August 1992. These were cancelled due to fraud, and subsequent primaries sched-

---

28 Kukah, Matthew , Human Rights in Nigeria, p. 8 Cf Major-General Ibrahim Babangida, national broadcast, 27 August 1985.
29 LIBRARY OF CONGRESS – Federal Research Division, Country Profile: Nigeria, June 2006, p 6.
30 NIGERIA, http://www.state.gov/r/pa/ei/bgn/2836.htm. Visited on 12.01.2008.

uled for September were also cancelled. All announced candidates were disqualified from again standing for president once a new election format was selected. The presidential election was finally held on 12 June, 1993, with the inauguration of the new president scheduled to take place on 27 August, 1993, the eighth anniversary of President Babangida's coming to power[31].

In the historic 12 June 1993 presidential elections that most observers considered to be Nigeria's fairest, early returns indicated that Chief M.K.O Abiola had won a decisive victory. However, on 23 June Babangida, using several pending lawsuits as pretence, annulled the election, thereby throwing Nigeria into turmoil. More than 100 persons were killed in riots before Babangida agreed to 'step aside' by handing power to an "interim government" on 27 August 1993. Without popular and military support, he was forced to hand over to Ernest Shonekan, a prominent non-partisan businessman. Chief Shonekan was to rule until new elections, slated for February 1994. Although he had led Babangida's Transition Council since early 1993, Shonekan could not reverse Nigeria's ever-growing economic problems nor was he able to defuse lingering political tension.

With the country sliding into chaos, Defence Minister Sani Abacha quickly assumed power and forced Shonekan's resignation on 17 November 1993. From November 1993 on, Abacha served as military dictator until his death in 1998. During his rule, he suppressed dissent and failed to follow through with a promised transition to civilian government. In 1995, as a result of various human rights violations, the European Union, which already had imposed sanctions in 1993, suspended development aid and Nigeria, was temporarily expelled from the Commonwealth. Corruption also flourished, and Abacha was later found to have siphoned off oil revenues into personal bank accounts in Switzerland.[32] It was during his regime that Nigerians suffered great inhuman brutality and violence. As we shall see later in this work, it was during his era that the human development problems in the Niger Delta region became unbearable and thus escalated into crises. He ignored all appeals for clemency from heads of state, intergovernmental bodies and human rights groups worldwide, including that of the Pope John Paul II and went ahead to execute the leader of the Movement for the Survival of Ogoni People (MOSOP) Ken Saro Wiwa and eight other compatriots for demanding from government justice, social and human development and environmental concern for the Niger Delta region.

The execution of Ken Saro Wiwa and his eight compatriots exposed the reality of the human development condition in the region to international spectacle. The

---

31   NIGERIA, http://www.state.gov/r/pa/ei/bgn/2836.htm. Visited on 12.01.2008.
32   Library of Congress – Federal Research Division, Country Profile: Nigeria, June 2006, p. 6.

official reason why government reacted so sharply in defiance of world opinion was that the activities of MOSOP threatened the territorial integrity of Nigeria.[33]

Under the military regime of Abacha, Nigeria experienced the worst military dictatorship ever, which contributed to military rule's complete loss of legitimacy. Despite the brutal dictatorship of the Abacha regime, people's desire and clamour for democracy could not be suppressed. Such groups like National Democratic Coalition (NADECO), a group established to oppose military rule and to ensure that Chief M.K.O. Abiola, the supposed winner of the annulled June 12, 1993 election, be sworn in as President of Nigeria were growing stronger. Others are Labour Unions, Civil Liberty Organization (CLO), Committee for the Defence of Human Rights (CDHR), The Justice Development and Peace Commission (JDPC) of the Catholic Church and Campaign for Democracy (CD). Other socio-cultural organizations also emerged to protect the interests of their ethnic groups from systematic extermination or at least from the systematic elimination of all notable opinion leaders that were opposed to perpetual military rule. Such groups as the Movement for the Survival of Ogoni People (MOSOP), *Afenifere* – Yoruba council of Elders and the Odua People's Congress (OPC), Movement for the Survival of the Sovereign State of Biafra, and the Bakassi Boys among others became very prominent in agitating for democracy and the rule of law.

Generally, the era of military rule saw the complete abuse of the rule of law, over-concentration of power at the centre, and general dissatisfaction among the people. The civil society's clamour for a democratic system of government, combined with the diplomatic isolation of the country, added to the momentum which set in motion the process for democratic elections.[34]

1.2.7 Transition to Civilian Rule (1999-2007)

It was only expedient in June 1998 as General Abdusalam Abubakar succeeded Abacha that he immediately put in place a transition programme that saw a new constitution and a new democratic government when a new president, Olusegun Obasanjo was sworn in on 29 May 1999. Fifteen years of military rule had come to an end, and Nigeria entered the longest period of civilian rule since Independence. In 2003 Obasanjo was re-elected. Midway into his second term he and his supporters in the Peoples Democratic Party sought a constitutional change that would permit him to run for a third term in 2007 and probably become a life

---

33 Yemi Akinseye-George, Pumping Oil and Pumping money: Impact on Local Cultures in the Niger Delta region of Nigeria. Cf. http://www.usos.be/download.aspx?c. Visited on 15.10.2007.

34 Ali-akpajiak, Sofo C. A. and Pyke, Tony, Measuring Poverty in Nigeria, Oxfam working Paper, 2003, p. 20.

president. In May, the Senate, to the delight of most democracy-loving Nigerians, rejected a constitutional amendment that would have permitted a third term. And so, on 29 May 2007 Obasanjo handed over to President Musa Yar'adua marking the second peaceful transition to yet another civilian government in the history of Nigeria.

1.2.8 Evaluation of Nigeria's Political Development

Since Nigeria became independent, her political development has been fraught with instability and inconsistency in development policy. It is true that she is endowed with wealth and considerable economic potentials, but because Nigeria has had a chequered political history, she has not as yet succeeded in effectively translating its potentials into economic growth, human development and overall social transformation.[35] Nigeria's colonial legacy and subsequent political instability have undermined its development.

In the 50 years since independence, Nigeria has endured civil war lasting from 1967 to 1970. Frequent military coups and prolonged military regimes have not afforded the nation adequate opportunity of internalising and appreciating the true culture of democracy. This is because the prolonged military rule, spanning altogether 28 years out of Nigeria's five decades of independence, has led to the repeated supplanting of constitutional provisions by military decrees.

The military coups were supposedly meant to correct the ills of the civilian government with the soldiers returning shortly thereafter to their barracks and to be dedicated to their professional constitutional duty to the nation. But they stayed put in power, having tasted power and gained access to the wealth of the nation and dwindled on the return to democratic rule for several decades.

Like other countries on the continent of Africa, Nigeria has experienced a great deal of violent changes in government since its independence from colonial rule in 1960. The almost 30 years of military dictatorship has not only repressed the psychic of the people, it has also denied the country its full potentials. The era of military dictatorship denied Nigerians their political rights and compromised their universal human rights. As noted by the series of military coups and the counter accusation of mismanagement by the different coup leaders, the theft of government resources by Nigerian leaders has plunged the people deeper into poverty and caused great damage to Nigerian society. It has earned Nigeria, in 1999, the

---

35   UNDP Country Report, 2003. P.21.

notoriety of being one of the four most corrupt countries in the world, ranked by Transparency International at 1.9 on a scale where 10 is the least corrupt.[36]

It is a popular knowledge that lack of democracy and popular participation is one of the reasons for the prevalence of poverty in Africa. Further analysis would show that the economic downturn in Nigeria is to a large extent the result of the long years of military rule. According to Sofo Ali-Akpajiak and Tony Pyke, "poverty usually flourishes in societies deprived of human freedom. Such societies are engulfed in a series of vicious circles of poverty. There is no further obstacle to development than the lack of basic human freedom."[37] This description aptly fits the Nigerian scenario during the years of military rule. In fact, summarising the military era, Omeje says:

> Nigeria has spent a longer part of its post-independence history under military dictatorship as opposed to civilian democracy. The consequences of frequent military intervention in Nigerian politics have been devastating – human rights repression, militarization of society and the political landscape, abuse of the rule of law, gross indiscipline, arbitrary proliferation of sub-national States and local government areas, aggravation of ethnic politics, destruction of the productive sectors of the economy and monumental corruption.[38]

Admittedly, since Obasanjo took over as the President of Nigeria, the government has already made improvement in tackling corruption and in ensuring civil and political rights, through the establishment of several bodies such as the anti-corruption commissions, the Human Rights Commission, and the Niger Delta Development Commission. Also, the government has made attempts to address the country's poverty by approving strategies such as the Poverty Alleviation Programme (PAP) and the National Poverty Eradication Programme (NAPEP). The government has issued a Poverty Reduction Strategy Paper (PRSP) which has also been developed into the National Economic Empowerment Development Strategy (NEEDS). Until his death, the late President Umar Ya'ardua was promoting a seven-point development agenda and attempts were being made to harmonise the seven-point agenda with the NEEDS to be known as NEEDS 2 spanning from 2008-2011. Despite all these efforts, the reality of general poverty and underdevelopment is still staring one on the face in the country.

---

36 Ali-akpajiak, Sofo C. A. and Pyke, Tony, Measuring Poverty in Nigeria, Oxfam working Papers, 2003, p. 3 Cf. also Central Bank of Nigeria/World Bank 1999, p. 15.

37 Ali-akpajiak, Sofo C. A. and Pyke, Tony, Measuring Poverty in Nigeria, Oxfam working Paper, 2003, p. 20.

38 Omeje, Kenneth C., High Stakes and Stakeholders, p. 27.

1.3 The Economy

On a positive note, Nigeria's economy is struggling to leverage the country's wealth in fossil fuels in order to displace the crushing poverty that affects about 70 percent of its population. Economists refer to the coexistence of extreme wealth due to vast natural resources and extreme personal poverty in developing countries like Nigeria as the "paradox of plenty"[39] or the "curse of oil". It is delighting to note, on the one hand, that Nigeria's exports of oil and natural gas at a time of peak prices have enabled the country to post merchandise trade and current surpluses in recent years. On the other hand, it is equally disheartening to know according to World Bank, that as a result of corruption 80 percent of energy revenues benefit only 1 percent of the population.[40] Karl Terry has shown in his work *The Paradox of Plenty* that there is a connection between the framework of decision-making (political power) and the leading export sector. This is why the political exigencies of Nigeria cannot be separated from her economy. We shall address this point in some details later when we shall be considering the political analysis of the causes of development problems.

In the light of political instability coupled with inconsistency in policies of the various regimes both military and civilian, one cannot expect any miracle in the economic sector. Despite having the seventh largest oil and gas reserves in the world and being the world's sixth largest exporter of crude oil, Nigeria's GDP per capita annual growth rate in real terms has been negative or zero for more than two decades.[41]

The National Economic Empowerment and Development Strategy (NEEDS) prepared by the Nigerian National Planning Commission in broad consultation with stakeholders and development partners, including staff of the World Bank and the IMF acknowledges the fact that "Nigeria's rich human and material resource endowments give it the potential to become Africa's largest economy and a major player in the global economy."[42] However, the same document paints the reality of the Nigerian economy and the challenges of development as follows:

> Per capita GDP in Nigeria was among the lowest in the world during the 1980s and 1990s, costing it decades of development. Annual per capita GDP remained stagnant in the 1990s,

---

39   Karl, Terry Lynn, The Paradox of Plenty – Oil Booms and Petro-States, Berkeley, University of California Press, 1997, xvi.

40   LIBRARY OF CONGRESS, Nigeria, June 2006, p. 10.

41   UNDP, Country Evaluation: Assessment of Development Results – Nigeria, 2003, p. 22.

42   http://www.imf.org IMF Country Report No. 05/433 Nigeria: Poverty Reduction Strategy Paper – National Economic Empowerment and Development Strategy (NEEDS) 2005 p. 7.

and it grew just 0.8 percent between 1999 and 2003 – far lower than the 4.2 percent per capita growth needed to significantly reduce poverty.[43]

Compared with other African and Asian countries, especially Indonesia, which is comparable to Nigeria in most respects, Nigeria's economic development has been disappointing. With GDP of about $45 billion in 2001 and per capita income of about $300 a year, Nigeria cannot be said to have quit the group of poor and less developed countries in the world. As at 2000 it had earned about $300 billion from oil exports since the mid – 1970s, but its per capita income was 20 percent lower than in 1975. Meanwhile, the country has become so heavily indebted – external and domestic debt amounted to about 70 percent of GDP – that it has serious difficulty servicing debt.[44] There is regional and sectoral unevenness in growth performance. The real sector is still dominated by the primary production. Agriculture, predominantly small farmers with low and declining productivity, accounts for 41 percent of the real sector, while crude oil accounts for 13 percent. The secondary sector, especially manufacturing, has been stagnating at about 5-7 percent of GDP.[45] This shows that industrialization in Nigeria is still quite low.

Services have been the fastest-growing sector since independence. Between 1975 and 2000 Nigeria's broad macroeconomic aggregates-growth, the terms of trade, the real exchange rate, government revenue and spending were among the most volatile in the developing world. Over the past three decades, high macroeconomic volatility has become a key determinant – as well as a consequence – of poor economic management. The economy has been caught in a low growth trap, characterized by low investment (at less than 20 percent).[46] Industrialization and exports remain low. With an average annual investment rate of barely 16 percent of GDP, Nigeria is far below the minimum investment rate of about 30 percent of GDP required to unleash a poverty-reducing growth rate of at least 7-8 percent per year.

In the 50 years since Independence, Nigeria has never grown at 7 percent or above for more than three consecutive years.[47] Because of perceptions of risks and the high cost of business operation, private agents keep the bulk of their

---

43   NEED document, p. 7.
44   In 2005 Nigeria's external debt was an estimated US$37.5 billion, but at midyear Nigeria and a group of international creditors known as the Paris Club agreed to eliminate all US$31 billion of the country's bilateral debt. Under the agreement, the Paris Club would write off US$18 billion of bilateral debt, and Nigeria would pay back the remainder. Non-bilateral debt owed to multilateral development banks and commercial banks was not affected by the agreement. Cf. Library of Congress – Federal Research Division, Country Profile: Nigeria, June 2006 p. 14.
45   NEEDS document, p. 8.
46   NEEDS document, p. 9.
47   NEEDS document, p. 9.

assets abroad, and more than 2 million Nigerians (mostly highly educated) have migrated to Europe, Asia and the United States of America. Most foreign direct investment into the country goes into the oil and extractive sectors. Only since 1999 has foreign direct investment in the non-oil sectors begun to rise significantly. This is particularly evident in the private mobile telephone sector.[48]

Nigeria's economic structure remains highly undiversified. Oil exports account for 95 percent of total exports, while manufacturing accounts for less than 1 percent. Since the 1970s Nigeria has lost international market share even in its traditional (agricultural) exports. To this effect Okonta and Douglas say that "at independence in 1960, Nigeria was virtually self-sufficient in food, and agricultural products accounted for 97 percent of export revenue."[49] Today Nigeria has become a food-importing nation. Macroeconomic policy has been highly circumscribed by inefficient, highly volatile, and unsustainable public sector spending and by unusual volatility of major macroeconomic aggregates. Fiscal decentralization has proved a challenge to effective macroeconomic stabilization and efficient public finance management. There has been lack of policy coherence between the states and the federal government and even among the various agencies of the federal government. The traditional instruments of economic management – the national plan and budgeting processes – have been rendered ineffective.[50]

The very low productivity of the private sector and the lack of diversification of the economy are due mainly to the prevailing business environment. The constraints to businesses include infrastructure deficiencies, poor security of lives and property, corruption and rent-seeking, low access to and the high cost of finance, weak institutions, poorly defined property rights and enforcement of contracts, and unstable macroeconomic policies, especially fiscal and trade policy.[51] Although these conditions have begun to improve since 1999, significant obstacles need to be addressed. Nigeria's urbanization rate – about 5.3 percent a year – is one of the fastest in the world with a stagnant secondary sector; urban unemployment and its attendant problems of slums, crime, and socio-political tensions is usually high.

In March 1999, 23.2 percent of the rural labour force and 12.4 percent of urban dwellers were without jobs. By March 2003 the rural unemployment rate had dropped to 12.3 percent and the urban rate to 7.4 percent, yielding a composite unemployment rate of 10.8 percent.[52] Nigeria faces the challenge of meeting the Millennium Development Goals. The statistics from the 1996 survey indicate that pov-

48 http://www.bertelsmann-transformation-index.de/fileadmin/pdf, Nigeria. Accessed on 5.9.2007.
49 Okonta, Ike and Oronto, Douglas, Where Vultures Feast, Shell, Human Rights, and Oil, London, Verso 2003, p. 24.
50 NEEDS document, p. 9.
51 NEEDS document, p. 10.
52 NEEDS document, p. 10.

erty is deep and pervasive, with an estimated 70 percent of the population living in poverty. The educational system is dysfunctional as graduates of many institutions cannot meet the needs of the country. According to the NEEDS document,

> Institutions are in decay, strikes and cultism are common, and corruption has become rampant. Youth militarism has now gone beyond the walls of schools to the heart of society. Despite efforts to promote a private sector-led, competitive market economy framework, Nigeria still faces the fundamental challenge of transition from statism and rent-seeking in an economy dominated by the public sector. The deep vested interests that profit from the system have proved resilient. They are strengthened by evidence of weak institutions. As a result, implementation failures in Nigeria are persistent.[53]

1.4 The Niger Delta Region: Land and People

The region is situated in the southern part of Nigeria and bordered to the south by the Atlantic Ocean and to the east by Cameroon. It has a surface area of about 112,110 square kilometres. It represents about 12% of Nigeria's total surface area.[54] The region extends along the coast from Benin River on the west to the Imo River on the east. The provisional census figure released in March 2006 by the National Population Commission gives the total population of the region to be 31,224,577 million inhabitants. The region comprises nine of Nigeria's constituent States: Abia, Akwa Ibom, Bayelsa, Cross River, Delta, Edo, Imo, Ondo, and Rivers, with 185 local governments. These States are not only oil-producing areas but also are considered relevant for reasons of administrative convenience, political expediency and development objectives.[55]

The region spreads over a number of ecological zones: sandy coastal ridge barriers, brackish or saline mangroves, freshwater (permanent and seasonal) swamp forest, and lowland rain forest (SPDC, 2002:9). More than half of the area consists of fragile mangrove and fresh water swamp forests. The Delta is a vast floodplain interspersed with network of creeks and tributaries that drain the River Niger into the Atlantic Ocean along the Gulf of Guinea. According to Kenneth Omeje, "The high rainfall and river discharge during the rainy season

---

53 The NEEDs document, Chapter 2, pp. 7-10. During 2003-2007 Nigeria attempted to implement an economic reform program called the National Economic Empowerment Development Strategy (NEEDS). The purpose of NEEDS is to raise the country's standard of living through a variety of reforms, including macroeconomic stability, deregulation, liberalization, privatization, transparency, and accountability.

54 Niger Delta Regional Development Master Plan, 2006, p. 49. This document and the UNDP Human Development Report serve as our major source of information for this section of the work.

55 Niger Delta Human Development Report 2006, p. 19.

combined with the low, flat terrain and poorly drained soils, cause widespread flooding and erosion: over 80 percent of the Delta is seasonally flooded."[56] Only selected elevated areas of the Niger Delta remain dry for a greater part of the year. This is because the copious rainfall coupled with the low relief and high water table produces frequent flooding. This topography explains the several small settlements found in the Niger Delta region. According to the NDDC master plan, there are about 13,000 small settlements of less than 5,000 inhabitants.

The Delta ecosystem is characterised by a dynamic equilibrium between flooding, erosion, and sediment deposition. Apart from the Niger River, the other major rivers in the region include the Cross, Imo, Qua Iboe and Orashi in the east and the Benin, Oluwa and Siluko in the west. The Niger Delta has a semi-hot, humid equatorial climate with wide variations from one part of the region to another.

The Niger Delta is the bedrock of Nigeria's crude oil production. All the nine states of the Niger Delta are oil-bearing with Bayelsa and Rivers accounting for 75% of oil production and over 50 percent of gross government revenue.[57] The region could be rightly referred to as the oil and natural gas capital of Nigeria, where most of the petroleum and natural gas is currently exploited. Oil and natural gas production in Nigeria account for about 95 percent of the country's foreign exchange earnings, and generates about 80 percent of total national revenue,[58] that is, the GDP of the country.

1.4.1 The People

The Niger Delta region is extremely heterogeneous with respect to culture and ethnicity. There are five major linguistic and cultural groups in the region, namely; Ijaw, Edo, Delta Cross, Yoruba and Igbo. Each of the groups is composed of numerous sub-groups. The Ijaws are the most complex linguistically. Each of the several clans of this group has some linguistic and cultural distinctiveness. In certain cases, villages in the same clan have linguistic variations. This group which occupies virtually the whole of Bayelsa State is also found in Rivers, Akwa Ibom, Delta, Edo and Ondo States.[59] The Edo group is made up of the

56 Omeje Kenneth C, High Stakes and Stakeholders, p. 31.
57 ANEEJ 2004, p. 1.
58 Atakpu, Leo, Resource-Based Conflicts: Challenges of Oil Extraction in Nigeria, A Paper presented at an European Conference Hosted by the German EU Council Presidency 2007, Berlin, March 29-30, 2007 Cf. http://www.adelphi-consult.com/ECC2007/downloads/Atakpu_WG_1_Day_1.pdf. Accessed on 19.9.2007.
59 ANEEJ 2004, p. 2.

Isoko and Urhobo of Delta State, the Edo of Edo State, the Engenni and Apie-
Atissa of Bayelsa State, and the Degema of Rivers State. Even within these groups,
several sub-groups exist; many claim to have their own individual identity.[60] For
example, among the Urhobo groups we have the Okpe and Uvbie. The Delta
Cross comprises mainly the Ogoni, Ogba, Abua, Odual and Obolo/Andoni in
River State and the Ibibio, Oron and Ibeno of Akwa Ibom State. The most well
known, especially internationally, is the Ogoni because of its agitation for resource control and autonomy. The ethno-cultural complexity of the Niger Delta
region is vividly illustrated by the fact that even a small ethnic group like the
Ogoni (about 500,000 people) is made up of at least four cultural groups: the
Khana, Gokama, Tai and Eleme.[61]

The main Yoruba groups are the Itsekiri of Delta State and the Ilaje and Ikale
in the borderlands of Ondo State. The main Igbo groups are the Ikwerre, Ndoni,
Egbema, Ogba and Ekpeye in Rivers State and the Ukuwani in Delta State. Before modern times, there was considerable interaction among the groups of the
Niger Delta region, especially those of the core Niger Delta (Bayelsa, Delta and
Rivers States). This interaction has always been in terms of trade and inter-group
marriages.[62] One major system of exchange is the trade between the Ijaws, who
fish, and the agricultural Urhobos. Until recently, Itsekiri female traders were
important facilitators of this trade. Intergroup marriages have been so significant,
particularly among the Urhobo, Itsekiri and Western Ijaws, that a large proportion of families in some areas are multicultural. These close interactions notwithstanding, owing to shortage of resources, particularly agricultural land there have
always been inter-ethnic conflicts among the ethnic groups in the Niger Delta
region. It must be added though, that inter-ethnic conflicts are not limited to the
Niger Delta region alone.

Inter-ethnic conflict is a common phenomenon in regions wherever multi-
ethnic groups are. However, the intensity of conflicts in the region is further
accentuated by the emergence of petroleum on the scene. There is no doubt that
the incidence of conflicts may have been considerably less if there had been no
oil and gas in the region.

Of all the zones, the lowland rainforest zone provides the best places for settlement. Of all the over 13 thousand settlements only 98 or one per cent, can be
regarded as urban centres based on their population. Factors responsible for the
small settlements are: first, the environment provides limited space for human
settlement, given the fragmentation of land into islands and the occurrence of dry

---

60   Niger Delta Human Development Report 2006, p. 21.
61   Niger Delta Human Development Report 2006, p. 22.
62   Niger Delta Human Development Report 2006, p. 22.

land in isolated pockets. Most settlements are small and dispersed. Secondly, fishing communities characteristically dwell in small fishing villages close to their fishing grounds. Thirdly, as indicated above, the Niger Delta is a home to many small minority groups, each of which is composed of numerous clans. Each clan cherishes its own private space.[63] There is no doubt that size plays an important role in the promotion of development, be it economic or human. For this reason, the prevalence of small settlements, topography and a swampy landscape in the Niger Delta make the task of sustainable human development much harder and challenging.

1.4.2 Population Growth and Demographic Characteristics

At the time of the 1991 census the total population for the Niger Delta Region was about 20 million, or about 23% of Nigeria's total population. Projections by government departments using an annual growth rate ranging between 2.0% and 2.9% indicated that the total population in 2005 would be nearly 27 million. However, the Master Plan Baseline sample survey, conducted in 2003, shows that the average annual rate of population growth in most communities, based on the household fertility and mortality data, is about 3.1%. This would mean that in 2004 the population of the Niger Delta Region would amount to about 30 million. Projected to 2015 it is expected therefore that population will increase to between 41.5 and 48 million, depending on the growth rates applied.[64] The average population density in the Niger Delta Region is currently 265 people/km² compared to the national average of about 255 people/km². There are, however, significant regional variations. Imo State, for example, has more than 700 persons per km² while in some other States the density is comparatively low, such as Cross River State where there are 120 persons per km². The differences in density reflect the topography.

1.4.2.1 Demographic Characteristics

The age structure of the population in the region reveals that over 62% are young people below the age of 30 (15-29) years. Adults in the age group 30-69 years make up only 36% while those aged 70 years and above constitute just 2% of the

---

63   Niger Delta Human Development Report 2006, p. 23. Cf. also Niger Delta Regional Development Master Plan p. 53.
64   NDR Master Plan, p. 56.

population. According to the UNDP Niger Delta Report, "A youthful demographic structure means many people remain outside of the working age bracket and are in their formative years, when social investment is heaviest."[65] According to the Master Plan, there are more males (54%) than female (46%) in the Niger Delta Region. Furthermore, there are overwhelmingly more male (93%) heads of households than females (7%). On the average, there are 6 persons per household, though there are variations in individual states, local government areas and senatorial districts. The household sizes tend to be larger in the rural communities with an average of 8 persons per household.[66]

1.4.2.2 Population Structure in the Niger Delta

As already indicated, because of the topography of the Niger Delta, each settlement enjoys a certain degree of autonomy, there was and is still no central authority over all the settlements traditionally. So, the organisational structure of the settlements varies from one to the other. However, there is a general pattern common to all the settlements or communities.

Like all other African societies, the Niger Delta region is also generally patriarchal and male-chauvinistic. Nevertheless, women are not left out of the traditional governance of the society. Age plays a significant role in the traditional political structure. There is the council of elders, to which men above the age of 60 belong. As the highest institution, the council prescribes the moral principles and the rules of conduct. A well recognised member of the council is chosen to take charge as the president or chairman of the council and traditional ruler. The council of elders is particularly very important because it makes decisions on matters relating to the community land and property.

The internal structures of a small community living in a single settlement and the structures of the community belonging to a larger village community spread out over several settlements are typically the same. Both men and women of most communities are subdivided into the youth and the elders, the latter being committed persons who are more advanced in age and have actively contributed to the development of the of the community and have to be recommended by other elders or the chiefs/traditional rulers. The "elders" (women and men) have a high status in the community because of their experience and they often make the decisive contributions regarding important activities at the community

65   Niger Delta Human Development Report, p. 24.
66   NDRD Master Plan, p. 56.

level.[67] Of significance and importance are the age groups into which young men are organised according to their age.

Most coherent are the women groups comprising of married women. Apart from their role of raising children, the women are most active in the agricultural sector. They are equally involved in petty trading while the men would go off to neighbouring towns in search of jobs or employment. In traditional political setup, the women may not be so influential like the council of elders but they have a significant role in determining the fate of a reigning traditional ruler. In rare spectacular cases, they possess unusual possibilities of dethroning or deposing any traditional ruler or chief. Today, the youth group between the ages 15 to 20 present the most radical and serious violence prone segment of the population in the Niger Delta region.

The chiefs and council of elders have no more efficient means of authority or sanctions as these have been taken over by the government. Due to lack of income opportunities in the villages, the chiefs and community leaders are easily susceptible to all forms of corruptions which are constantly being offered to them by government institutions and oil companies seeking their support to ensure peace and nip ensuing protests or crisis in the bud in the respective communities.

Though it appears that the democratic election of representatives at the local, district, and ward levels has subordinated the traditional structure of government, it needs to be pointed out that the traditional cultural values and practices of the people do not give way so easily to modernization. This explains why even till the present time in the Niger Delta region as elsewhere in the country, "every community is still headed by a chief or king. The chiefs of all the clusters form the council of chiefs, headed by a king/traditional ruler (officially recognized by the Nigerian Government)."[68] It must be added that because of the permanence in office of a traditional ruler in a community or a cluster of communities, no political office holder normally takes the risk of underestimating the political influence of a traditional ruler. In addition to the structure already described above are the various associations and groups such as the women groups, age groups, associations of the different artisans and cooperative societies as well as township unions of sons and daughters of communities in the Diaspora.

The social situation in the Niger Delta is characterised by high population growth, stagnating agricultural productivity and higher population density in areas that are habitable and economically viable. The per capita income is lower than that of the other parts of the country; the presence of some highly paid workers in the oil and gas sector has not improved the per capita income of the

---

67   NDRD Master Plan, p. 52.
68   NDRD Master Plan, p. 52.

region because of capital flight as most of them are non-indigenes. This is made more acute by the fact that the cost of living is one of the highest in the country. The level of education is below the average compared with other parts of Nigeria and the unemployment rate particularly among youths is high. One of the most serious social and health problems is the insufficient supply of clean drinkable water. 80% of recorded illnesses can be traced to the problem of unclean and untreated water. It is estimated that only about 20% of the population have access to clean drinkable water. Not only that there are no community water works, neighbouring flowing rivers serve as waste disposal depot. The problem of water pollution is worsened by oil spillage, and added to this is the fact that many villages in the Niger Delta live on rivers that flow from one village to the other. Majority of the villages have neither access to electricity nor any sanitary facilities. Education and health systems like in the rest of the country are problematic. The frustration and disappointment arising from the devastation of the host communities through pollution and other environmental problems caused by oil exploration and gas flaring have generated intense conflicts and instability in the sub region and beyond.[69]

Conclusion

From our brief presentation, the human development situation and problems in the Niger Delta can best be imagined. In the third chapter, we shall present in more details, with statistical support, the human development problems in the region which is actually the focus of this work. An attempt has just been made to give an overview of Nigeria generally and the Niger Delta region in particular.

---

69 Yemi Akinseye-George, Pumping Oil and Pumping money: Impact on Local culture in the Niger Delta Region of Nigeria. Cf. http://www.usos.be/download.aspe?c. Accessed on 15.10.2007.

2. Theoretical Framework of Development Concept

2.1 The Concept

The concept of development means different things to different people, depending on their background. Even within the same academic discipline its application and meaning vary. For instance, in the field of biology, we have animal development, plant development, developmental genetics, etc. 'Development' is an ubiquitous term in daily language. It can refer to the emergence or elaboration or evolution or improvement of almost anything: an idea, a paper, a project, a musical theme. It refers too to the unveiling and fulfilment of an inner potential, as of the images hidden within exposed photographic film; it is the opposite of envelopment.[70] It is expedient, therefore, to delineate the usage of the concept of development by various scholars at different epochs. This will enable us to arrive at a working definition for the purpose of our work.

To develop means that something grows or changes over a period of time and usually becomes more advanced, complete and severe. This implies, in a general sense, that development is a movement from one position to another in time and the movement is for the better.[71] The *Encyclopaedia Britannica* describes development as "the act, process or result of developing; the state of being developed: a gradual unfolding by which something is developed. It is the whole process of growth and differentiation by which the potentialities of something are realised. It is the gradual differentiation of an ecological community or a natural group; a gradual advance or growth through progressive changes (evolution)."[72] According to the World Bank Group, "Development is process of societal transformation that takes place over time."[73]

---

70 Des Gasper, The Ethics of Development, Edinburgh, University Press, 2005 p. 27.
71 Nwankwo. O. Peter, Social Development in Rural Communities in South-Eastern Nigeria, Frankfurt/M, IKO Verlag 2006 p. 27.
72 Encyclopaedia Britannica, Vol. I, Inc. Chicago 1986, p. 618.
73 THE WORLD BANK GROUP, Partners in Transforming Development: New Approaches to Developing Country-Owned Poverty Reduction Strategies, March 2000. http://www.imf.org/external/np/prsp/pdf/prspbroc.pdf . Visited on 19.02.2009.

Discussing the meaning of development Des Gasper points out that "development is a seductive term which has had connotations historically of the unfolding of a necessary path of progress. Its usage has often combined ideas of necessity, influenceable change and fundamental improvement. Taking different aspects of this historical package of ideas give different definitions."[74] For Des Gasper, therefore, development should be defined from a historical perspective.

For Goulet, development is a process of economic, technological, social, political and especially value change. He says, "development is above all else a question of human values and attitudes, goals self-defined by societies, and criteria for determining what are tolerable costs to be borne, and by whom, in the course of change."[75]

Similarly in answering the question 'what do we mean by development?' Barnett presents three meanings and three problem areas. First, he talks of 'development from within': this view says that "any object – a plant, an animal, a society – has the tendency to change its form. When we talk about societies in this way, we assume that the possibilities and the direction of change are the result only of processes within that society."[76] Secondly, he sees development as interaction: this view says that "development of anything results from the interaction of an object and its environment. Thus, an animal or a society changes because of a combination of the qualities and potentials within the object and the opportunities and resources available in the environment."[77] Thirdly, Barnett considers "development as interpenetration: this view says that we cannot really draw a sharp distinction between an object and its environment."[78] We can sum up development to mean the improvement of human conditions and his environment. We shall treat what constitutes development in details in the course of this work.

2.2 Historical Background of the Concept

In his work on the 'Theories of Development' P.W. Preston points out that the idea of development is very modern. It dates back to the post-Renaissance period of European history and it is associated with the idea of progress and perfection.

---

74 Des Gasper, The Ethics of Development, Edinburgh, University Press 2005, p. 5.
75 Goulet, Denis, Development Ethics at Work, London, Routledge Taylor and Francis Group 2006, p. xvii.
76 Barnett, Tony, Sociology and Development, p. 8.
77 Barnett, Tony, Sociology and Development, p. 8.
78 Barnett , Tony, Sociology and Development, pp. 8-9.

Relying on Passmore[79], Preston opined that it is the idea of the perfectibility of man and this idea of perfection originated from the Greek philosophers, which were later taken up by Christian theologians. In this regard Passmore summarised the idea of perfection in three ways: It is natural rather than a metaphysical process; it is attained with the help of other people rather than by God's grace or individual efforts; and a shift from an unrealisable purity of motive towards doing the maximum of good.[80]

While Nohlen and Nuscheler agree with Preston that development is a modern concept, they both seem to go beyond Passmore's claim that it is a natural rather than metaphysical process. They trace the origin of the concept to anthropology and theology. It is embedded in salvific historical teleology and entelechy.[81] Leibnitz gave the concepts *evolutio, developpment* and *envelopment* a meaning that shows headway, that is, the unwrapping of something wrapped up, something latent but still hidden, the unfolding of a talent. Development means movement, process, change and liberation.[82]

The concept is connected with that of optimism in the progressive philosophy of the 18th and 19th century, which claimed that individuals and societies were capable of producing a continually better world through their own effort. According to Kant, "all natural talents of a creature are ordered to completely and purposefully unwrap themselves, but the human beings must bring development to realisation through their effort."[83] This theorem can be applied to the current debate on development by implication: development cannot be developed; rather it means to develop oneself.

Nonetheless, both authors (Nohler and Nuscheler) point out that the concept already got a transitive meaning in the doctrine of justification of imperialism which was then taken up in 1945 by the modernisation theory, developed further and transformed into universal structure: that non-western societies should be developed (civilised) through transfer of economic, political and cultural forms of western life. This cultural imperialism, however well intended and packaged it might have been, replaced colonialism through a cultural disdain of 'primitive societies' which were believed to be incapable of any development without foreign aid.

---

79 In tracing the origin of the idea of development, Preston made use of Passmore's idea of perfectibility. Cf. PRESTON P.W., Theories of Development. London, Roughtledge & Kegan Paul 1982, p. 18.

80 Nwankwo, O. Peter, Social Development in Rural Communities in South-Eastern Nigeria, pp. 27-28 Cf. P.W. Preston, Theories of Development, pp. 18-19.

81 Nohlen, Dieter und Nuscheler, Franz (Hrsg), Was heißt Entwicklung? In Handbuch der Dritten Welt Bd 1, Bonn, J.H.W. Dietz Nachof 1993, p. 58.

82 Nohlen, Dieter und Nuscheler, Franz (Hrsg), Was heißt Entwicklung? p. 58.

83 Nohlen, Dieter und Nuscheler, Franz (Hrsg), Was heißt Entwicklung? p. 58.

Development in this sense was an after birth of colonialism. The original notion of development as unwrapping and unfolding of one's own capacities and abilities became revitalised after the realisation of the 'delusion of development' following the failure of development strategies, which tried to bring about development through the transfer of capital, personnel and know-how from outside.

A concise systematic presentation of the history of the concept of development by Langhorst appears very useful at this point. He points out that a new world-view is being recognised by the realisation since the end of World War II that we are all on the way to a common goal which is expressed in the concept "development". The establishment of the United Nations (UN) on the 24.10.1945 by the allied forces initiated by the United States indicates the willingness to be united.[84] The idea of development was brought into the vacuum of international political relations, which arose after the World War II, by the US President Harry S. Truman. In his declaration on 20 January 1949 he stated: "We must embark on a bold new program for making the benefits of our scientific advances and industrial progress available for the improvement of *underdeveloped areas.*"[85]

It is clear that not only is the standard given, but also here development means to transfer American and furthermore Western European model of society to the whole world, and with it to the entire humanity, a model that is based on the values and ideals of rationalistic enlightenment. The USA considered itself as the new world power that was in a position to create the model of a new global order, after the war.

According to Truman's development theory, the world is a unitary space to be united not through war, hegemony or military-political domination, rather on peaceful basis, through economic interdependence. On the basis of the American-European influenced worldview, development means equation with economic growth, accompanied by the cultural obligation in the sense of a civilizing model. In this sense, development means economic mobilization. Thus, the level of civilization of a country is measured by the level of its economic production. It holds then that development is the economic-cultural yardstick for civilization and pure capitalization as well as industrialization of former colonies. Langhorst points out further that the countries of the South that have become independent are adjusting first to this teleological world view: to overcome underdevelopment, one wants to adapt to the industrial nations; the outcome is the concept of 'developing country'.[86]

---

84 Langhorst, Peter, Kirche und Entwicklungsproblematik, Paderborn Ferdinand Schöningh 1996, p. 13.
85 Langhorst, Kirche und Entwicklungsproblematik, p. 14. Cf. also Staley, Eugene, The Future of Underdeveloped Countries. Political Implications of Economic Development, New York, 1961, p. 32.
86 Langhorst, Kirche und Entwicklungsproblematik, p. 14.

As reaction to the cold war between the power blocks in the East and the West in the 1950s, a process of self-consciousness set in. In April 1955, 29 Afro-Asian countries met at the Brandung Conference. These countries considered themselves as progenitors of the free block nations, as the third power/force in the world. In the context, the concept Third World became prevalent. From this period on many developing countries started to draw up development plans and models with the assistance of experts from industrialised countries.[87]

Since the 1960s, critique on the understanding of development as economic and social progress has proven it to be a fiction. However, the model of development has not been compromised. Instead, its scope has been expanded to include issues like agriculture, education, health, sport, family, religion as well as poverty eradication, unemployment, hygiene, etc. These are issues that concern the human person in his social and cultural context and converge in new development theories and strategies. The understanding is gradually gaining acceptance among scholars and development practitioners (particularly in the UN Human Development Reports since 1990s) that not only the economy or economic structures are to be regarded as key issues in development, but rather the human person is at the centre and the subject of every development.[88]

2.3 Historical Controversy: Modernization vs. Dependency Theories

Following President Truman's call for America to make the benefits of their scientific advancement and industrial progress available for the improvement of *underdeveloped areas*, some development experts seem to lay claim to a process of modernization or Americanization of the Third World countries as a development theory and strategy while others, the dependency theorists, think that such a theory and practice continue to make developing or underdeveloped areas dependent on industrialized countries like North America and core Western European countries. For dependency theorists, modernization theory is part of the causes of underdevelopment in the developing countries since particularly these countries were former colonies of the industrialized countries. The evolution of the controversy between these theories is our concern in this section. The work of Alvin Y. So is

---

87 Langhorst, Kirche und Entwicklungsproblematik, p. 15.
88 Langhorst, Kirche und Entwicklungsproblematik, p. 15.

instructive for this part of the work.[89] In other words, there are two main theories of development that are competing for attention or dominance, namely; modernization and dependency theories.

2.3.1 Modernization Theory

It is a description and explanation of the processes of transformation from traditional or underdeveloped societies to modern societies. It evolved from two ideas about social change developed in the nineteenth century: the conception of *traditional vs. modern societies,* and *positivism* that viewed development as societal evolution in progressive stages of growth. According to S.N Eisenstadt, "historically, modernization is the process of change towards those types of social, economic and political systems that have developed in Western Europe and North America from the seventeenth century to the nineteenth and have then spread to other European countries and then in the nineteenth and twentieth centuries to the South American, Asian, and African continents."[90] In other words, the hindrances to development are to be found in the heads, attitudes, and behaviours of people as well as in the social structures and value systems of traditional societies. Modernization simply says that the developing countries are underdeveloped because they are not able to free themselves from the chains of tradition. They have to be like, think, behave, produce and consume like the Western world.[91]

Similarly, Johannes Müller observes that the modernization theory holds that development means that traditional societies overcome their "backwardness" to modern societies. Modernization which is often equated with industrialization is synonym for development. On the other hand, traditionalism equally means backwardness and underdevelopment. Behind this idea is the conviction that modernization is an aimed, continuous and global historical process, which more or less follows the same procedure everywhere and which traditional societies cannot avoid continually.[92]

Given the historical context of this theory, Alvin noted that it was a historical product of three crucial events in the post-World War II era. First, there was the

---

89 So, Alvin Y., Social change and Development, Modernization, Dependency and World-System Theories, London, Sage Publication 1990. He is a Chinese Professor of sociology at the University of Hawaii, Manoa.

90 Eisenstadt, S.N. 1966: Modernization, Protest and Change, Englewood Cliffs, p. 1 Cf. Also http://www.bookrags.com/research/modernization-theory-eos-03/. Visited on 07.10.2008.

91 Nuscheler, Franz, Lern- und Arbeitsbuch Entwicklungspolitik, Bonn: Dietz 6·2005, p. 214.

92 Müller, Johannes, Entwicklungspolitik als globale Herausforderung – Methodische und ethische Grundlegung, Stuttgart: Kohlhammer 1997, p. 59.

rise of the United States as a superpower. While the other Western nations (like Great Britain, France, and Germany) were weakened by World War II, the United States emerged from the war strengthened, and became a world leader with the implementation of the Marshall Plan to reconstruct war-torn Western Europe. In the 1950s, the United States practically took over the responsibility of managing the affairs of the whole world. Second, there was the spread of a united world communist movement. The Soviet Union extended its influence not only to Eastern Europe, but also China and Korea in Asia. Third, there was the disintegration of the European colonial empires in Asia, Africa, and Latin America, giving birth to many new nation-states in the Third World. These nascent nation-states were in search of a model of development to promote their economy and to enhance their political independence. In such historical context, it was natural that American political elites encouraged their social scientists to study the Third World nation-states, to promote economic development and political stability in the Third World, so as to avoid losing the new states to the Soviet communist bloc.[93]

As a follow up, notable sociologists like Marion Levy Jnr.[94] approached modernization process by differentiating between Relatively Modernized and Relatively Non-modernized Societies. This is similar to Emile Durkheim's distinction between organic solidarity and mechanical solidarity in his study of social solidarity in the society. According to Emile Durkheim (1858-1917) in his work on the division of labour there are two principal sources of social cohesion or forms of solidarity: "archaic society dominated by mechanical solidarity or solidarity by similarities"[95] and "the modern society ruled by organic solidarity or solidarity arising from the division of labour"[96]. The latter finds the basis of her cohesion "on the increasing role differentiation and the attendant social interdependence."[97] For Durkheim the two kinds of solidarity by means of which any society coheres is reflected in the law of that society: "Life in general within a society cannot enlarge in scope without legal activity simultaneously increasing in proportion. Thus we may be sure to find reflected in the law all the essential

---

93 So, Alvin Y., Social Change and Development – Modernization, Development, and World-System Theories, New Dehli , Sage Publications 1990, p. 17.
94 Levy Marion J. Jr. (1918 – 2002). An American sociologist noted for his work on modernization theory. Levy was an advocate of structural functionalism in sociology. He was Professor of sociology at Princeton, a student of Talcott Parson.
95 Durkheim, Emile, The Division of Labour in Society, London: The Free Press, 1997, p. 31. Emile Dukheim is believed to be the father of modern sociology.
96 Durkheim, The Division Labour in Society, p. 68.
97 Prüller-Jagenteutel, Solidarität, p. 30.

varieties of social solidarity."[98] The varieties of social solidarity notwithstanding, it has always to do with a mutual interdependent and participation in a collective or common duty.

For Levy then, modernization is the process of moving from relatively non-modernized society to relatively modernized one. By borrowing initial expertise in planning, capital accumulation, skills and pattern of organisation, etc. without the cost of invention from relatively modernized society, the relatively non-modernized society can move up to the high level of the relatively modernized society.[99]

In the same vein, the sociologist, Neil Smelser[100] makes a sociological structural differentiation of the society. For Smelser, modernization generally involves structural differentiation because through the modernization process a complicated structure that performed multiple functions is divided into many specialized structures with each performing just one function. The new collection of specialized structures, as a whole, performs the same functions as the original structure, but the functions are preformed more efficiently in the new context than were in the old.[101]

Smelser gives the example of the structural functions of the traditional family and the functions of new modern structures and institutions. In the past, the traditional family had a complicated structure – it was large and multigenerational, with relatives living together under one roof. In addition, it was multifunctional. It was responsible not only for reproduction and emotional support, but for production (the family farm), for education (informal socialization), for welfare (care of the elderly), and for religion (ancestral worship). In the modern society, the family institution has undergone structural differentiation. It now has a much simpler structure – it is small and nuclear. The modern family has a lot of its old functions as well.

The corporate institution has taken over the employment function, the formal education institutions now provide schooling for the young, and the government has taken over the welfare responsibilities, and so on. Each institution specializes in just one function, and the new institutions collectively perform better than did the old family structure. Modern society is more productive, children are better educated, and the needy receive more welfare than before. He admits that struc-

98   Durkheim, The Division of Labour in Society, p. 25.
99   So, Alvin Y., Social Change and Development, pp. 23-26.
100   Smelser Neil J. (1930-) is an American sociologist, ex-director of the Center for Advanced Study in Behavioral Sciences (1994-2001) and Prof. emeritus of the University of California.
101   So, Alvin Y., Social Change and Development, p. 26 Cf. also Smelser, Neil, Toward a Theory of Modernization. In: Etzioni, Amitai and Etzioni, Eva (eds.) Social Change, New York, Basic Books, 1964, pp. 268-284.

tural differentiation is often accompanied by the problems of integration (i.e. coordinating the activities of the various new institutions) and social disturbances arising from the lack of integration among differentiated structures and concludes that modernization is not necessarily a smooth and harmonious process. He says this framework serves to draw attention to the examination of the problems of integration and social disturbances that are so common in the Third World countries.[102]

From the perspective of economics, W.W Rostow[103] presents modernization theory of development with his five Stages of Economic Growth. These five stages of economic development begin first with traditional society where the economy is dominated by subsistence activity and output is consumed by producers rather than traded. Any trade is carried out by barter, where goods are exchanged directly for other goods. Agriculture is the most important industry and production is labour-intensive, using only limited quantities of capital and tools. Resource allocation is determined very much by traditional methods of production.[104]

Second, the Transitional stage (the preconditions for take-off) is characterised by the rise of new entrepreneurs, the expansion of markets, the development of new industries, and so on. This is only a precondition stage because, even though economic growth has begun to take place, there is also a decrease in death rate and expansion of population size. There is little momentum for self-sustained economic growth because the large population size has, to a certain extent, consumed the entire economic surplus. Thus Rostow argues that a stimulus is needed in order to propel Third World countries beyond the precondition stage. This could take the form of political revolution that restructures major institutions or a favourable international environment with rising export demands and prices.[105]

Third, the Takeoff stage is attained when a country reaches a self-sustained economic growth. Such a country must have capital and resources must be mobilized so as to raise the rate of productive investment to 10% of the national income, otherwise economic growth cannot overtake the rate of population growth.

Fourth, Drive to Maturity: At this stage the economy is diversifying into new areas. Technological innovation is providing a diverse range of investment op-

---

102 So, Social Change and Development, pp. 26-29.
103 Rostow W. W (1916 – 2003) was an economist and political theorist who served as special assistant for National Security Affair to U.S President Lyndon B. Johnson. He developed the Rostovian take-off model of economic growth, one of the major historical models of economic growth.
104 So, Social Change and Development, p. 29.
105 So, Social Change and Development, p. 29. Demands for exported products with better prices from the Third World could propel fasten or propel modernization process.

portunities. The economy is producing a wide range of goods and services and there is less reliance on imports.

Fifth, High Mass Consumption: This stage is characterized by growth in employment opportunities, increase in national income, rise in consumer demands, and formation of a strong domestic market.[106]

Based on his five-stage model of growth (traditional society, precondition for takeoff, takeoff, drive to maturity and high mass-consumption), Rostow has found a possible solution for the promotion of Third World modernization. According to Rostow, if the problem facing Third World countries lies in their lack of productive investment, then the solution lies in the provision of aid to these countries in the forms of capital, technology, and expertise.[107] This model of Rostow is not without some limitations. Many development economists argue that his model was developed with Western cultures in mind and not applicable to Less Developed Countries.

In addition, its generalised nature makes it somewhat limited. It does not set down the detailed nature of the pre-conditions for growth. In reality policy makers are unable to clearly identify stages as they merge together. Thus as a predictive model it is not very helpful. Perhaps its main use is to highlight the need for investment. Like many of the other models of economic developments it is essentially a growth model and does not address the issue of development in the wider context. We shall return to this point later when we shall be evaluating modernization theory as a whole.

On the political dimension of modernization theory, Coleman[108] takes up the trend of thought similar to that of Smelser's process of differentiation. Firstly, Coleman refers to differentiation as the process of progressive separation and specialization of roles and institutional spheres in the political system. He gives as example, that political differentiation includes the separation of universalistic legal norms from religion, the separation of religion and ideology, and the separation between administrative structure and public political competition. The products of this process are: greater functional specialization, more structural complexity, and a higher degree of interdependence of political institutions. Secondly, he argues that equality is the ethos of modernity. And therefore, the politics of modernization is the quest for and the realization of equality.

What constitute equality are the notion of universal adult citizenship (distributive equality), the prevalence of universalistic legal norms in the government's

---

106   So, Social Change and Development, pp. 29-30.
107   So, Social Change and Development, pp. 29-30.
108   James Coleman (1926-1995) was an American sociologist and a Professor at the department of Social Action at the John Hopkins University.

relations with the citizenry (legal equality), the predominance of achievement criteria in the recruitment and allocation of political and administrative roles (equality of opportunity), and popular involvement in political system (equality of participation).[109] Thirdly, Coleman asserts that the quest for differentiation and equality may lead to the growth of political capacity of the system. Accordingly, modernization is considered by Coleman to be the progressive acquisition of political capacity for the system of government.

In sum, modernization theorists posit that the reasons for success or failure of development are to be found in the concerned societies. How good a society develops depends on a multiple of factors; from infrastructure, life styles of the people (motivation to work, diligence, educational level etc.), legal security, system of government, as well as economic conditions like the rate of savings and investment, etc. It follows that a state of backwardness or underdevelopment should be reduced or minimized by catching up with development in the sense of industrialization, democratization, building up of markets, organization of a solid education and training, as well as establishing effective state structures. For the modernization theorists, the European development process since the end of the 18th century would serve as paradigm.[110]

From whichever perspective modernization may be viewed, it is obvious that it considers development from the standpoint of the United States and other Western European countries. And such understanding of development is projected to the Third World countries. Modernization theory presumes that Western countries are modern while Third World countries are traditional. In order to develop, "Third World countries must drop their traditional traits and acquire Western traits."[111]

2.3.2 Dependency Theory

Just as the modernization school can be said to examine development from the point of view of the United States and other Western countries, the dependency school can be said to view development from a Third World perspective. According to Alvin So, "The dependency school presents the voices from the pe-

109 So, Social Change and Development, 31. Cf also "Modernization: Political Aspects." In: Davi L. Sills (ed.) International Encyclopedia of Social Sciences (Vol. 10), New York: Macmillan, 1968, pp. 395-402.

110 Kesselring, Thomas, Ethik der Entwicklungspolitik, Gerechtigkeit im Zeitalter der Globalisierung, München: C. H. Beck, 2003, p. 134.

111 So, Social Change and Development, p. 52.

ripheries that challenge the intellectual hegemony of the American modernization school."[112]

The idea of dependency was initiated by the first director of United Nations' Economic Commission for Latin America (ECLA), Raul Prebisch in the 1950s. But its greatest exponent and co-founder was the German economic historian and sociologist, André Gunder Frank (Berlin, February 29, 1929 – Luxemburg, April 23, 2005) with his work "Development of Underdevelopment" published in 1966. Another prominent scholar on dependency theory is the former Brazilian President Fernando Henrique Cardoso.

In the 1950s, the dependency theory was elaborated by the United Nations Economic Commission for Latin America (ECLA or CEPAL),[113] responsible for studying the development problems from an underdeveloped perspective (Cardoso 1972; Janvry and Garramon 1977a). André Gunder Frank[114] simplified and popularized many of the ideas of dependency produced by ECLA through his work published in English. The ECLA neo-Marxist economists blamed the declining terms of trade as the key reason why Latin America remained less developed than wealthier nations. Since the value of manufactured goods has a tendency to rise, and the value of food and raw materials to decline, poor countries had to sell more and more goods to get less and less in return. For the dependency theorists, Latin America's development situation was a result of capitalist development, just as industrialization in the North was a result of this process.[115]

Although dependency theory was largely applied to Latin America, the concepts of dependency were also applied to other parts of the world. For example, Walter Rodney's book *How Europe Underdeveloped Africa* (1972) argued that the interference of European powers in African social, economic and political processes throughout the nineteenth century created a situation of dependency and led to the impoverishment of African peoples. In contrast to the modernization theory, the dependency theory states that underdeveloped countries could not follow the same path of development as the industrialized countries due to the heritage of colonialism. The formal colonies still maintain their economic dependency on their colonial masters long after they had attained independence.

---

112 So, Social Change and Development, p. 91.
113 So, Social Change and Development, 93. Under the ECLA program, Latin America was asked to produce food and raw materials for the great industrial centres and in return, Latin America would receive industrial goods from these centres. But as it turned out, reliance on exports of food and raw materials would inevitably lead to a deterioration of Latin America's terms of trade, which would further affect its domestic accumulation of capital.
114 Gunder, Frank, Andre, Latin America. Underdevelopment or Revolution, New York: Monthly Review Press 1969.
115 Willis, Katie, Theories and Practices of Development, New York: Routledge 2008, p. 69.

The dependency theorists view unfavourable external influences as the causes of the backward development of the less progressive or less developed societies. The argument of the dependency theorists is based on the fact that despite their attainment of independence, former colonies still persist in economic dependency in a double sense: partly, dependency on former colonial masters, and partly, dependency on the unpredictable wave of world market, whereby in many countries, particularly in Latin America, the structures of dependency are extended into the society.[116]

The protagonists of dependency theory argue that the most important obstacle to national development is not lack of capital, entrepreneurial skills, or democratic institutions; rather, it is to be found outside the domain of the national economy. The historical heritage of colonialism and the perpetuation of the unequal international division of labour are the greatest obstructions to the national development of Third World countries. The world economic condition ensures the flow of economic surplus from Third World countries to Western capitalist countries. Thus Third World countries generally suffer from declining terms of trade with Western countries. It is opined that the underdevelopment of the Third World countries is caused by the continued influx of economic surplus from there to the Western countries. Thus underdevelopment in the periphery and development in the core are two aspects of a single process of capital accumulation, leading to regional polarization in the global economy.[117] For the dependency theorists, as long as the world economic system remains unchanged and development is measured only in terms of economic growth, the countries at the periphery will never develop.

2.4 Continuation of the Debate in the Era of Globalization

We have, in the last section, tried to picture the theoretical controversy between modernization and dependency theories of development from a historical perspective. In this section, we shall examine how the debate between these theories is being carried out today, in this era of globalization. In other words, how is the problem of poverty and underdevelopment to be addressed in this era of globalization? We shall, as first step, consider what globalization is and what it means for

---

116 Kesselring, Ethik der Entwicklungspolitik, p. 134.
117 So, Social Change and Development, 104. Periphery are the countries of the Third World while core the industrialized countries of Europe and North America.

development of the Third World. Second, we shall look at the issues in Washington-and Post-Washington Consensus. Third, we shall treat the most recent Poverty Reduction Strategy Paper (PRSP) coming from the Britton Wood Institutions.

2.4.1 The Process of Globalization

Globalization is a current issue that imposes itself on everyone directly or indirectly. It refers to a complex phenomenon consisting of a rapid expansion of global interaction and interdependence in areas of economics, finance, trade, labour, travel, transportation, communications and technology, culture, and the arts. Various authors have attempted to describe it as a process, a situation, a structure, a force, and an era. The term has generated an enormous literature across many disciplines. Globalization can be defined as "the closer integration of the countries and peoples of the world which has been brought about by the enormous reduction of costs of transportation and communication, and the breaking down of artificial barriers to the flows of goods, services, capital, knowledge, and (to a lesser extent) people across borders."[118]

Among several literatures, we consider the publication by the German Bishops' Conference Research Group on the Universal Tasks of the Church[119] as instructive for this section of our work. Not only that the study presents a concise understanding of globalization and its workings, it also discusses how globalization can be made to benefit the poor people in the industrialized countries as well as bring about the desired development in the countries of the Third World.

The publication points out that the process of globalization is reflected in its manifestations and causes. Its manifestations on the economy show that there has been increase in world-wide production capacities, growth in world trade, growth in Foreign Direct Investment (FDI) and joint ventures as well as integration of the international capital movements. Not to be overlooked too are the regional imbalances of globalization. The study shows, for example, that on the one hand, the share of East and South East Asia has almost quadrupled since 1980, largely influenced by China's demand for international capital. The share of FDI in developing countries taken up by Latin America fell in the years from 1980 to 1995, on the other hand. The study shows further, that countries in Central and Eastern Europe are those that largely benefited from inflow of foreign

---

118   Stiglitz, Joseph, Globalization and its discontents, London: Penguin Books, 2002, p. 9.
119   German Bishops' Conference Research Group on the Universal Tasks of the Church, The many faces of globalization – Perspectives for a humane world order – Study of the Group of Experts "World Economy and Social Ethics" and the church agencies Adveniat, Caritas international, Misereor, Missio Aachen, Missio München and Renovabis, 2000.

capital because they have price stability. Africa, the continent with the largest population after Asia, only attracted about 3 per cent of world-wide FDI in 1995, as against 6 per cent in 1988. The fall in the economic balance of this continent as against the rest of world is attributable to globalization. This proves that the continent of Africa is almost entirely excluded from the trend towards greater integration of the world's economy.[120]

From the socio-cultural dimension, globalization follows the model of Western civilization with all its effects on the economy, politics and its attendant impact on the environment. For many people in the developing nations, "the term globalization has replaced that of 'dependency', so familiar in the seventies."[121]

In spite of the success stories of globalization, not only that the gap between the rich the poor is getting wider, there are also new forms of poverty and underdevelopment as evidence in the increasing incidents of migrations from the South to the North, drug trafficking and human trafficking particularly of youth and women, increasing wave of crimes and terrorism. While unskilled workers in industrialized nations are being marginalized, millions of people in the Third World countries are still hungry, with no access to portable water, health care facility, and basic goods and services. These phenomena are not unconnected with the logic of globalization, which is the drive for economic growth and prosperity. The study reveals that globalization has great potential for providing opportunities for progress. But it lacks a moral and ethical compass. We need to take charge of and steer the globalization process in a direction that promotes economic and social inclusion – not exclusion. In order that the globalization will be of benefit to all, the study under consideration proposes an ethical orientation that should be based on the dignity of the human person everywhere and not just economic growth and prosperity for its sake. We shall return to the socio-ethical dimension of globalization in the third part of this work.

2.4.2 The Washington- and Post-Washington Consensus

Since the early 1970s many developing countries, particularly in Latin America, had begun to feel the pinch of failure of the Import Substitution Industrialization (ISI) strategy of development and the malfunctioning of centrally planned economies which they have adopted since the 1950s and 1960s. The basis of ISI was that foreign aid should support the large-scale modern industries that governments of developing countries nurtured through trade protection, directed credits

---

120   German Bishops' Conference, The many faces of globalization, pp. 15-20.
121   German Bishops' Conference, The many faces of globalization, p. 11.

and subsidies. ISI was characterized by strong government intervention in the market. Over the subsequent two decades, however, the dominant development assistance strategy changed significantly twice, away from the government-centred ISI toward the market and away from market toward non-market institutions. The market-centred strategy is referred to as the Washington Consensus and it emerged to counter the disappointing results of ISI. The Washington Consensus was a paradigm that focused on economic growth and advocated the market as a universally efficient mechanism to allocate scarce resources and promoter of economic growth. Under its influence the international financial institutions, the World Bank and IMF, actively encouraged governments to dismantle controls on the market. Scarcely a decade later, in the mid-1990s, the Washington Consensus was replaced by a contrasting paradigm, termed post-Washington Consensus that emphasized the need of different institutions for different economies and recog-nized cases in which government's market interventions can play a positive role. The post-Washington Consensus focused on poverty reduction, emphasizing the need of delivery by government and civil society to the poor, of social services, such as education and health care and advocated the initiative ("ownership") of aid-receiving communities.[122]

2.4.2.1 Washington Consensus

The term "Washington consensus" was coined in 1989 by J. Williamson, senior Fellow, Institute for International Economics, to describe a set of market-oriented reforms that the sluggish state-directed economies of Latin America could adopt to attract private capital to the region following the crippling debt crisis of the "lost decade" of the 1980s.[123] It is called Washington consensus because it expresses the convictions of the two Bretton Wood institutions – the World Bank and the International Monetary Fund – that the recommended eco-nomic strategies would address the problems of poverty and underdevelopment in Latin America, as well as other developing countries.

According to Williamson, the ten reforms that constituted the Consensus were: (a) Fiscal Discipline (b) Reordering Public Expenditure Priorities (c) Tax Reform (d) Liberalizing Interest Rates (e) A Competitive Exchange Rate (f)

---

122 Yujiro Hayami, From the Washington Consensus to post-Washington Consensus: Recent Changes in the Paradigm of International Development Assistance, pp. 2-3. Cf. also http://www.fasid.or.jp/daigakuin/fa_gr/kyojyu/pdf/s. Visited on 15.4.2008.

123 Clift, Jeremy, Beyond the Washington Consensus. In: Finance & Development September 2003, p. 9. Cf. also http://www.imf.org/external/pubs/ft/fandd/2003/09/pdf/clift. pdf. Accessed on 9.3.2008.

Trade Liberalization (g) Liberalization of Inward Foreign Direct Investment (h) Privatization (i) Deregulation (j) Property Rights[124]

Williamson merely coined the term Washington Consensus in 1989 but the content has been in the practice of the World Bank since early 1980s. Discussing the shifts of emphasis in development aid from 'Poverty to Structural Adjustment' (SAP), Waeyenberge traces it to the early 1980s when the World Bank started the Structural Adjustment Program.[125]

The objectives of the SAP and that of Washington Consensus, which is the expression of the conviction of the Britton Wood institutions, were aimed at economic policy reform with the purpose of eliminating all obstacles to a 'perfect market' as the presumed optimal path to growth. What came to be referred to as the 'Washington Consensus' proposed (or rather imposed) stabilization of the economy through control of money supply, and enhancement of growth through a set of supply-side measures aimed at boosting private sector.[126]

The hope that WC would bring economic growth to Latin America as well as to the Third World countries remains unfulfilled. In fact, in less than a decade it started to be bombarded with an avalanche of criticisms from within and outside of Washington, both positive and negative. Such criticisms have led some scholars to ask the question: Is it Washington Consensus or Washington confusion?[127] Others like the (former) President of the World Bank J. Wolfensohn and Simon Maxwell have declared the Washington Consensus dead[128] while others like

---

124 Williamson, J, A Short History of the Washington Consensus. Paper commissioned by Fundacion CIDOB for a conference "From Washington Consensus towards a new Global Governance", Barcelona, September 24-25, 2004 Cf. http://www.petersoninstitute.org/publications/papers/williamson 0904-2.pdf accessed on 17.3.2008.

125 Waeyenberge, Elisa Van, From Washington to Post-Washington Consensus – Illusions of Development. *In*: Jomo, K.S and Fine, Ben (eds.), The New Development Economics After the Washington Consensus, London: Zed Books 2006, p. 24. He says: "The turn of the decade saw a set of events that were to affect the development scene dramatically: as second oil shock provoked another oil price hike, interest rates followed suit [...] and right-wing administrations came to power in the major OECD (Organization for Economic Cooperation and Development) countries. The last implied political hostility to aid, and the former two resulted in a dramatic increase in the financial needs of developing countries. Furthermore, inside the Bank, concern mounted with regard to the limited influence of project lending over policy.".

126 Waeyenberge, Elisa Van, From Washington to Post-Washington Consensus, p. 26.

127 Naim, Moises, Fads and Fashion in Economic Reforms: Washington Consensus or Washington Confusion?, IMF, Washington, 1999. Cf also http://www.imf.org/external/pubs/ft/seminar/1999/reforms/Naim.HTM. Accessed on 30.3.2008.

128 Maxwell, Simon, The Washington Consensus is dead! Long live the meta-narrative. Cf http://web.worldbank.org/WBSITE/EXTERNAL/EXTABOUTUS/ORGANIZATIONAL//o,,contentMDK:20206669~memPK. Accessed on 12.4.2008.

Joseph Stiglitz are more sympathetic by proposing the Post-Washington Consensus.[129] The criticisms against WC were not unconnected with its affiliation to SAP. The occasion of the fiftieth anniversary of World Bank in 1994 provided a lot of individuals and organizations the opportunity to demonstrate their grievances against World Bank and IMF. Such protests are summed up in the phrase: "50 years is enough".[130] The myriad of criticisms is put together by Colens Parkins when he says:

> It has long been the object of criticism from outside the charmed circle of global policy makers, where SAPs is associated with 'a sharp increase in unemployment, a fall in the remuneration of work, an increase in food dependency, a grave deterioration of the environment, a deterioration in healthcare systems, a fall in admission to educational institutions, a decline in the productive capacity of many nations, the sabotage of democratic systems, and the continued growth of external debt.[131]

2.4.2.2 Post-Washington Consensus

All these criticisms against World Bank, IMF and Washington Consensus took a dramatic turn when an insider, Joseph Stiglitz, a onetime chief economist and senior vice-president of the World Bank and former chairman of President Clinton's Counsel of Economic Advisors delivered the 1998 WIDER annual lecture in Helsinki, Finland titled "More Instruments and Broader Goals: Moving Towards the Post-Washington Consensus".

To begin with, Post-Washington Consensus is a constructive criticism and improvement on the Washington Consensus. Stiglitz begins his critic of the Washington Consensus by questioning its goal, which is economic growth he says:

> The Washington Consensus held that good economic performance required liberalized trade, macroeconomic stability and getting prices right. Once the government handled these issues – essentially, once the government "got out of the way" – private markets would produce efficient allocations and growth. To be sure, all of these are important for markets to work. It is very difficult for investors to make good decisions when inflation is running at 100 percent annually. But the policies advanced by Washington Consensus are hardly complete and sometimes misguided. Making markets work requires more than just low inflation, it requires sound financial regulation, competition policy, and policies to facilitate the transfer of technology, and transparency, to name some fundamental issues neglected by the Washington Consensus[132].

129   Stiglitz, Joseph, More Instruments and Broader Goals: Moving Toward the Post-Washington Consensus, Cf. http://www.globalpolicy.org/socecon/bwi-wto/stig.htm. Accessed on 12.4.2008.
130   See http://www.50years.org.
131   Colen, Parkins, A Post-Washington Consensus? Cf http://www.cseweb.org.uk/downloads/parkins.pdf accessed on 11.4.2008 see also Amin, S., Capitalism in the Age of Globalization, London: Zed Press 1997, p. 13.
132   Stiglitz, More Instruments and Broader Goals: Moving Toward the Post-Washington Consensus, Cf. http://www.globalpolicy.org/socecon/bwi-wto/stig.htm. Accessed on 12.4.2008.

Stiglitz argues to debunk the claim that 'once the government got out of the way – private markets would produce efficient allocation growth' by pointing to the successful East Asian development stating that: "after all here was a cluster of countries that had not closely followed the Washington Consensus prescriptions but had somehow managed the most successful development in history. To be sure many of their policies – like low inflation and fiscal prudence – were perfectly in line with the Washington Consensus. But many, especially in the financial sector, were not."[133] He further points out that this observation was the basis for the World Bank's East Asian Miracle study (World Bank 1993) as well as a stimulus for the recent rethinking of the role of the state in economic development. He disagrees with those who claim that the system of state intervention in the economy is the root of East Asia financial crises by referring to the "not inconsiderable success of the past three decades, to which the government, despite its occasional mistakes, has certainly contributed. These achievements are real."[134] He then makes a case for government's involvement in financial regulation and corporate governance.

Emphasizing on making the markets work better, Stiglitz reviews the experience of Latin American countries in the 1980s which catalyzed the Washington Consensus by showing that many countries that have adopted the Washington Consensus as packaged by IMF and World Bank were not faring better. He then concludes that "the origins of the current financial crises are elsewhere and the solutions…will not be found in the Washington Consensus either."[135] Stiglitz is of the view that the major sources of the macroeconomic instability are weak financial sectors. According to him:

The focus on freeing up markets, in the case of financial market liberalization, may actually have had a perverse effect, contributing to macro-instability through weakening of the financial sector. More broadly, the focus on trade liberalization, deregulation, and privatization ignored other important ingredients required to make an effective market economy, most notably competition: competition, in the end, may be more important than these other ingredients in determining long-term economic success. I will also argue that there were other ingredients that are essential to economic growth that too were left out or underemphasized by the Washington Consensus; one has been widely recognized within the development community, education, but the others, such as the improvement of technology, have perhaps not received the attention they deserve.[136]

133 Stiglitz, More Instruments and Broader Goals: Moving Toward the Post-Washington Consensus. Cf. http://www.globalpolicy.org/socecon/bwi-wto/stig.htm. Accessed on 12.4.2008.
134 Stiglitz, More Instruments and Broader Goals, pp. 3-6.
135 Stiglitz, More Instruments and Broader Goals, pp. 3-6.
136 Stiglitz, More Instruments and Broader Goals, pp. 3-6.

Furthermore, for him, in successful financial markets, regulations serve four purposes: maintaining safety and soundness (prudential regulation), promoting competition, protecting consumers, and ensuring that underserved groups have some access to capital. He then points out that "Washington Consensus developed in a context of highly regulated financial systems, while many of the regulations were designed to limit competition, not to promote of the four legitimate objectives of regulation. But all too often the dogma of liberalization became an end in itself not a means to a better financial system."[137]

Concluding his discussion on making markets work better, he emphasizes the need to broaden macroeconomic policy beyond a single minded focus on inflation and budget deficits. He says "the set of policies which underlay the Washington Consensus are neither necessary nor sufficient either for macro-stability or long-term development; but the agenda for creating sound financial markets should not confuse means with ends; financial liberalization is not the issue – redesigning the regulatory system should be."[138] The fundamental Theorems of Welfare Economics, the results that establish the efficiency of a market economy, have two basic assumptions: private property and competitive markets. Many countries – especially developing and transition economies – are lacking in both.

Stiglitz's criticisms of the goals of the Washington Consensus and his suggested enlargement (Broadened Goals of Development) which also reflect his own Post Washington Consensus are put succinctly as follows:

> The Washington Consensus advocated a set of instruments (including macroeconomic stability, liberalized trade, and privatization) to achieve a relatively focused goal (economic growth). The Post-Washington Consensus begins by recognizing that broader set of instruments are necessary to achieve those goals. I have discussed some of the most important instruments, including financial regulation, competition policy, investments in human capital, and policies to facilitate the transfer of technology ... the post – Washington Consensus also recognizes that our goals are much broader. We seek increases in living standards – including improved health and education – not just increases in measured GDP. We seek sustainable development, which includes preserving our natural resources and maintaining a healthy environment. We seek equitable development, which ensures that all groups in society enjoy the fruits of development, not just the few at the top. And, we seek democratic development, in which citizens participate in a variety of ways in making decisions which affect their lives. Knowledge has not kept with proliferation of our goals. We are only beginning to understand the relationship between democratization, inequality, environmental protection, and growth. What we do know holds out the promise of developing complementary strategies that can move us toward all of these objectives.[139]

---

137 Stiglitz, More Instruments and Broader Goals, p. 7.
138 Stiglitz, More Instruments and Broader Goals, p. 8.
139 Stiglitz, More Instruments and Broader Goals, p. 16.

He illustrates his position by discussing four goals in some details, namely: Education (promoting human capital), Environment, Investments in Technology and Participation. He warns that "unless the economy is competitive, the benefits of free trade and privatization will be dissipated in rent seeking, not directed towards wealth creation. And if public investments in human capital and technology transfers are insufficient, the market will not fill the gap."[140] Elsewhere he says:

> Trade liberalization *accompanied by high interest rates* is an almost certain recipe for job destruction and unemployment creation – at the expense of the poor. Financial market liberalization *unaccompanied by an appropriate regulatory structure* is an almost certain recipe for economic instability – and may well lead to higher, not lower interest rates, making it harder for poor farmers to buy the seeds and fertilizer that can raise them above subsistence. Privatization, *unaccompanied by competition policies and oversight to ensure that monopoly powers are not abused*, can lead to higher, not lower, prices for consumers. Fiscal austerity, *pursued blindly*, in the wrong circumstances, can lead to high unemployment and a shredding of the social contract.[141]

With the Post-Washington Consensus, not only has poverty reduction become an immediate objective of development assistance to the Third World or developing countries, there is now emphasis on the indispensable role of non-market institutions such as government and the civil society in development efforts.[142]

2.4.3 Poverty Reduction Strategy Paper

It seems that the Post-Washington Consensus has made the World Bank to become conscious of its motto "Our dream is a world without poverty". Since 1999 the WB and IMF have adopted a new approach to development designated as "Comprehensive Framework for Development" (CFD); and at their annual congress in autumn the same year they decided on a new condition for debt cancellation for highly indebted poor countries as well as pre-condition for access to new development aid. This condition is tagged the "PRSP – Poverty Reduction Strategy Paper" which should be a comprehensive, detailed document prepared by a developing country explaining its own plan for reducing poverty as its development program.

The PRSP must include four core elements: (1) a description of the country's participatory process; (2) a poverty diagnosis; (3) targets, indicators, and monitoring systems; and (4) priority public actions, which should be summarized in tabular form for a three year time horizon. PRSPs are the basis for concessional

---

140 Stiglitz, More Instruments and Broader Goals, p. 18.
141 Stiglitz, Globalization and its discontents, p. 84.
142 Yujiro, Hayami, From the Washington Consensus to the post-Washington Consensus, p. 21.

assistance from both the IMF and the World Bank, including debt relief under the HIPC (Heavily Indebted Poor Countries) Initiative so that its acceptance by the joint WB/IMF assessment committee is very important.[143] The PRSPs are prepared by member countries in broad consultation with stakeholders and development partners, including the staffs of the World Bank and the IMF.[144] The insistence on participatory process in the formulation of the document was to insure the ownership of the document by each country, particularly to ensure the involvement of the poor people in the formulation and implementation of the document. PRSP is supposed to shift attention from mere economic growth to the well-being of the people which is being hindered by poverty.

Theoretically, the idea behind PRSP is laudable. But since its commencement critics have expressed doubt if in practice the poor people will benefit from it. The criticisms are based on the assumption that if the poor people would benefit from PRSP then it must be seen and noted that the poor actually participate in its preparation and implementation – a fact that is hard to ascertain. Indeed, an appraisal of PRSP after five years carried out by VENRO (Verband Entwicklungspolitik deutscher Nichtregierungsorganisationen e. V.), the network of German NGOs in the field of development cooperation in collaboration GKKE (Gemeinsame Konferenz Kirche und Entwicklung), Joint Conference of Church and Development, in 2005, titled "Fighting Poverty without the Empowering the Poor" has given credence to these doubts. According to the report, in most of the countries examined, the poverty reduction strategies are dominated by an alliance of technocrats of respective governments and influential international institutions, in particular, the IMF, the World Bank and a handful of bilateral donors. The appraisal concludes by saying that: "Significant improvements in the effects of the PRSP approach can only be reckoned with if more scope is given for societal involvement and, above all, if an empowerment of the poor sections of the population themselves is attained."[145]

In 2004 Nigeria produced its own document termed National Economic Empowerment and Development Strategies (NEEDS). The document is a brainchild of the Presidential Economic Team made up of the then Chief Economic Advisor to the President and the chief salesman of the reform Professor Charles Soludo (later Governor of the Central Bank of Nigeria up to May 2009), Dr. Ngozi Okonji-Iweala, the Finance Minister, Mrs Oby Ezekwesili, the Special Assistance

143   Yujiro, From the Washington Consensus to the post-Washington Consensus, p. 24.
144   2005 International Monetary Fund, Nigeria: Poverty Reduction Strategy Paper – National Economic Empowerment and Development Strategy, IMF Country Report No. 05/433. Cf. http://www.imf.org. Accessed on 6.1.2008.
145   VENRO/GKKE, Fighting Poverty without Empowering the Poor? Cf. http://www.venro.org/fileadmin/publikationen/E. Visited on 7.1.2010.

on Budget and Due Process, Mallam El-Rufai, the Minister of the Federal Capital Territory (FCT) Abuja, and a sundry of Abuja technocrats. At the launch of the program ex-President Obasanjo expressed the hope that Nigeria will be great again. His hope is that NEEDS would catalyze a process of economic growth, poverty reduction and value re-orientation in Nigeria.[146]

In the meantime some state governments have also replicated the document to reflect the needs of their respective states and tagged it SEEDS – State Economic Empowerment and Development Strategies and local governments too are expected to have done the same with Local Economic Empowerment and Development Strategy – LEEDS.

By 2006 the NEEDS document fulfilled one of the conditions for debt relief and further loans from WB and IMF to Nigeria and so the Paris Club worked out a package that relieved Nigeria $30 billion out of her then $35 billion debt, leaving her with just $5 billion outstanding. What has happened to NEEDS since its publication, how far NEEDS has contributed to poverty reduction in Nigeria and more importantly how far have the poor benefited from the strategies are questions for further research. Now that most of those who drew up the document are no longer in government, and knowing the problem of continuity in Nigeria, it is doubtful whether the document would continue to be implemented.

2.5 Normative Concepts of Development

Here we shall address the following questions: How should development be carried out? What should constitute development? What should be the achievement of development? In doing this we shall consider some normative concepts of development that aim to answer the questions. We shall consider the concepts of sustainable development, attacking poverty, the magic pentagon of development, the human development and measuring development.

2.5.1 Sustainable Development

In 1972 a human environment conference was held in Stockholm. During the course of the conference, the idea of "sustainable development" was developed. While this ambiguous term initially referred to the importance of linking development and

---

146　Amadi, Sam, Contextualizing NEEDS: Politics and Economic Development. *In*: Amadi, Sam, Ogwo, Frances (eds.), Contextualizing NEEDS: Economic/Political Reform in Nigeria, Lagos, HURILAWS & CPPR 2004, p. 1.

environmental protection, over time this definition expanded and its significance has grown. In 1983 the United Nations set up an independent organization called The World Commission on Environment and Development (WCED) chaired by the then Prime Minister of Norway, Gro Harlem Brundtland. The aim of WCED was to examine the problems of the environment and development facing the world and to consider possible solutions. These solutions should be considered not just for current generations, but with an awareness of long-term issues.[147] In 1987 the WCED published its findings in a report titled, *Our Common Future*, in which the Brundtland Commision laid out the environmental challenges facing the world, and examined how environmental destruction would limit forms of economic growth, but also how poverty and disadvantage contribute to environmental destruction. The report stressed the importance of 'sustainable development' as a goal towards which the international community should work. According to the WCED, 'sustainable development' is "development that meets the needs of the present generation without compromising the ability of future generations to meet their own needs."[148] This definition refers to the belief that although the main goal of development is to improve living conditions for the poor, if underdeveloped countries follow the current resource-based development process, development will be environmentally unsustainable.

The WCED's thesis of sustainable development posits that the present generation has been reckless and wasteful in both its exploitation and use of natural resources by pursuing a series of socioeconomic and industrial policies which endanger global environmental security. Viewed as a doctrine of qualitative societal change, sustainable development underlines the perils of global environmental degradation – oil spills, deforestation, acid rain, ozone depletion, toxic waste, etc. – and calls for the creation of policies that would lead to the reduction of damage to the environment, meet the "needs" of the present generation and also allow "future generations" to meet their own needs. To achieve the above objectives, the WCED urged governments to pursue a new developmental strategy that can both ensure continued economic growth and ecological stability with less exploitation and use of natural resources.[149] Thus there has to be a balance between development and environmental degradation. Consequently, this model of development promotes a standard of consumption that lies within the limits of what is ecologically feasible. In other words, sustainable development is

147 Willis, Katie, Theories and Practices of Development, p. 158.
148 World Commission on Environment and Development (WCED), Our Common Future, New York: University Press 1987, p. 43.
149 Igho, Natufe, The Problematic of Sustainable Development and Corporate Social Responsibility: Policy Implications for the Niger Delta, A Conference Paper, http://www.urhobo.kinsfolk.com/Conferences/SecondAnnualConference/ConferenceM. Visited on 22.5.2007.

a process that fulfils current human needs without endangering the opportunities of future generations.

To further stress the importance of sustainable development, the United Nations' international conference in Rio de Janeiro in 1992 was focused on ways in which sustainable development could be achieved. Sustainable development has become a key element in development theorizing and policy-making. For example, the 2003 World Development Report is titled Sustainable Development in a Dynamic World: Transforming Institutions, Growth and Quality of Life (World Bank 2003). We are of the view that there is the need for an ecological ethics that would bring into focus intergenerational, global and environmental justice. We shall address this point later in part three.

2.5.2 Attacking Poverty

The simplest and commonest equation of underdevelopment says: Underdevelopment = Hunger + Disease + Ignorance (illiteracy).[150] This constitutes the concept of absolute poverty which the former President of the World Bank, Robert McNamara described in his famous Nairobi speech in 1973 as situation of such degrading conditions of life like, illness, illiteracy, undernourishment and neglect. The description of underdevelopment as a survival question and empty stomach brings the concept into proper focus.

It is not enough to describe underdevelopment as poverty. There is the need to clarify what constitutes poverty precisely. During the World Summit for Social Development in Copenhagen 1995, certain clarifications were made between overall poverty, absolute poverty and relative poverty. In the final declaration of the summit, overall poverty was defined in the following terms to differentiate it from absolute poverty:

Poverty has various manifestations, including lack of income and; productive resources sufficient to ensure sustainable livelihoods; hunger and malnutrition; ill health; limited or lack of access to education and other basic services; increased morbidity and mortality from illness; homelessness and inadequate housing; unsafe environments; and social discrimination and exclusion. It is also characterised by a lack of participation in decision-making and in civil, social and cultural life. It occurs in all countries: as mass poverty in many developing countries, pockets of poverty amid wealth in developed countries, loss of livelihood as a result of economic recession, sudden poverty as a result of disaster or conflict, the poverty of low-wage workers, and the utter destitution of people who fall outside family support systems, social institutions and safety-nets. *Absolute* poverty is a condition characterised by severe deprivation of basic

---

150 Nohlen, Dieter & Nuscheler, Franz, Was heißt Unterentwicklung? *In*: Handbuch der Dritten Welt 1, p. 31.

human needs, including food, safe drinking water, sanitation facilities, health, shelter, education and information. It depends not only on income but also on access to social services[151].

Relative poverty defines poverty in terms of its relation to the standards which exist elsewhere in society. This is understood primarily in terms of inequality. According to Roach and Roach (1972:23) relative poverty is applicable to 'the bottom segment of the income distribution'. Townsend (1979:915) refers to poverty as a form of relative deprivation, which is the absence of or inadequacy of those diets, amenities, standards, services and activities which are common or customary in society.[152]

The World Bank's World Development Report 2000/2001 is titled "Attacking Poverty". The report is based on the earlier result of a research carried out by the World Bank on the situations and views of 60,000 poor people in 60 countries, titled the "Voices of the Poor".[153] As the title indicates, the report discusses the causes of and ways to attack poverty in all its forms – relative, absolute and overall. Specifically, chapter two focuses on "Causes of Poverty and a Framework for Action". According to the report, the poor people have highlighted the dimensions and causes of poverty as follows:

• Lack of income and assets to attain basic necessities – food, shelter, clothing, and acceptable level of health and education.
• Sense of viocelessness and powerlessness in the institutions of state and society.
• Vulnerability to adverse shocks, linked to an inability to cope with them.[154]

Though it is conventional, while discussing the causes of poverty, to mention such things as climatic conditions, imbalance of trade, political bias against the poor and rural areas, colonial heritage, rural-urban migration etc., the effects of all these are summed up in the three main causes listed above.

It is a fact that poverty is an outcome of economic, social, and political processes that interact with and reinforce each other in ways that can worsen or ease the deprivation poor people face every day. It is for this reason that the World Bank suggests that "to attack poverty requires promoting opportunity, facilitating empowerment, and enhancing security – with actions on local, national, and global levels. Making progress on all three fronts can generate the dynamics for sustain-

151 Gordon, David & Spicker Paul, The International Glossary on Poverty, London: Zed Books 1999, p. 98. Cf. also The Copenhagen Declaration and Programme of Action: World Summit for Social Development 6-12 March 1995, New York: United Nations Department of Publications.
152 Gordon, & Spicker, The International Glossary on Poverty, p. 113.
153 World Development Report 2000/2001, Attacking Poverty, p. 3.
154 World Development Report 2000/2001, Attacking Poverty, p. 34.

able poverty reduction."[155] In other words, any action geared towards attacking poverty must go beyond the motto 'think globally and act locally', rather, thought and action must be carried out on the three levels of local, national and global. Though the stories and conditions of poor people all over the world are similar, the specific strategic approaches and priorities to be adopted in attacking poverty need to be worked out in each country's economic, socio-political, structural, and cultural context – indeed, each community's. But even though choices depend on local conditions, it is generally necessary to consider scope for action in all three areas – opportunity, empowerment, and security – because of their crucial complementarities.[156]

Promoting opportunity for the poor "means jobs, credit, roads, electricity, markets for their produce, and the schools, water, sanitation, and health services that underpin the health and skills essential for work."[157] These material opportunities are central to the life of the poor and therefore any strategy or approach at attacking poverty must offer these opportunities to them.

In facilitating empowerment of the poor, it must be noted that "the choice and implementation of public actions that are responsive to the needs of poor people depend on the interaction of political, social, and other institutional processes. Access to market opportunities and to public sector services is often strongly influenced by state and social institutions, which must be responsive and accountable to poor people. Achieving access, responsibility, and accountability is intrinsically political and requires active collaborations among poor people, middle class, and other groups in society."[158] This again requires changes in governance that make public administration, legal institutions, and public service delivery more efficient and accountable to all citizens. In addition, there is the need to strengthen the participation of poor people in political processes and local decision-making. Of no less importance is removing the social and institutional barriers that result from distinctions of gender, ethnicity and social status.

Attacking poverty demands enhancing security for poor people, by reducing their vulnerability. Reducing vulnerability – to economic shocks, natural disasters, ill health, disability, and personal violence – is an intrinsic part of enhancing well-being and encourages investment in human capital and in higher-risk, higher-return activities. This requires effective national action to manage the risk of economy-wide shocks and effective mechanisms to reduce the risks faced by poor people, including health- and weather-related risks. It also requires building

---

155   World Development Report 2000/2001, Attacking poverty, p. 37.
156   World Development Report 2000/2001, Attacking Poverty, p. 37.
157   World Development Report 2000/2001, Attacking Poverty, p. 7.
158   World Development Report 2000/2001, Attacking Poverty, p. 7.

the assets of poor people, diversifying household activities, and providing a range of insurance mechanisms to cope with adverse shocks – from public work to stay-in-school programs and health insurance.[159]

Each of the strategies (opportunity, empowerment and security) affects underlying causes of poverty and therefore they are complementary. For example, promoting opportunity through assets and market access increases the independence of poor people and thus empowers them by strengthening their bargaining position relative to state and society. It also enhances security, since an adequate stock of assets is a buffer against adverse shocks. Similarly, strengthening democratic institutions and empowering women and disadvantaged ethnic and racial groups – say, by eliminating legal discrimination against them – expanding the economic opportunities for the poor and socially excluded. Strengthening organizations of the poor can help ensure service delivery and policy choices responsive to their needs and can reduce corruption and arbitrariness in state actions as well. Helping poor people cope with shocks and manage risks put them in a better position to take advantage of emerging market opportunities.[160]

The basic strategy (opportunities, empowerment and security) for attacking poverty and underdevelopment notwithstanding, we think that since the simple illustration of poverty and underdevelopment is = hunger + disease + ignorance, attacking poverty should begin with fighting hunger through provision of sufficient food by the way of promoting agriculture, at the same time the provision of health facilities with the essential drugs as well as provision of educational facilities to enable people have access to basic education. This is because hungry children must be fed before they can go to school. Hungry adults must eat before they can work. Sick people (those who are not terminally ill) must recover their health before they can make a contribution to society. In such cases of extreme poverty and poor health, economic development becomes temporarily a second priority, until the basic human needs are satisfied. And because the majority of poor people all over the world live in rural areas and are generally engaged in agriculture, efforts at attacking poverty and underdevelopment must be focused on agriculture and rural development, while not losing sight of the urban poor.

2.5.3 The Magic Pentagon of Development

Attempt is being made to ascertain some normative notions of development. We have taken cognizance of sustainable development and attacking poverty according

159 World Development Report 2000/2001, Attacking Poverty, p. 7.
160 World Development Report 2000/2001, Attacking Poverty, p. 7.

to the World Bank. In this section we shall dwell on the magic pentagon of development as a normative concept.

In his attempt to answer the question "what is development?" Dudley Seers proposes the "Magic Triangle" of development as its goal, namely: Food, Labour, and Social Equality.[161] Similarly Charles Elliot (1970) describes development in a trilogy to mean Growth, Social Equality, and Independence. In like manner, the economist Michael Todaro raised another three core goals of development to be "satisfying the basic needs, self respect of the person, freedom from internal and external foreign determination – in the more fundamental sense of freedom or emancipation from alienating material conditions of life and from social servitude to nature, ignorance, other people, misery, institutions, and dogmatic beliefs."[162] Dieter Nohlen and Franz Nuscheler, relying on a work by Senghaas, present the Magic Pentagon of Labour, Growth, Equality/Justice, Participation and Independence as complementary aspects and goal of Development.[163] This understanding of development is multidimensional.

2.5.3.1 Labour

Labour is an unavoidable core element and not just an independent variable of development. Labour is the most essential resource for the development of any society. Not only is this available in abundance in developing countries, its potentials are not yet exhaustive. From an individual perspective, the condition should be created, which enables the people in the Third World to overcome poverty on their own efforts or at least be able to satisfy their basic needs.[164] It is in this sense that the slogan being promoted by ILO – International Labour Organisation is tenable, 'development through labour' or development through creation of employment opportunities. Through labour or gainful employment not only is one able to create economic value to the society, one's self-fulfilment or self-realization is guaranteed as well.

2.5.3.2 Economic Growth

Economic growth is a necessary, but not sufficient condition for development. Besides quantitative components, growth that is agreeable with development

---

161 Langhorst, Kirche und Entwicklungsproblematik, p. 41. Cf. also Seers, Dudley, Was heißt Entwicklung? In: Peripherer Kapitalismus, 37-67.

162 Nohlen & Nuscheler, Was heißt Entwicklung? In: HDW, Bd 1, p. 65. Cf. alsoTodaro, M.P., Economic Development in the Third World, 4th ed. New York: 1989, p. 90.

163 Langhorst, Kirche und Entwicklungsproblematik, p. 41. Cf. also Nohlen &Nuscheler, Was heißt Entwicklung? pp. 54-67.

164 Langhorst, Kirche und Entwicklungsproblematik, pp. 41-42.

must fulfil qualitative claims. That is to say, growth that conforms to development is connected with qualitative conditions: First, its usefulness to the increment of overall societal welfare, in other words, poverty alleviation. Second, on the condition that it is not at the cost of the fundamental natural source of livelihood.[165] For example, any industry or sector of the economy that renders the havoc of environmental degradation is not acceptable. In the light of sustainable human development, growth must take cognisance of human welfare and his natural habitat. Ecological consideration is part and parcel of development.

2.5.3.3 Equality/Justice

Development entails in itself the idea of material well-being, human dignity, security, justice and equality.[166] The postulate of justice creates the necessary qualitative correction to growth, in order to avoid growth without development. Development demands both the production as well as the just distribution of society's multiple products; this is because experience has shown that differences in income do not necessarily lead to higher savings or investment, rather to consuming luxury goods, unproductive accumulation of property and capital flight. Considered from the perspective of its ethical desirability, distributive justice must not prevent growth.[167] Injustice is not based on economic circumstances rather it is based on political power. Thus, all those who hold political power must see to it that economic systems or structures serve the benefit of all or at least the majority in the society.

2.5.3.4 Participation

Here development is understood to be a complete socio-cultural process, which must lead to a social system, on which the most possible number of members of a social institution partake in its formation and achievement made possible through co-consultation, co-decision making and execution of decision. Participation is the opposite of marginalisation or exclusion. It demands the active involvement of all in process of securing and distribution of the political, social, cultural and material goods of a given society. The basic needs strategy demands a development politics for the poor, a development through the poor; it means grassroot democratic development from below. It is against all forms of unnecessary bureaucracy and pre-packaged decisions and orders from above. According to Nohlen und Nuscheler, "Development takes place when people and communities

---

165   Nohlen & Nuscheler, Was heißt Entwicklung? p. 67.
166   Nohlen & Nuscheler, Was heißt Entwicklung? P. 70 Cf. also Brandt Bericht 1980, p. 65.
167   Nohlen & Nuscheler, Was heißt Entwicklung? p. 70.

act as subjects and are not treated as objects; when they claim their autonomy, self-reliance and self-confidence, when they plan and execute projects. Development means to be and to change, and not to have."[168]

2.5.3.5 Independence

Some synonyms for independence are sovereignty, self-reliance, autonomy, etc. Each of these concepts is the opposite of structural dependency. Independence and sovereignty encompass a catalogue of demands: greater internal and external political freehand to operate in the course of governmental sovereignty, self-determination over societal and political constitution, cultural identity, domestic decolonisation and overcoming of structural heterogeneity as heritage of colonialism.[169] This implies that governments' policy decisions, and other public institutions like the parliament's freedom of choice and decisions may not be influenced or imposed by foreign powers. Neither should the existence of a state and the self development of the citizenry entrusted to it be endangered nor its political independence and territorial integrity be jeopardised in any way. Viewed from this perspective, "development is a process, which enables people to develop their capacities, to gain self confidence and lead a life fulfilled with dignity. Development is a process that liberates people from fear of poverty and exploitation. It is escape from political, economic or social oppression. Political independence receives its ideal meaning through development...Therefore development is equated with growing of individual and collective self-reliance."[170] Even when the fact of interdependence in the world politics tends to overtake the value of independence, small states still have a right to autonomous development, and thus freedom from servitude. This point is necessary in view of the conditionalities of Structural Adjustment Program (SAP), the Washington- and Post-Washington Consensus, etc., in this era of globalization as earlier discussed.

2.5.4 UNDP Concept of Human Development

The UNDP defines the basic objective of development as creating an enabling environment for people to enjoy long, healthy, and creative lives. And it sees human development as a process of enlarging people's choices.[171] Enlarging people's choices is achieved by expanding human capabilities. Essentially the

---

168 Nohlen & Nuscheler, Was heißt Entwicklung?, p. 71. Cf. also IFAD-Dossier, 17/1980.
169 Langhorst Kirche und Entwicklungsproblematik, p. 43.
170 Nohlen & Nuscheler, was heißt Entwicklung?, p. 73.
171 UNDP Human Development Report 1990, pp. 9-10. Cf. also UNDP HDR 1995.

three capabilities for human development are for people to lead long and healthy lives, to be knowledgeable and to have access to the resources needed for a decent standard of living and be able to participate in the life of the community. If these basic capabilities are not achieved, many choices are simply not available and many opportunities remain inaccessible.[172] Beyond all these are other areas of choice that people equally value. These are political, economic and social freedom, opportunities for being creative and productive, enjoying self-respect, empowerment and a sense of belonging to a community and guaranteed human rights.[173] It is in this sense that the UN human development report since 1990 has been focusing on the need to consider the other side of human development that cannot be captured in monetary terms or income alone.

Series of Human Development Reports since 1990 have demonstrated that there are two basic sides to human development. One is the formation of human capabilities, such as improved health, knowledge and skills. The other is the use that people make of their acquired capabilities for productive purposes, for leisure or for being active in cultural, social and political affairs. It is obvious that the concept of human development is much broader than the conventional theories of economic development. Economic growth models deal with expanding GNP rather than enhancing the quality of human lives. It means that all development must have the well-being of the human person as its goal.

2.5.5 Measuring Development

Measuring development is no doubt problematic just as defining it is. However, whichever way development is defined, there is the need for its actors to measure development for obvious reasons. For example, policy makers may want to find out what the social development position (as defined by the policy-makers) of a population is in order to have informed policy formulation. Government and international agencies may want to assess the impact of a particular development initiative and therefore want to have measurements from both before and after the project.[174] Similarly, NGOs, academicians or campaigning organizations seeking to improve living conditions for marginalized groups, may want information about the nature of marginalization, etc.

In ascertaining the development level of a country, it is conventional to measure its economic development by looking at the Gross National Product

---

172   Human Development Report 2001, p. 9.
173   Human Development Report 1990, box 1.1.
174   Willis, Katie, Theories and Practices of Development, London: Routledge 2005. p. 13.

(GNP) per capita. GNP or national income is divided by the total population, which gives an average income for a country as a whole. This is widely used as an indicator of development and national poverty. Also in use to measure economic growth is the Gross Domestic Product (GDP); the difference between them is that GDP is the sum total of internally generated revenue, while GNP includes all foreign income.[175] Other indicators associated with GNP as a measure for economic growth include human capital formation, human resource development, human welfare or basic human needs.

Theories on which GNP and the likes are based, view human beings primarily as means rather than as ends. To this end, the UNDP Human Development Reports 1990 observes that, "they are concerned only with the supply side – with human beings as instruments for furthering commodity production. True, there is a connection, for human beings are the active agents of all production. But human beings are more than capital goods for commodity production. They are also the ultimate ends and beneficiaries of this process. Thus, the concept of human capital formation or human resource development captures only one side of human development and not its whole."[176] There are several statistical problems such as those regarding the informal sector and exclusion of the household sector in GNP. This makes Mahbub ul Hag to point out that "GNP reflects market prices in monetary terms. Those prices quietly register the prevailing economic and purchasing power in the system – but they are silent about the distribution, character or quality of economic growth. GNP also leaves out all activities that are not monetized – household work, subsistence agriculture, and unpaid services. And what is more serious, GNP is one-dimensional: it fails to capture the cultural, social, political and many other choices that people make."[177]

It is obvious then that there is the need for another set of measurement that is not necessarily confined to money and income as index or yardstick. Such set of measurement must focus on the human beings who are the subjects or end users of money and income. In the light of the foregoing, UNDP has in its human development reports developed the following measurement to reflect the other side of GNP. The measurement entails the following elements:

- **Human Development Index (HDI)** which measures the overall achievement in a country in three basic dimensions of human development – longevity, knowledge and decent standard of living. It is measured by life expectancy,

175 David Gordon and Paul Spicker (eds.), The International Glossary on Poverty, London: Zed Books, 1999, p. 72.
176 UNDP Human Development Reports 1990, p. 11.
177 Mahbub ul Hag, The Birth of the Human Development Index. In: Fukuda-Parr, Sakiko & Shiva, A.K., Readings in Human Development, New York: Oxford Press 2006, p. 127.

educational attainment (adult literacy and combined primary, secondary and tertiary enrolment) and adjusted income.

- **The Human Poverty Index (HPI):** While the HDI measures overall progress in a developing country in achieving human development, the human poverty index reflects the distribution of progress and measures the backlog of deprivations that still exists. The (HPI)[178] measures deprivation in the same dimensions of basic human development as the HDI. The HPI-1 measures poverty in developing countries. The variables used are the percentage of people expected to die before age 40, the percentage of adults who are illiterate, deprivation in overall economic provisioning – public and private – reflected by the percentage of people without access to health services and safe water, and the percentage of underweight children under five.

- **HPI-2** measures human poverty in industrialized countries. Specifically, HPI-2 is for 17 Organization for Economic Cooperation and Development (OECD) countries (Northern countries) and HPI-1 for 88 developing countries.[179] Because human deprivation varies with the social and economic conditions of a community, this separate index has been devised for industrialized countries, drawing on the greater availability of data. It focuses on deprivation in the same three dimensions as HPI-1 and one additional one, social exclusion. The variables are the percentage of people likely to die before age 60, the percentage of people whose ability to read and write is far from adequate, the proportion of people with disposable incomes of less than 50% of the median and the proportion of long-term unemployed (12 months or more).

- **Gender-related Development Index (GDI)** measures achievements in the same dimensions and variables as the HDI, but captures inequalities in achievement between women and men. It is simply the HDI adjusted downward for gender inequality. The greater the gender disparity in basic human development, the lower a country's GDI compared with its HDI. To calculate HDI, indicators from the various dimensions are converted to an index from 0 to 1 to allow for equal weighting between each of the three dimensions. Once an index value has been calculated for each dimension, they are averaged and the final figure is the HDI. The higher the value the higher too is the level of human development.

---

178   The UNDP's 1997 Human Development Report introduced the Human Poverty Index. This draws heavily on Amartya Sen's capability concept (capabilities and characteristics) and defines poverty as 'the denial of choices and opportunities for a tolerable life'. The HPI attempts to operationalise this concept by focusing on those groups whose choices are heavily constrained in each of the three areas used in HDI.

179   Willies Katie, Theories and Practices of Development, London, Routledge 2005, p. 14.

- **Gender Empowerment Measure (GEM)** reveals whether women can take active part in economic and political life. It focuses on participation, measuring gender inequality in key areas of economic and political participation and decision-making. It tracks the percentages of women in parliament, among administrators and managers and among professional and technical workers – and women's earned income share as a percentage of men's. Differing from the GDI, it exposes inequality in opportunities in selected areas.[180] These measures do not reflect such items as roads, water, electricity and appropriate waste management which are necessary to determine the quality of life of citizens.

Conclusion

From the foregoing, there is the need for another development politics that would focus on the welfare of the people or rather put the human person at the centre stage of economic activities. There is the need for a development politics that would consider the human being as subject, beneficiary and end in itself and not just as means to attain economic growth.

---

180 Ali-Akpajiak, Sofo C.A. & Pyke, Toni, Measuring Poverty in Nigeria, Oxford: Oxfam 2003, p. 7.

3. The Development Problems in Niger Delta

3.1 Introduction

Attempts have been made in the previous chapter to examine the concepts of development, the theories as well as measurement and some normative understanding of development. In the following, attention will be focused on the existential problems of development confronting the people of the Niger Delta region in Nigeria. Without doubt, the main problem facing the people in the Niger Delta region is that of poverty and underdevelopment. This fundamental problem is compounded by environmental pollution associated with exploration and exploitation of oil and gas in the region. Concomitant with the presence of oil and gas industry is the phenomenon of HIV/AIDS in the region. Another major factor that is heating up the society is the legal framework put in place by the Nigerian government and the oil companies to secure the control of the oil. The conflicts in the region are partly the consequences of the biting effects of poverty and underdevelopment, the environmental problem, the HIV/AIDs problem and the legal and regulatory framework of the government and the oil companies.

The Nigeria government has been responding to these problems by setting up development commissions to address the problem of poverty and underdevelopment in the region. On the one hand, the commissions have undertaken some infrastructural development projects, on the other hand, bedeviled by the problems of the composition of the membership, undue politicization, shortage of fund, corruption and mismanagement, the commissions have not been able to address the poverty and underdevelopment adequately in the region. The above argument seeks to give answer to the classical "Niger Delta Question", that is: why abundant human and natural resources have had so little impact on poverty alleviation in the region and why past development planning efforts have failed to address the region's needs. We shall rely on the UNDP's Niger Delta Human Development Report (HDR) 2006. Our choice of the HDR is informed by the fact that it is the first comprehensive sub-regional human development report on the region.[181]

181　No doubt, there have been several reports by organizations including those by Environmental Rights Action (ERA), Institute of Human Rights and Humanitarian Law (IHRHL), Movement for the Survival of Ogoni People (MOSOP), Human Rights Watch, African Network of Eco-

The development problems of the region have always been an issue in Nigerian politics.[182] However, the Niger Delta problem has taken a dramatic national and international dimension since the 1990s. Many scholars[183] on the Niger Delta have demonstrated that several attempts have been made in the past by minority groups in the Niger Delta to articulate the development problems but with little success. It is commendable on the part of the minority groups to have made the region's development problems both national and international issues since the 1990s.[184] Issues that have been the main concern of the minority groups in region are political (exclusion from the government of Nigerian State), social (non-

nomic and Environmental Justice (ANEEJ), Centre for Law Enforcement Education (CLEEN), Women Aid Collective (WACOL), Niger Delta Environmental Survey (NDES), Niger Delta Wetland Centre, Centre for Advanced Social Sciences (CASS) and Centre for Democracy and Development (CDD). The uniqueness of the report is that from conception to implementation, emphasis was placed on challenges of the region as articulated by people of the region. From the lead consultant (Environmental Resources Managers Ltd) to the participants at the stake-holders' consultative meetings in Abuja, Port Harcourt and Calabar, there was high level participation by citizens of the region. Cf. Otive Igbuzor, A Review of Niger Delta Human Development Report 2006, Cf. also http://akanimoreports.blog.co.uk/2006/09/22/nigeria_activist_takes_on undp_over_niger_ delta. Accessed on 17.11.2007.

182 The Niger Delta development problem predates Nigeria's Independence. This is evidenced by the Willink's Commission of 1957 set up by the British Colonial Government to look into Niger Delta regional issues. The commission acknowledged that the region deserves special attention; the Niger Delta Volunteer Force (NDVF) led by Isaac Adaka Boro to create the Niger Delta republic, but without success in 1966 and the activities of MOSOP led by Ken Saro Wiwa and other 8 judicially murdered Ogonis, etc.

183 For example, Ukeje, Charles, "Oil Capital, Ethnic Nationalism and Civil Conflicts in the Niger Delta of Nigeria", unpublished PhD thesis, Faculty of Administration, Obafemi Awolowo University, Ile-Ife, 2004. Others are Omoweh Daniel, Shell Petroleum Development Company, the State and Underdevelopment of Nigeria's Niger Delta – A Study in Environmental Degradation, African World Press, Trennton, New Jersey, 2005 and Obi Cyril, The Changing Forms of Identity Politics in Nigeria under Economic Adjustment – The Case of the Oil Minorities Movement of the Niger Delta.

184 Activities of such groups as the Movement for the Survival of Ogoni People (MOSOP), particularly its articulation of the concerns of the Ogoni people in the famous Ogoni Bill of Rights (OBR) presented to the government of General Ibrahim Babangida in 1990, its continuous agitations for their right that was climaxed by judicial the killing of the "nine Ogonis" in 1995 by the government of late General Sani Abacha; the Ijaw people, through the instrumentalism of the All Ijaw Youth Congress have also made a declaration called The KAIAMA DECLARATION at the end of the All Ijaw Youth Conference which was held in the town of Kaiama on the December 11, 1998 Others include the Charter of demands by the Movement for the Payment of Reparations to Ogbia (MORETO), the Ogbia Charter, the Isoko Youth Charter (why we struck), the Resolutions of Urhobo Economic Summit, the Communiqué of the Itsekiri Patriots General Conference, the Aklaka Declaration of the Egi people etc. All these Charters, Declarations and Communiqué follow more or less the same pattern and practically address the issues of development in the Niger Delta.

availability of social infrastructure like, road, drinkable water, electricity, educational facility, and healthcare services), economic (lack of employment opportunities, shortage of land and food, etc), and environmental pollution. These issues can be summed up in the problem of poverty, which concerns basically the condition of the human person in the society.

3.2 Underdevelopment

The previous chapter describes the theoretical framework and the normative concepts of development. Generally, it is clear that development is the opposite of poverty and underdevelopment. To bring the theoretical framework and the normative concept to bear on the Niger Delta situation, it is necessary to find out the nature and the extent of the poverty and underdevelopment in the region. This can be presented through indicators of poverty and the incidence of poverty in the region.

3.2.1 Poverty: Meaning and Forms

Indicators of poverty reflect the various levels and forms of poverty. Owing to the fact, that different people associate different things with the term poverty, it is difficult to offer a universally acceptable definition of poverty. However, Scholars[185] have made distinction between six pairs of understanding poverty as follows:

1. Absolute poverty	Relative poverty
2. Material poverty	Non-material poverty
3. Objective poverty	Subjective poverty
4. Primary poverty	Secondary poverty
5. Voluntary poverty	Non-voluntary poverty
6. Permanent poverty	Temporary poverty

---

185 German Bishops' Conference, Social Security Systems as Elements of Poverty Alleviation in Developing Countries, Study by the Group of Experts on „World Economy and Social Ethics", Bonn 1998, p. 13.

Absolute poverty describes the conditions of life like illness without medical care, illiteracy, undernourishment and neglect. It is condition characterized by severe deprivation of basic human needs, like food, safe drinking water, sanitation facilities, health, shelter, education and information. It is lack of income and access to social services. In other words, absolute poverty is the absence of basic necessities of life; food, clothing and shelter. **Relative poverty** describes a situation of inequality in a given society. It is based on comparing the standards which exist elsewhere in the society. Relative poverty is a poverty measure based on a poor standard of living or low income relative to the rest of the society. Unlike absolute poverty, it does not necessarily mean that those concerned cannot lead a dignified life; it merely means that because of the existing distribution structures, individual people and groups are at a disadvantage when compared with others.[186] It may lead to social exclusion. In other words, someone is considered to be in relative poverty when he or she appears to have more than someone who is in absolute poverty yet has less than others have in terms of income, property, and other resources.[187] Relative poverty is applicable to 'the bottom segment of the income distribution'. It is a form of relative deprivation, which is the absence of or inadequacy of those diets, amenities, standards, services and activities which are common or customary in a given society.[188] In addition, it describes a way of life characterized by low calorie intake, inaccessibility to adequate health facilities, low quality education system, low life expectancy, high infant mortality, low income, unemployment and underemployment and inaccessibility to various housing and societal facilities.[189] Common to both absolute and relative poverty is the fact that those concerned are at a disadvantage.

Material poverty is the situation in which the disadvantage refers to aspects of meeting material needs. It covers that aspect of poverty which is defined by access to goods which serve to ensure physical existence. **Non-material poverty** entails other aspects of the quality of life, such as social, ethical, religious and cultural values. It also includes aspects of political system to which the persons and groups are subjected, like political freedom and human rights.[190]

Objective poverty covers the disadvantages to individual persons and groups, irrespective of whether they are perceived as such by those concerned. It describes observable conditions like of level income, the standard of consumption or a basket of goods. **Subjective poverty** is the perception of poverty by those concerned, notwithstanding whether poverty exists in objective terms or

---

186   German Bishops' Conference, Social Security Systems, p. 13.
187   Ali-Akpajiak & Pyke, Measuring Poverty in Nigeria, p. 6.
188   Gordon & Spicer, The International Glossary on Poverty, p. 113.
189   Ali-Akpajiak & Pyke, Measuring Poverty in Nigeria, p. 5.
190   German Bishops' Conference, Social Security Systems, p. 14.

not. According to the group of experts from German Bishops' Conference, subjective poverty entails "the feeling of shortage with regard to elements of the standard of living which are regarded as being primarily very much characterized by the individual perception, or by the perception influenced by members of certain groups within society (e.g. in access to material goods, to education, to the possibility to live a certain lifestyle, and so on). It is also based on the standard which people set for themselves."[191]

Secondary poverty is the result of the inability to utilize sufficiently available resources efficiently to prevent poverty. In other words, the state of poverty would not have occurred to the persons or groups if they had used the sufficient available resources efficiently. It means that access to sufficient resources does not necessarily guarantee escape from absolute poverty. For instance, alcoholism and drug addiction could prevent sufficient nutrition and healthcare for addicted family members, not minding the fact that sufficient resources are actually available. **Primary poverty** occurs when the available resources do not suffice to prevent poverty, even if they were managed efficiently.[192]

Non-voluntary poverty arises when those concerned are unable to overcome poverty in spite of all their efforts. This could be because their resources are insufficient to obtain the goods required in order to meet their basic needs. **Voluntary poverty** is a result of a decision taken by those concerned themselves. It is not the case that there are no sufficient opportunities and resources to provide for the basic needs, rather they have refrained from doing so and have opted to utilize the available resources for other purposes. For example, people may opt for material poverty in order to able to attain non-material values which they may consider to be of higher value. The Gospels provide an example of the condition for Christ's discipleship as that of voluntary poverty (Mark 10, 17-31 and Luke 14, 25-33).[193]

Temporary or transitory poverty describes a period of lack of resources due to a season of low income or periodic poor climatic condition. This could be of a regular nature (e.g. seasonal, related to cyclical changes in the economy) or irregular (e.g. unemployment, illness or natural disasters). In the period of sufficient high income, it is possible theoretically, for people to protect themselves against the risks associated with the period of low income by preserving their surplus through savings or insurance. They may also incur debt to make up during the low income period. **Permanent poverty** is a situation of continuous period of low income for persons or groups such that those concerned are constantly at subsistence level of existence.

191 German Bishops' Conference, Social Security Systems, p. 14.
192 German Bishops' Conference, Social Security Systems, p. 14.
193 German Bishops' Conference, Social Security Systems, p. 15.

In the light of the distinctions made above, one may safely state that people are poor if they do not have a minimum income which suffices to cover their basic nutritional and other needs. As we shall see in the section that follows, the phenomenon of mass poverty in the Niger Delta region demands that attention be focused on addressing the problems of absolute, material, objective and non-voluntary poverty. This is because these forms of poverty are 'sufficiently' available in the region.

In light of the foregoing, it is imperative to highlight the level of poverty in the Niger Delta region. There is a certain level of development in the Niger Delta region, but there is also the reality of poverty and underdevelopment. To demonstrate this, we shall limit our examples to the general incidence of poverty in Nigeria as whole, the HDI and the HPI-1 for the region as indicators. That is not to say that the GDI and the GEM are less important.

3.2.2 Incidences of Poverty

Table 1: Incidence of Poverty in the Niger Delta, 1980-2004[194]

	1980	1985	1992	1996	2004
Nigeria	28.1	46.3	42.7	65.6	54.4
Edo/Delta	19.8	52.4	33.9	56.1	Delta 45.35
					Edo 33.09
Cross River	10.2	41.9	45.5	66.9	41.61
Imo/Abia	14.4	33.1	49.9	56.2	Imo 27.39
					Abia 22.27
Ondo	24.9	47.3	46.6	71.6	42.15
Rivers/Bayelsa	7.2	44.4	43.4	44.4	Rivers 29.09
					Bayelsa 19.98

Source: National Bureau of Statistics 2004.

The National Bureau of Statistics does not give any definition of poverty; it however provides a description of the dimensions of poverty in its Nigeria Poverty Profile 2010. It states: "The scourge of poverty goes beyond mere measurement of a household's expenditure or welfare. Poverty has many dimensions and may include inadequate access to government utilities and services, environmental issues, poor infrastructure, illiteracy and ignorance, poor health, insecurity, social and political exclusion. In urban areas, the burden of demand of services has effects on school enrolment, access to primary health care, growth of unsanitary urban slums. Also in rural areas, poverty manifests itself more in the agricul-

---

194   NDHDR, p. 35 Cf. National Bureau of Statistics 2004.

tural sector and food security. For any meaningful economic growth and poverty reduction, there is the need to enhance and improve access to social services, including health and education."[195]

Following the indices (see table 1) of poverty in the Niger Delta region, it is evident that poverty in the region has increased since 1980. The Niger Delta Human Development report 2006, reveals that poverty incidence (table 1) in Nigeria was 28.1 percent in 1980. It rose to 46.3 percent in 1985. It declined slightly to 42.7 per cent in 1992, before soaring dramatically to 65.6 per cent in 1996. Estimates from the Central Bank of Nigeria (1999) were even higher, with the Bank putting the overall poverty rate for the country at 69 per cent in 1997.[196]

In the Niger Delta, the situation is similar to that at the national level as shown above. Except for Rivers and Bayelsa states where poverty incidence seems to have stabilized at around 44 per cent after an initial jump from 7.2 percent, the poverty level increased between 1980 and 1996 (44.3%). In line with national estimate, poverty incidence declined between 1996 and 2004.

Table 2: HDI for the Niger Delta States, 2005[197]

State	Life Expectancy	Education Index	GDP Index	HDI
Abia	0.492	0.578	0.560	0.543
Akwa Ibom	0.506	0.683	0.540	0.576
Bayelsa	0.455	0.523	0.520	0.499
Cross River	0.556	0.630	0.565	0.584
Delta	0.587	0.636	0.621	0.615
Edo	0.579	0.602	0.600	0.594
Imo	0.503	0.546	0.591	0.547
Ondo	0.501	0.575	0.512	0.529
Rivers	0.563	0.590	0.620	0.591
Niger Delta	0.527	0.596	0.570	0.564
Nigeria				0.470
Indonesia				0.728
Venezuela				0.792

Source: ERML fieldsurvey 2005

---

195 http://www.nigerianstat.gov.ng/uploads/latestRelease/46e10622a9d47f73d5ea082c4ca7cc53b c734016.pdf.

196 Niger Delta Human Development Report 2006, p. 35.

197 To calculate HDI, indicators from the various dimensions are converted to an index from 0 to 1 to allow for equal weighting between each of the three dimensions. Once an index value has been calculated for each dimension, they are averaged and the final figure is the HDI. The higher the value the higher too is the level of human development. Cf. www.photius.com/rankings/human_develop men_index_1975-2005.

A Comparison of the Niger Delta's HDI of 0.564 with that of Nigeria's 0.470 shows that the Niger Delta region is slightly better that than Nigeria as whole: however, comparing the Niger Delta region with other oil producing countries or regions that are in similar situation with Nigeria, like Idonesia's 0.728 and Venezuela's 0.792 indicates that the region is lagging behind.

Table 3: HPI-1 Index for Niger Delta region in 2004/5[198]

State	HPI-I	State	HPI-1
Abia	29.169	Edo	23.399
Akwa Ibom	30.649	Imo	28.949
Bayelsa	33.826	Ondo	35.442
Cross River	29.3	Rivers	26.53
Delta	22.355	Niger Delta	28.847
Indonesia	17.8	Nigeria	38.8
Venezuela	8.8		

The average HPI-I for the Niger Delta States is 28.8 percent for 2005 compared with 38.8 percent for Nigeria as a whole. This means that the Niger Delta outperformed the rest of the country. But the Niger Delta average HPI-I of 28.8 percent is by far worse than those of other oil producing countries of Indonesia (17.8 percent) or Venezuela (8.8 percent).

3.3 Environmental Degradation and Development Nexus

We have already addressed the interconnection between the environment and sustainable human development (2.5.1). The environment is equally important to the Niger Delta people. This is a region "where nearly 60 per cent of the population depends on the natural environment – living and non-living for their livelihoods."[199] Admittedly, population growth accentuated by the influx of people from other parts of the country in search of employment in the oil industry has consequences on the environment, the ecosystem is further stressed by the fact that, "industrialization, urban development, and oil and gas exploration and exploitation have infringed on the people and their environment, leading to the opening up of previously pristine ecosystems. This has resulted in the alteration of habi-

---

198   NDHDR 2006, p. 58.
199   Niger Delta Human Development Report 2006, p. 74.

tats, biodiversity loss, deforestation and pollution."[200] A more detailed account of environmental pollution and its consequences for the poverty and underdevelopment of the ND region has been provided by Daniel Omoweh.[201] Suffice it for us to state briefly the reality on ground.

Perhaps environmental problems would have been minimal if regulatory laws were in place and effectively enforced in due time. Unfortunately, the oil companies, particularly *Shell Petroleum*, have operated for over 30 years without appreciable control or environmental regulation to guide their activities. The Federal Environmental Protection Agency (FEPA) did not come into being until 1988 and all the environmental quality standards on emissions and effluent discharge, and the laws requiring an environmental impact assessment for every major project did not come into effect until early 1990s. By that time, the Niger Delta environment had suffered much damage at the hands of the oil companies. Even now, it is doubtful whether the government's environmental monitoring agencies can adequately control the activities of the oil companies.[202]

It is instructive to know how the environmental base of oil-producing areas is being depleted as a result of oil production activities. To this effect, Anyakwe Nsirimovu (2000: 97) says:

> For example, during exploration, drill cuttings drilling mud and fluids are used for stimulating production. The major constituents of drill cuttings such as barites and bentonitic clays when dumped on the ground prevent local plant growth until natural processes develop new topsoil. In water these materials disperse and sink and may kill local bottom-living plants and animals by burying them...In addition to the pollutants introduced into the environment from exploration and exploitation operations, refinery wastes also have characteristics which constitute potential land, water and air pollutants...Further, flaring of natural gas has also been identified by several studies to damage the environment.[203]

Similarly, the Inspectorate Division of the Nigerian National Petroleum Corporation (NNPC) admitted in 1983 that environmental problems were caused by the activities of oil companies in the Niger Delta. The inspectorate, for instance, spoke of "the slow poisoning of the waters and the destruction of vegetation and agricultural land by spills which occur during petroleum operations", and went on to observe that "since the inception of the oil industry in Nigeria, there has been no concerted effort on the part of the government, let alone the oil operators, to control the environmental problems associated with the industry."[204]

---

200 Niger Delta Human Development Report 2006, p. 74.
201 Omoweh, A. Daniel, Shell Petroleum Development, the State and Underdevelopment of Nigeria's Niger Delta – a Study in Environmental Degradation, pp. 126-160.
202 Niger Delta Human Development Report 2006, p. 81.
203 ANEEJ, Oil of Poverty, 2004, p. 13.
204 ANEEJ, Oil of Poverty, 2004, pp. 13-14.

Unfortunately, should local people seek redress under existing laws demanding compensation for damages caused by oil companies to their crops or farmland, they are either poorly compensated or they have no means to seek redress at all. This is because: "Existing laws prescribe that aggrieved persons can only seek redress against the oil and other big multinational companies engaged in the oil industry in the Federal High Courts. To the local people, this is another case of collusion between the oil companies and the Government. The courts are located in the state capitals, putting them out of the easy reach of most rural inhabitants. The litigation process is fraught with many technicalities, requiring the services of legal practitioners that most people cannot afford."[205] The current restiveness in the region is a pointer to the fact that "lack of appropriate avenues for redress is one of the major causes of the conflicts in the region."[206]

Consequently, the manifestation of the environmental problems includes flooding, siltation and occlusion[207], shortage of land for development, canalization, oil spills, gas leaks and flares, depletion of forest resources, erosion, effluent and waste from oil operations. Finally, the negative social impacts of the environmental problems can be highlighted to include, among others, the frustrations of the local people with oil companies and multinational corporations on the one hand and the three tiers of government and regulatory agencies on the other. Again, according to the Niger Delta Human Development Report 2006, "The issues at stake include rapid and uncontrolled urbanization, occupational changes, the loss of fishing grounds, the disappearance of livelihoods and land shortages, among others. These changes have in turn threatened cultures, traditional systems and values, and the authority structure in the region."[208] With the condition of the environment as depicted by the above scenario, sustainable human development can only remain an illusion without concrete efforts and strategies aimed at improving the environment.

205   Niger Delta Human Development Report 2006, p. 83.
206   Niger Delta Human Development Report 2006, p. 83.
207   Siltation and occlusion happens when silt carried as water velocity slacks in the more sluggish waters of the Niger Delta. Siltation reduces channel capacity, narrows creeks and reduces water depths. This increases the rate at which aquatic plants grow on waterways. The weeds occlude the navigable sections of waterways and hamper fishing. Niger Delta Human Development Report 2006, p. 75.
208   Niger Delta Human Development Report 2006, p. 81.

3.4 HIV and AIDS as a Development Problem

The phenomenon of HIV and AIDS was first reported in Nigeria in 1986. Its prevalence was recorded at 1.8 per cent in Nigeria in 1990. In 2001, a federal survey showed that 5.8 per cent of the population or 7.5 million people had tested positive for HIV.[209] Experts and scholars are of the consensus that HIV and AIDS belong to the category of Sexually Transmitted Infections (STIs) and Sexually Transmitted Diseases (STD). Other modes of transmission include blood transfusion. These media are encouraged by heterosexual intercourse with multiple partners, socio-cultural practices like female genital mutilation (FGM), widowhood rites, widow inheritance, polygamy, early marriage, etc. The effects of the virus on its patients are psychologically devastating (stigmatization) and corporally agonizing, as it renders patients terminally ill. Though there is no cure yet, there is however, anti-retroviral therapy (ART) to alleviate the pains and thus prolong the life of people living with HIV&AIDS (PLWHA). The drugs are in most cases expensive and unaffordable to poor people who are mostly affected.

Owing to the continued deterioration of the state of poverty in Nigeria, many women and young girls are forced to prostitution or multiple sexual partners for commercial gains in order to escape from their state of impoverishment. This social behaviour has contributed in no small measure to the spread of HIV and AIDs in Nigeria generally and in the NDR in particular. The HIV&AIDS pandemic poses a significant threat to government planning in Nigeria and with specific reference to the region, the Niger Delta Human Development Report 2006 says:

> In the Niger Delta, when combined with the prospects for an eco-catastrophe, the crisis is potentially devastating. The epidemic impedes sustainable human development by destroying the family as the basic unit of society; weakening the educational system, which nurture the next generation of leaders; threatening agricultural productivity and food security; impeding industrial capacity; and overwhelming the health care system. The disease erodes human capacity, which is a principal building block for development, by raising attrition among farmers, teachers and other groups to rates that cannot be managed.[210]

The report shows that the prevalence of HIV and AIDS in the Niger Delta is among the highest in the country, higher than the average for Nigeria as a whole. According to the report, "The 2003 sentinel survey rated the South-South region as having the second highest prevalence (5.8 per cent), after the North Central zone with seven per cent. This result is alarming compared to the South-West at

---

209 Niger Delta Human Development Report 2006, p. 93.
210 Niger Delta Human Development Report 2006, p. 93.

4.2 per cent."[211] It is evident that prevalence of the decease in the Niger Delta region is not unconnected with a heavy concentration of oil production. The impact of HIV&AIDS has been particularly harsh in the Niger Delta. It is well known that the disease wreaks greater havoc where there is poverty, social inequity and general political marginalization – all of which afflict the Niger Delta.[212]

3.5 Legal and Regulatory Framework to Secure Oil Control

Laws regulating mineral resources in Nigeria date back to the colonial era.[213] However, since Independence in 1960, the key laws governing oil production activities in Nigeria were all made under military rule since the military ruled for the greater part of the period thereafter. The laws were made without consulting the Nigerian people. Such relevant laws are the Land Use Act, the Petroleum Act, the Oil and Pipelines Act, the Minerals Act and the Petroleum (Anti-Sabotage) Decrees.[214] Besides taking away the right of ownership of land from the traditional owners, that is, the communities these laws guarantee to the federal government the access to and control of the use of land, oil revenues, royalties and proceeds. For instance, the 1978 Land Use Act decreed under General Obasanjo, included in the 1979 Constitution and adopted by subsequent constitutions including the one of 1999 set up under the military rulership of General Abubakar provides that:

> The entire property in and control of all minerals, mineral oils and natural gas in, under or upon any land in Nigeria or in, under or upon the territorial waters and the Exclusive Economic Zone of Nigeria shall be vested in the Government of the Federal and shall be managed in such matter as may be prescribed by the National Assembly.[215]

To ensure that land is always made available for the construction of oil facilities and proper control of land, the Act states further that "All land comprise in the

---

211 Niger Delta Human Development Report 2006, p. 94.
212 Niger Delta Human Development Report 2006, p. 95.
213 Cf. Jedrzej, Georg Frynas, Oil In Nigeria – Conflict and Litigation between Oil Companies and Village Communities, Münster, Lit Verlag 2000. The author provides details of the oil-related legal arrangements in history of Nigeria beginning from 1914 to the end of the Military era.
214 Constitutional Rights Project, 1999, p. 35. Cf. also Neu, Elke M., An Analysis of Constellation of Interests Regarding the Conflict in the Niger Delta, Nigeria. Abschlußarbeit zur Erlangung der M.A im Fach Politologie, im Fachbereich Gesellschaftswissenschaften der Johann Wolfgang Goethe-Universität, Frankfurt am Main, 2000, p. 43.
215 HRW 1/1999, Ch. III, p. 7.

territory of each State in the Federation are [sic] hereby vested in the Governor of the State and such land shall be held in trust and administered for the use and common benefit of all Nigerians"[216].

This law provides that the state governor has control and management over land in urban areas, grants "statutory rights of occupancy" to any land, issues "certificate of occupancy" and demands payment of rental for that land. Local governments grant "customary rights of occupancy" to land other than in urban areas. Yet, the right of occupancy can be revoked in case of "overriding public interest" for land required for activities regarding mining purposes and oil related activities. Above all, the Land Use Act provides that "... no court shall have jurisdiction to inquire into any question concerning or pertaining to the amount or adequacy of any compensation paid or to be paid under this Act"[217].

In addition to that, the 1979 Constitution itself, and again the 1999, provide that nothing in the Constitution shall invalidate the Land Use Decree[218]. Thus, all the provisions discussed above which were written into the 1979 constitution were taken over into the Constitution of 1999. If compensation for acquired land for mining purposes provided under the Land Use Act (provision under the Minerals Act or the Mineral Oils Act which is now superseded by the petroleum Act) is due to a community, it is paid "to the community", or "into some fund specified by the Military Governor for the purpose of being utilised or applied for the benefit of the community"[219].

However, contrary to that is the Petroleum Act of 1969 that makes no provision for compensation to be paid for land acquisition. It requires holders of oil exploration licenses, oil prospecting licenses or oil mining leases only to pay "fair and adequate compensation for the disturbance of surface or other rights" to the owner or occupier of any land or property.[220] Thus, the rent for properties acquired since the implementation of the Land Use Act is paid to the federal government only. With oil being federal property, land occupiers are not entitled to any royalties for oil extracted from their land. Before 1978, under the Public Land Acquisitions (Miscellaneous Provisions) Act 1976 and other laws, compensation was to be paid for the land acquired itself.

Against this background, the reactions of the local communities to these laws alienating and de-enfranchising the people of the right to their ancestral heritage

---

216 Section 1, Decree No. 6 of 1978, Cap. 202, Laws of the Federation of Nigeria. *In*: HRW 1/1999, Ch V, p. 10.

217 Section 27, Land Use Act. *In*: HRW 1/1999, Ch V, p. 10.

218 Article 274(5) of the 1979 Constitution. This provision is repeated in Article 346(5) of the draft 1995 Constitution. *In*: HRW 1/1999, Ch. V, p. 10.

219 HRW 1/1999, Ch. V, p. 10.

220 HRW 1/1999, Ch. V, p. 10.

can best be imagined. It is evident that the expropriation of the land for the oil industry leaves the people whose livelihoods may be destroyed with no effective due process. The people affected have no right to voice opposition to the acquisition; they cannot present their opposition before an impartial court in order to obtain adequate compensation[221]. The oil companies operating in Nigeria before 1978 recognized the indigenous communities as the owners of the land and negotiated terms including payment of rents with them.

Thus, with their sudden loss of land rights, rent ceased to be paid, and entitled compensation was only for the loss of use but does not cover the loss of economic activities. The fact is that the losses are not adequately addressed by either the compensation paid or the system of paying compensation. "In this situation, the people become antagonistic. They have been deprived of their main stay, and yet the damage is not paid for. Because they are not adequately compensated, the slightest misunderstanding is conflict", says J. Fenine Fekunor, dean of the Faculty of Law at the Rivers State University of Science and Technology, Port Harcourt[222].

Scholars are agreed that agitations for resource control began to pick up momentum gradually from the time of the enactment of the Land Use Act, although, other factors also contributed to the tensions which have snowballed into constant protests and agitations since the 1990s. Such factors as the Structural Adjustment Program (SAP) introduced by Gen. Babangida in 1986, the protracted transition to civilian rule by the military regimes, but more importantly the annulment of the election of June 12, 1993. It needs to be added that this legal framework also provides the state legal backing to the use of brutal force against protesters in the interest of state security. In short, the legal framework concerning land ownership and oil production has no regard for the quality of life and concerns of the human persons living in the communities.

3.6 Violent Conflicts

Scholars are agreed that conflict is a common phenomena arising "around people and relationships."[223] In his field investigation, A.Onuoha indentifies eight kinds of conflict in the Niger Delta namely: land, chieftaincy, community leadership tussle, oil spill and pipeline explosions, compensation, citing of community de-

---

221   HRW 1/1999, Ch. V, p. 10. Cf. also Omotola, J.A, Essays on the Land Use Act, 1978, Lagos: Lagos University Press 1984, Ch.5.
222   Neu, Elke M. An Analysis of Constellation of Interests Regarding the Conflict in the Niger Delta, Nigeria, p. 48.
223   Onuoha A., From Conflict to Collaboration, p. 110.

velopment projects, on/offshore oil dichotomy and resource control. He further discusses the responses to these conflicts from the perspective of the government, communities, oil companies and NGOs[224]. It is probably appropriate to refer to these eight kinds of conflicts as eight sources or causes of conflicts. This is because conflicts are often surrounding these issues.

Historical evidences situate the reality of conflicts in the Niger Delta region way back to the pre-colonial period and it was always over resources. At that time, the major trade was in palm oil in which the kings and middlemen in the region were very much involved. The Royal Niger Company, in addition to its trading activities, was already virtually in charge of governance on behalf of the British. The Niger Delta Human Development Report 2006 notes that "Its attempt to monopolize the trade in palm oil to the exclusion of the Niger Delta kings and middlemen was to result in the first major rebellion in the region against injustice"[225]. Before the advent of oil in commercial quantities, the production of palm oil, palm kernels and timber earned considerable income for the region and Nigeria. The generality of the people were gainfully employed in the agricultural sector.

Though the reality of conflicts dates back to the pre-colonial period and the post-Independence crisis that ended up in a civil war, the major difference between then and now is that the region has become far more volatile, a situation brought on by the limited access to an array of resources. Unemployment is high, especially among youth. Social services (education, health, recreation, etc.) and physical infrastructure (roads, electricity, water, sewers, etc.) are poor everywhere. The problem of poverty in the midst of ballooning oil revenues has spawned discontent and disillusion. Several angry groups have taken up the fight for equity through agitations for resource control or at least, enhanced allocations in the federally shared revenues from the oil industry. The Niger Delta is virtually in a state of siege.[226] The severe pollution of rivers and soils and the overall environmental degradation wrought by oil have led to the decline of crops and fishing, thus making agriculture unattractive. This has made the UNDP's Niger Delta Human Development Report to conclude, that "the loss of the once vibrant agricultural and fishing sectors and very limited access to benefits from today's oil resources has set the stage for violence in the region."[227] This is because years of deprivation have pushed citizens into anger, hopelessness, cynicism and violence.

---

224 Onuoha A., From Conflict to Collaboration, pp. 151-176.
225 Niger Delta Human Development Report 2006, p. 111.
226 Niger Delta Human Development Report 2006, p. 112.
227 Niger Delta Human Development Report 2006, p. 112.

3.6.1 Repressions and Intimidations by the State

Kenneth Omeje[228] and A. Onuoha (2005) have aptly documented in details the causes and nature of the conflicts in the Niger Delta region as well as the extent of state responses with violent repression. Omeje has particularly argued to refute the theory of the state and transnational oil companies (TNOCs) hegemonic alliance in the use of force and repression against the Niger Delta region – the oil-producing communities as it is being proected by some scholars. While he admits the fact that there is excessive use of force by the state against the oil protesters, such use of force is not limited to the Niger Delta alone, it is the peculiar way that the state responds to protesters generally in the country. Our concern is the extent to which brutal force against oil-producing communities has been a hindrance to the human development of the region.

While the state is offering institutionalized development programmes as response to the yearnings for development in the Niger Delta region on the one hand, it is also responding on the other hand with brutal force and repressions to most protests in the region, be it peaceful or otherwise[229]. The various reports of Human Rights Watch (HRW) and other notable NGOs as well as scholars have documented the nature and intensity of such brutal repressions by agencies of the state with the connivance and, sometimes financial backing of oil multinationals operating in the region. Wale Adebanwi notes that: "The Nigerian state responded by imposing a reign of terror. Between 1993 and 1998, when the struggle was at its peak, the military regime of the late General Sani Abacha deployed a military task on Ogoni land to "keep the peace". Lieutenant Colonel Paul Okuntimo, the task-force commander, boasted that he knew 103 ways to kill. For many Ogoni, this was no mere boast, for the soldiers ravaged villages, raped women, and randomly killed men, women, and children in a sadistic manner. The infamous hanging of Ken Saro-Wiwa and eight Ogoni compatriots by the Abacha regime in November 1995 marked the height of the repression"[230].

The hope of reaping the dividends of democracy for the Niger Delta region dampened when a few months after the inauguration of the civilian government

---

228 Omoje, Kenneth C., High Stakes and Stakeholders: Oil Conflict and Security in Nigeria, London: Ashgate 2006.

229 Most of the occupations or other disruptions of production are ended peacefully by negotiation between oil companies and protesters. However, in some cases security force action leads to deaths and injuries among protesters – of whom some are armed but many are not – and among others targeted for collective punishment.

230 Adebanwi, Wale, Nigeria: Shell of a State. *In*: Dollar and Sense magazine, July/August 2001. Cf. also http://www.thirdworldtraveler.com/Africa/Nigeria_Shell_State.html. Accessed on 18.12.2007.

of President Obasanjo military repression was visited on the town of Odi. To this effect, Human Rights Watch reports that: "in November 1999, the Nigerian army destroyed the town of Odi in Bayelsa State, killing hundreds of people, a more serious single incident than any in the delta under the military regime. Army, navy, and paramilitary Mobile Police personnel are still widely deployed across the delta, mostly at oil facilities...Security force abuses against civilians continue across the delta on more-or-less routine basis."[231] Furthermore, HRW notes that "in virtually every community, there have been occasions on which paramilitary Mobile Police, the regular police, or the army, have beaten, detained, or even killed those involved in protests, peaceful or otherwise, or individuals who have called for compensation for oil damage, whether youth, women, children, or traditional leaders. In some cases, members of the community are beaten indiscriminately, irrespective of their role in any protest"[232]. It must stated, though, that there are cases of hoodlums and armed criminals hiding under the cloud of protests to steal, vandalise and killed innocent civilians and oil workers alike in the region. All the same, heavy-handed responses by the security forces contribute to a generally repressive atmosphere in which people become afraid to protest peacefully.

The situation of state repressions and violence has led to what A. Ikelegbe describes as "Economy of Conflict" in the oil-rich Niger Delta. He says: "The region is generally restive, with pockets of insurrection and armed rebellion. Decades of oil exploitation, environmental degradation and state neglect has created an impoverished, marginalized and exploited citizenry which after more than two decades produced a resistance of which the youth has been a vanguard. A regime of state repression and corporate violence has further generated popular and criminal violence, lawlessness, illegal appropriation and insecurity. The Niger Delta is today a region of intense hostilities, violent confrontations and criminal violence. It is pervaded by a proliferation of arms and institutions and agencies of violence ranging from the Nigerian Armed Forces to community, ethnic and youth militias, armed gangs and networks, pirates, cultists and robbers."[233]

As alternative to peaceful demonstrations and protests, people now resort to hostage-taking of oil workers and prominent indigenous politicians, occupation of oil installations, etc. For instance, several hundred Itsekiri women from the nearby Igborodo community occupied from July 8 to 18, 2002 the large *ChevronTexaco*

---

231   Human Rights Watch, The Niger Delta: No Democratic Dividend, 14,7A (2002) 6. Cf. http://www.hrw.org.
232   Human Rights Watch, The Price of Oil, 1999, pp. 10-11.
233   Ikelegbe, A., The Economy of Conflict in the Oil rich Niger Delta Region of Nigeria. *In:* Nordic Journal of African Studies 14,2 (2005) 208-234.

(previously *Chevron*) terminal at Escravos, on the Atlantic coast in Delta State. Initially, more than 700 workers at the terminal were prevented from leaving by the women, who occupied the heliport and dock area; after five days, 300 of the oil workers were allowed to leave. About one hundred police and soldiers were sent to the terminal, but did not harm the women. The siege was eventually ended when *ChevronTexaco* acceded to some of the women's demands, including hiring local "youth," building schools, and providing electricity, water and other facilities.[234]

3.6.2 Types and Causes of Conflicts

There are four most common and vicious forms of conflict, in terms of lives lost and property destroyed, in the Niger Delta. These are: intra-community, inter-community, inter-ethnic and community and oil company conflicts.[235] The Niger Delta Human Development Report has aptly documented a catalogue of escalating violence in the Niger Delta region between 2003 and 2006 (pp. 113-114). There are also other forms of conflicts which can be described as inter-governmental and inter-multinationals. These latter forms do not necessarily fall within the scope of this work. However, the issues of poor (bad) governance and benefit captors or vultures (beneficiaries of the conflicts) are not unconnected with conflicts and poverty in the Niger Delta region.

3.6.2.1 Intra-community Conflicts

Intra-community conflicts arise most often from struggles over the sharing of benefits from oil. These involve members of a clan, village or ethnic group with some form of communal identity.[236] An example was the incident in Ogbogoro community where violence has flared since 1998 over claims to benefits from rents, contracts and jobs among local people by oil companies. A claim to such benefits by two rival traditional heads of the community has resulted to rampaging youths destroying properties worth millions of Naira. Similarly, the Membe episode – "Membe war", in Membe community *Shell* and *Agip* had negotiated with the chiefs on compensation, contracts and job opportunities. The chiefs were accused of short-changing the community by keeping most of the benefits to themselves. This provoked anger and disaffection among the people – a situa-

---

234 HRW, The Niger Delta, No Democratic Dividend, p. 7.
235 Niger Delta Human Development Report 2006, p. 113. See also Unuoha, A, From conflict to collaboration, pp. 89-116 and pp. 117-145.
236 Niger Delta Human Development Report 2006, p. 113.

tion that resulted to formation of rival youth groups visiting terror on the community. It further resulted to heavy loss of lives and property.[237]

It is evident, from these examples of intra-community conflict, that the struggles over sharing of benefits from oil have given rise to violent conflicts. At the centre of the conflicts are the traditional authorities, be they the ruler or the council of chiefs, which negotiate with the companies. They are considered to be lacking in transparency and inclusiveness. When some people perceive unfairness in the distribution of compensation, they organize to challenge the existing order and seek to overthrow it. This is one of the major causes of the breakdown of traditional authority in most oil-producing areas. Some traditional rulers have lost their legitimacy partly because of greed and partly because there is not enough money to satisfy everybody. We must add, though, that in some areas, such as the Ilaje communities of the Western Niger Delta (Ondo State), the elders and local chieftains still command much respect.

3.6.2.2 Inter-community Conflicts

Inter-communal conflicts are not new to the Niger Delta people and they do not always result in violence. As a mark of their long tradition of civility and respect for the rule of law the people are known for their patronage of the judicial system because a lot of inter-communal cases are settled in the law courts. The courts in such urban centres as Port Harcourt and Warri have a series of these cases.[238] However, troubles come when communities are dissatisfied with court verdicts. Often time, inter-communal conflicts arise as a result of communities attempting to assert their rights over disputed territories particularly if oil fields are located in such areas. There is no doubt that the oil economy is stressing the traditional communal relationships. Litigation over land is usually not a satisfactory means of resolving conflicts not only that the wheels of justice grind too slowly, and good counsel too expensive to hire, a land dispute often drag on for years in law courts. The benefits of being able to immediately assert rights over disputed territory are attractive. More important is the fact that the role of security agencies – police and the army, called to restore law and order between warring communities, can also aggravate the violence.

---

237 Niger Delta Human Development Report 2006, p. 115.
238 Niger Delta Human Development Report 2006, p. 115.

3.6.2.3 Inter-ethnic Conflicts

It is a fact that inter-ethnic conflict is not a strange occurrence in Nigerian society as indeed elsewhere in Africa. The episodes of Ife-Modakeke (in South-West), Zango-Kataf (in the Middle Belt), etc. are still fresh in the memory of many Nigerians. Karl Maier has aptly documented the conflicts in the various parts of the country in the contemporary time.[239] In spite of cultural affinities and interactions, inter-ethnic conflicts are common in the Niger Delta region. The inter-ethnic conflicts, particularly in Delta State, are well documented by Imobighe T.A et al.[240] Among notable inter-ethnic conflicts in the Niger Delta are the Ijaw vs. Itsekiri (Delta State), Urhobo vs. Itsekiri (Delta State), Ogoni vs. Okrika (Rivers State), Ogoni vs. Andoni (Rivers State) and Ilaje vs. Ijaw (Ondo State).

What is obvious about inter-ethnic conflicts is that not all inter-ethnic conflicts are related to oil exploration. For example, the case of Warri conflicts has more to do with laying claims to territorial integrity and political rights by the main ethnic groups (Ijaw, Itsekiri and Urhobos) that make up the city. It is certain that sustainable development cannot be attained in the face of constant conflicts and fighting.

3.6.2.4 Communities and Oil Companies

A cursory look at the various Bills of Rights (Oron and Ogoni), Declarations, Charters, etc. reveals that generally, the communities are dissatisfied with the effects of oil operations. Besides committing their legitimate grievances against the state and oil multinationals to documentation and presenting it to the government and the public, the communities' dissatisfaction is expressed in various forms, including violent demonstrations against oil companies, blockades of their operations, the sabotage of pipelines and other oil installations, and hostage-taking.

The oil companies, especially the *Shell Petroleum Development Company*, are accused of not assisting their host communities enough. Other accusations include, among others, oil companies' failure to adequately provide infrastructure such as water systems, health facilities, roads and electricity grids. They point to the fact that "their own staff live in estates that meet international standard and are adjacent to the deprived host communities."[241] The term "Where Vultures

---

239 Maier, Karl, This House has Fallen – Nigeria in Crisis, Oxford: Westview Press, 2000.
240 Imobighe, T.A, et al., Conflict and Instability in the Niger Delta – The Warri Case, Ibadan: Spectrum Books 2002.
241 Niger Delta Human Development Report 2006, p. 121.

Feast" has been used by Okonta and Oronto[242] to describe the intrigues and the exploitations of the oil producing communities by the oil companies particularly *Shell* and the Nigerian State with the connivance of some state officials. The authors' analysis of the relationship between oil companies and the communities reveals that it "is not anywhere near the nice and cozy 'partner in progress' picture so assiduously promoted by the company's image makers."[243] Both authors picture the relationship thus:

> Oppressed, repressed, and denied their property rights in turn, the oil-producing communities of the Niger Delta have become living carrion on which successive regimes in Nigeria and their foreign collaborators, like insatiable vultures, have feasted, and are still feasting, without letup. This particular carrion would have nothing to lose if its tormentors were suddenly to leave her alone. It has its life to gain.[244]

The social impacts of the oil industry on the communities are blamed on the oil companies. Such impacts as the lifestyles of oil workers aggravate feelings of discrimination. The influx of young girls looking for livelihoods in the region has led to increasing incidence of prostitution and its attendant diseases such as HIV&AIDS. According to the Niger Delta Human Development Report 2006, "local young women and even school girls feel the pressure to join the race for petro-money to raise their own standards of living."[245]

An appraisal of the relationship between the oil-producing communities and the oil and gas industry or rather the oil multinationals reveals a number of salient socio-economic issues, for example: the industry is an exclusive economy, in the sense that it leaves out those who are not concerned with it. In this regard, the Niger Delta Human Development Report 2006 notes that "land is lost to oil exploitation, while the invasion of oil workers invariably raises the local cost of living. Most local people lack the skills required to be employed by the oil companies; if they are employed at all, it is in the most menial and poorly paid jobs, where they suffer the indignity of seeing outsiders arrive to take preeminence over them in the oil industry. Outsiders always occupy the higher echelons of the oil companies."[246] What is more baffling is the fact that none of the major oil companies is headquartered in the Niger Delta.

242 Okonta, Ike & Douglas, Oronto, Where Vultures Feast – Shell, Human Rights and Oil, London: Verso 2003.
243 Okonta & Douglas, Where Vultures Feast, p. 105.
244 Okonta & Douglas, Where Vultures Feast, p. 115.
245 Niger Delta Human Development Report 2006, p. 121.
246 Niger Delta Human Development Report 2006, p. 122.

3.7 Development Commissions

One of the stereotype responses of the State to people's clamour for development or protests for social justice has always been to set up a commission to look into what can the State do to pacify the people. In most cases such commissions end up drawing programs according to the mind of the State and not necessarily to address the actual needs or demands of the people. Those who constitute the membership of such commissions are often largely government representatives and their trusted agents on the local level. The real people concerned are often marginally represented if at all they are included. The performances of a commission depend to a large extent on whose interests its membership represents. This assertion is evident by the commissions discussed below.

3.7.1 Oil Mineral Producing Areas Development Commission (1992-1999)

Following growing discontent and restiveness in the oil producing areas, over a year after the presentation of the Ogoni Bill of Rights, the Babangida regime set up the Oil Mineral Producing Areas Development Commission (OMPADEC) with decree 23 in 1992, while the commission proper commenced operations in 1993.[247] The decree increased the 1.5 percent of oil proceeds allocated to the oil-producing communities to 3 percent, and transferred the fund to the new commission to administer on their behalf.[248] The fund was meant to be used to address the developmental needs of the areas. It was given the statutory responsibility to receive and administer, in accordance with the confirmed ratio of oil production in each state, the monthly allocation from the Federation Account. This was set aside for the rehabilitation and development of the mineral-producing areas and for tackling ecological problems that had arisen from the exploration of oil minerals. The overall goal was to determine and identify, through the commission and the oil-mineral-producing states, the actual oil-producing areas and foster the development of projects agreed upon with local communities in the oil-mineral-producing areas.[249] It was charged with several responsibilities, including: ad-

---

247   The OMPADEC was actually a direct product of an earlier recommendation of by the Justice Belgore Commission set up by government to identify the root causes of the incessant communal clashes and disaffection in the oil producing areas and to suggest the best way forward.
248   Okonta & Douglas, Where Vultures Feast, p. 32.
249   Ojameruaye, E., http://www.waado.org/Environment/Remediation/Chadian_model_niger _delta.htm. Accessed on 03.08.2007 Cf. Omotola, J. Shola, From the OMPADEC to the

dressing the problems of oil pollution, community development, securing accurate record of operation of NNPC.[250]

The announcement, establishing the Commission was greeted by the people with enthusiasm and high expectation, because they thought that respite had come their way at last. But their joy was short-lived. Though OMPADEC initially raised the spirit and hope of the people, it became inefficient and corrupt and ended up as another great disappointment.[251] It is on record, that "between 1993 and 1997, OMPADEC collected about N17.42 billion, a little over US$135 million. At first, OMPADEC was allocated three per cent of the Federation Account, but this was raised to 6 per cent in 1995."[252]

Commentators on the performance of OMPADEC are agreed that it provided electricity and pipe-borne water to some villages, but most of its funds were misappropriated.[253] Similarly Okonta and Oronto are of the view that:

> Since OMPADEC was under no supervisory authority other than the presidency, which in any case had "weightier" matters of state to engage its attention, inefficiency and financial mismanagement quickly set in. The World Bank team that studied OMPADEC's activities in the Niger Delta communities in 1995 concluded that it would be difficult for the commission to effectively fulfil its role as a development agency because (1) there was no emphasis on environmental sustainable development; (2) the commission did not have the requisite personnel to enable it to meet the its ecological mandate; (3) there was an absence of long-term planning; (4) there was little or no project assessment, and where projects were initiated, maintenance requirements were not built into them; and (5) there was no integrated approach to development planning, which should have involved the local communities and other government agencies in the area.[254]

Between 1992 and 1999 when it was scrapped, OMPADEC completed several projects but bequeathed numerous abandoned or unfinished projects and huge debts. There is no reliable information on the total amount the commission received from the Federation Account, but what is clear is that OMPADEC suffered from lack of focus, inadequate and irregular funding, and lavish spending by officials, corruption, and excessive political interference, lack of transparency

---

NDDC: An Assessment of the State Responses to Environmental Insecurity in the Niger Delta, Nigeria, Africa Today 54,1 (2007) 73-90.

250 Ukeje, Charles U., Oil Capital (Doctoral theses) 2004, pp. 274-275.
251 Ojameruaye E., http://www.waado.org/Environment/Remediation/Chadian_model_niger _delta.htm. 3.8.2007 Cf Omotola, J. Shola, From the OMPADEC to the NDDC: an assessment of the state responses to environmental insecurity in the Niger Delta, Nigeria, in: Africa Today – Bloomington 2007 Vol. 54. Nr. 1 pages 73-90.
252 Niger Delta Human Development Report 2006, p. 12.
253 Omotola, From OMPADEC to the NDDC, http://www.accessmylibrary.com/coms2/summary_0286-33385913_ITM. Visited on 27.5.2008.
254 Okonta & Douglas, Where Vultures Feast, p. 33.

and accountability and high overhead expenditure.[255] Other explanations for the failure of OMPADEC could be traced to the fact that "there were no available data for planning purposes, such as the crude oil production quota by state. OMPADEC had no means to cope with the volume of demands given decades of physical neglect and deprivation"[256] in the region. In fact, "most of its projects had little to do with poverty reduction and the vast majority of the people did not benefit from its activities. In brief, OMPADEC failed abjectly to abate discontent and restiveness in the Region."[257]

It needs to be said that the way and manner in which OMPADEC carried out its assignment in the region contributed to the conflicts between communities and ethnic groups in the region. Through its distributive policies OMPADEC was able to play one community against the other, pitch one ethnic group against the other, and place clients of the state: elite and traditional; in positions of advantage in the award of contracts and placement in powerful positions. Communities engaged themselves in low intensity conflicts over the location of OMPADEC projects, while others were practically torn apart over the choice of a project, or between those who rejected the project, and those who wanted it. OMPADEC in the tension-soaked environment went on to identify, and collect information on the activities of "troublemakers".[258]

It is worth noting that among the reasons for the failure of OMPADEC in the Niger Delta region are lack of participation or non-involvement of the oil producing communities in the decision-making process and the divide and rule tactics in its operation. According to Cyril Obi, "perhaps the greatest weakness of OMPADEC was that the people of oil producing communities were totally excluded from its decision-making process. This was further compounded by the corruption and its lack of accountability to the people of the oil producing communities. The lack of transparency and divide and rule tactics of its operations soon marked out OMPADEC as part of the infrastructure of federal hegemony in the Niger Delta. It to all intents and purposes became yet another local site in the Niger Delta for primitive accumulation, and intra-elite struggle for office, power and contracts."[259]

255 NDRD Master Plan, 102. Cf. Ojameruaye, E., Lessons From The Chadian Model, http://www. waado.org/Environment/Remediation/chadian_model_niger_delta.htm. Visited on 3.8.2007.
256 Niger Delta Human Development Report, p. 12.
257 NDRD Master Plan, p. 102.
258 Obi, Cyril I., The Changing Forms of Identity Politics in Nigeria under Economic Adjustment: the Case of the Oil Minorities Movement of the Niger Delta, Uppsala: Nordiska Afrikainstitutet 2001, p. 57. Trouble-makers are those considered to be critiques of the government and those who questioned the mode of operation of OMPADEC.
259 Obi, The Changing Forms of Identity, p. 58.

Though OMPADEC had succeeded in producing millionaires of a few contractors and members of the traditional ruling class in the oil producing areas, it had no positive impact on the wretched state of the oil communities. Again, Obi says that "the creation of a few millionaires and more office holders, did not positively affect the overall quality of life in the impoverished villages, it worsened matters, as the few rich elicited a mixture of envy, hatred, scorn and admiration. This combustible mix combined with existing rivalries, cleavages and perceptions of betrayal to explode into complex conflicts at the personal, intra-elite and national levels."[260] Rather than solving the development problems, OMPADEC created more problems in the Niger Delta.

One could say without mincing words that OMPADEC was "a contract rather than development outfit."[261] This situation may not be unconnected with the lack of regulatory mechanisms to monitor its activities. Omoweh, one of the experts in Niger Delta study, is of the view that, "as a political outfit, the commission is meant to play carrot and stick politics for the state in the Niger Delta. So, it is not really concerned with the desired development of the oil-producing area contrary to the view of many a Nigerian. As part of its politics, it believes in awarding portfolio contracts as a means of building up the needed political support in the area for the Babangida junta in need of civilizing itself."[262] Furthermore, he opines that "across the oil areas of the Niger Delta, therefore, there was (and still) complaints and grievances that the then chairman, A. K. Horsefall, a state security expert, awarded contracts to those seen to be allies of the state in the area, and others who are government officials' fronts who are from oil areas. He did what the state wanted him to do."[263] And not what the ND people desired and longed for.

From all reports and criticisms on OMPADEC it is clear that the issue of human development and poverty eradication did not come near its agenda in the span of its existence from 1992 to 1999 when it was replaced by NDDC. With the failure of the OMPADEC to make meaningful impacts on environmental and developmental concerns in NDR, there was the need to search for alternative institutional measures that could adequately address the issues at stake. One of the first actions of former President Obasanjo soon after his inauguration in May 1999 was to send a Bill to the National Assembly, seeking the abrogation of

260 Obi, The Changing Forms of Identity, p. 58.
261 Ovwasa, Lucky, Oil and the Minority Question. *In*: Saliu, A.Hassan (ed.), Issues in Contemporary Political Economy of Nigeria, Ilorin: Haytee Books 1999, p. 92.
262 Omoweh, Daniel, Shell Petroleum Development Company, The State and Underdevelopment, Trenton NJ: Africa World Press 2005, p. 172.
263 Omoweh, Daniel, Shell Petroleum Development Company, The State and Underdevelopment, p. 173.

OMPADEC and the establishment of the Niger Delta Development Commission (NDDC) to replace it.

3.7.2 Niger Delta Development Commission

The NDDC was inaugurated on December 21, 2000 with a vision "to offer a lasting solution to the socio-economic difficulties of the Niger Delta Region" and a mission "to facilitate the rapid, even and sustainable development of the Niger Delta into a region that is economically prosperous, socially stable, ecologically regenerative and politically peaceful."[264] The basic mandate of the NDDC was comprehensive, though essentially limited to addressing the environmental and developmental concerns of the delta. It is the most ambitious developmental enterprise embarked upon by any government in the Niger Delta.[265] The NDDC is expected to be funded by the Federal, States and Local Governments as well as the Oil Multis.

Report on its activities in first three years of its existence (2001 -2003) indicates that, the NDDC:

- Received N47 billion from all its funding sources.
- Awarded about 700 contracts of which 358 had been completed by June 2003.
- Undertook the construction of 40 road projects, 90 water projects, 129 electrification projects, 47 shore protection/jetty projects, 50 health centres, 205 new blocks of six classrooms each[266].

To date, a Master Plan (2007) has been produced outlining the development strategies for the region. This is a commendable achievement. With the production of a Regional Master Plan for the Niger Delta, the NDDC is at least poised for positive action on its founding objectives. This is because earlier body had never managed or bothered to produce a plan, whether at regional or sectoral levels.[267] Though the plan should cover the period from 2005 to 2020, it only came to light in 2007. We shall address the essentials of the master plan in later chapter of this work.

Though the NDDC appears promising, some critics still see it as an imposition from the Federal Government and a top-down approach to development

---

264 NDRD Master Plan, p. 103. Cf also Ojameruaye. http://www.wacado.org/Environment/Re mediation/chadian_model_niger_delta.htm. Accessed on 3.8.2007.
265 Ukeje, Oil Capital, p. 277.
266 NDRD Master Plan, p. 104.
267 Niger Delta Human Development Report 2006, p. 13.

planning and implementation. In fact the NDDC's philosophy is still development dumping. The local people had no say in determining its composition; it primarily comprises appointees of the Federal Government. As far as ordinary people are concerned, the loyalty of the NDDC is not to the Niger Delta people but to the Federal government and the oil companies that provide the bulk of its budget.[268] The operations of the commission continue to generate remarkable criticisms similar to those against its predecessors: that it is under-funded, badly managed, very partial in its allocation of funds for projects, lack of equitable distribution in terms of project implementation, poor quality of many projects, lack of adequate consultation with and input from local beneficiaries in the conceptualization and implementation of projects, indiscriminate use of funds to cultivate and strengthen patronage, excessive bureaucracy, politics and corruption. Another scathing criticism of the NDDC is that its enabling instrument ignored the substantive clamour for resource control and improved revenue allocation by oil producing areas.[269] It does mean that if the commission would receive acceptance from the local people, at least a similar commission must be replicated on the state or local government level to comprise the local community representatives as members. Ondo State has given an example of how the commission could work locally by its OSOPADEC.

3.7.3 Ondo State Oil-Producing Areas Development Commission

If the Federal government has responded to the yearning of the Niger Delta people for development with the establishment of NDDC for the whole region, such a commission ought to be replicated on the state level in order for the communities concerned to take ownership and ensure the effective implementation of the programmes of the commission. This logic informed the initiative of Ondo State government to set up OSOPADEC, though not without an initial legal tussle between Ondo State government and some concerned citizens of Oil producing communities.[270]

OSOPADEC was established by law on October 29, 2001 as an interventionist agency to cater for the development of the oil-producing areas of the Ondo state.

268 Niger Delta Human Development Report 2006, p. 13.
269 Ukeje, Oil Capital, p. 279.
270 African Network for Environment and Economic Justice (ANEEJ), Oil of Poverty in Niger Delta, Benin City: 2004, p. 31.

It was created as an institutional framework for the development of that part of the state. It was inaugurated in November 2001.

Since the establishment of OSOPADEC, resonances from the communities concerned have been to a large extent positive. This confirms that the pragmatic approach to the development of the oil-producing areas by the Ondo State government is paying off. According to the ANEEJ document, "like NDDC, most OSOPADEC's interventions are in the infrastructural development of roads, water supply, jetties and school classrooms while its board has representatives from oil-producing areas. But its board of representatives drawn from both the government and oil communities are far more effective than those of the NDDC."[271] It is also being reported that scholarships are being awarded to students from oil producing communities while credits are being given out to fishermen and women to enhance their economic performance in their respective occupations. Generally, the oil producing communities are satisfied with the performance of OSOPADEC since its inception. Though that is not say, that all communities are contented with their share of the oil revenue in form of projects, no community has complained that it has been completely left out in the scheme of things.

The good performance of OSOPADEC so far is attributed to the clarity of the legal framework establishing it. For example, the law establishing the OSOPADEC clearly states how its funds should be allocated and the share of each stakeholder, be it state and local governments or the oil communities. The enabling law thus make it easier for OSOPADEC to be held accountable by citizens of the state in line with human rights approach to good governance, transparency and accountability.[272] Besides the legal framework, the financial control mechanism put in place has equally reduced the incidence of abandoned projects. For example, bank guarantees are obtained from prospective contractors handling them. Monies, especially mobilisation fees paid are therefore recoverable from the banks should the contractors default. With this, the banks also set up their own monitoring team to ensure project performance by contractors.[273]

Of importance is the fact that most of those who constitute the membership of the commission are representatives of the oil producing communities who the local people trust and belief to represent their interests at the commission. Unlike the case of NDDC or OMPADEC whose membership are mostly handpicked by the government based on political patronage.

An appraisal of OSOPADEC's performance since its establishment in 2001 shows that the novel experiment, specifically its emphasis on the utilisation of a

271   ANEEJ, Oil of Poverty, p. 31.
272   ANEEJ, Oil of Poverty, p. 31.
273   ANEEJ, Oil of Poverty, p. 31.

proportion of the 13 per cent oil derivation fund for oil-producing areas of the state, is worthy of emulation by other states in the Niger Delta. This is because the approach brings visible benefits of oil money to oil-producing areas[274]. However, it needs to be pointed out that concentrating on provision of infrastructure only without paying sufficient attention to building human capacity cannot guarantee sustainable development in the region.

Conclusion

It is evident that the development trends and problems in the Niger Delta are complex and multifaceted. One should also expect the solutions to be multi-dimensional. The indicators and incidences of poverty reveal the state of underdevelopment in the region. We have shown that hindrances to the development of the region include environmental degradation resulting from oil explorations and exploitations, HIV and AIDS, the legal and regulatory framework to secure the oil control by the state and oil companies, violent conflicts aggravated by repressions and intimidation of the people by the state security forces, the divide and rule tactics of the oil companies towards the oil producing communities, as well as the top-down government organized development commissions that are ridden with corruption, ineptitude and lack of accountability to the local communities. The evidence of OSOPADEC has shown that development commissions could work to bring about the desired development if local communities are involved in their composition as well as in the determination of their project priority.

In sum, the presence of the oil industry has brought wealth and fame to a very few while at the same time, it has aggravated for the majority poverty and underdevelopment in the Niger Delta region by way of political marginalization, social exclusion and economic deprivation of the people within the Nigerian federation. However, all hope is not lost. A socio-economic and political analysis of the causes of these development problems could lead to solutions. We shall address this in the next part of this work.

---

274   ANEEJ, Oil of Poverty, p. 31. As a matter of fact, the former President Olusegun Obasanjo recommended OSOPAPEC to other states of the Niger Delta during his official visit to Ondo State in April 2006.

Part II
Socio-economic and Political Analysis

4. Socio-economic Analysis: Resource Curse Theory

4.1 Introduction

The previous chapter focused on the reality of the development problems in the Niger Delta region. It summarised the problems as those of poverty and under-development. In contrast to this situation is the fact that the region is home to abundant crude oil which has become a major source of revenue to the Nigerian government since its commercial production and export began in 1958. In between this period to date, Nigeria has recorded billions of dollars as revenue from oil export coming from the region. The question, which has come to be known as the Niger Delta question, is why the situation of poverty and underdevelopment persists in the region. What are the causes of these development problems?

Studies, like the work of the economists Jeffrey Sachs and Andrew Warner[275], have indicated that there is a connection between abundance of natural resources (e.g. Gold, Diamond and Petroleum etc.) and low or little economic growth. This connection is reflected in the phenomena which economists describes as paradox of plenty and seek to explain with the theory of resource curse. The "resource curse" in resource abundant states refers primarily to the negative socio – economic development and phenomena such as poverty and general economic decline.[276]

4.2 The Resource Curse Theory

Authors like Karl and Terry Lynn – Paradox of Plenty 1997, Gary, Ian, et al., Bottom of the Barrel 2003, Douglas A. Yates, The Rentier State in Africa 1996 and Paul Collier, The Bottom Billion 2007 etc., have discussed in details what consti-

---

275 Jeffrey D. Sachs and Andrew M. Warner: *Natural resource abundance and economic growth*, Center for International Development and Harvard Institute for International Development, Harvard University, Cambridge MA, 1997.

276 Basedau Matthias, Context Matters: Rethinking the Resource Curse in Sub- Saharan Africa. German Overseas Institute (DÜI), No 1 May 2005.

tutes the resource curse theory as it reflects in states endowed with abundance of natural resources. Resource curse refers to the paradox that countries and regions with an abundance of natural resources, like mineral and fuels, tend to have less economic growth and worse development outcomes than countries with fewer natural resources. In other words, the negative development outcomes associated with petroleum and other minerals are referred to as "resource curse."[277] The term resource curse thesis was first used by Richard Auty in 1993 to describe how countries rich natural resources were unable to use that wealth to boost their economies and how, counter-intuitively, these countries had lower economic growth than countries without an abundance of natural resources.[278] The term further entails the negative effects of the mismanagement of abundance of revenues accruable from the natural resources on the people and environment by governments of countries endowed with such resources like petroleum or solid minerals like gold or diamond. It is the failure of the government to translate the abundant revenues from oil exports into socio-economic growth, human development and general welfare of the people in the country particularly in the region where such resources are located.

The following negative phenomena constitute the resource curse theory as they are observable in the countries concerned: the Dutch Disease, oil as enclave economy, debt accumulation, dictatorship and corruption, neglect of human capital development and other sectors of the economy, rentier economy, political instability and armed conflicts as well as environmental destruction and poverty. We shall discuss each of these phenomena and afterwards indicate Nigeria as an oil exporting country. In the second part of this chapter we shall treat in some details how corruption in Nigeria is affecting the development of the Niger Delta region.

4.2.1 Dutch Disease

It describes the negative effects which dominant exports of primary goods could have on the economy of such raw materials exporting countries. The Dutch Disease takes its name from the situation in the 1970s when booming North Sea gas exports pumped massive rents into the Netherlands. The gas export revenues appreciated the Dutch Guilder against other currencies. This makes the country's other export activities uncompetitive.[279]

---

277 Gary & Karl, Bottom of the Barrel, p. 21.
278 Auty, Richard M. Sustainable Development in Mineral Economies: The Resource Curse Thesis, London, Routledge, 1993.
279 Collier Paul, The Bottom Billion, p. 39.

It works in such a way that the high price of raw materials or the discovery of new deposits gives rise to an export boom. The sudden and massive inflow of foreign currency from the exported raw materials leads to over valuation of the local currency and to loss of ability for competition and this invariably has negative effects on the processing and manufacturing industries and well as the agricultural sector.[280] This situation provokes a rapid, even distorted, growth of services, transportation, and construction, while simultaneously discouraging some industrialisation and agriculture. It is a pathology that has been observed in the oil-rentier economies afflicted by price shocks. The Dutch Disease afflicts countries with booming oil sectors by distorting the patterns of growth in the agricultural and other tradable productive sectors of the economy.[281] As noted above, the inflow of capital leads to an appreciation of the currency, making imports cheap and exports expensive.

Because it is cheap to import, imported goods, including food items, become more attractive or valuable than locally produced goods to the people, particularly the middle class and elites. This in turn discourages local productions. Local industries, which have hitherto provided employment opportunities for many people, are forced to fold up as they are not able to compete favorably with imported goods. One consequence of the large amount of external rent available in a rentier economy is that its state tends to relax constraints on foreign exchange. The availability of foreign currency in such relative abundance means that the rentier states can acquire foreign goods without the usurious costs of exchange. It also means that imported goods have the tendency to replace domestically produced goods, particularly in agriculture and manufacturing, which often cannot compete with foreign goods produced under economies of scale. The state purchases foodstuffs, which then compete with domestically produced foodstuffs on the local markets[282]. Little wonder then, that the Nigerian state has not been focusing adequate attention on agriculture and manufacturing.

4.2.2 The Enclave nature of Oil Economy

Enclave describes the part of an economy of any developing country that is dominated by the most modern foreign technology and capital, thus producing mainly for the world market with little or weak connection with other sectors of the local economy. In this case, the control of the technology and the capital are

280 Schuldt &Acosta, Ölrenten und Unterentwicklung, 64. Cf. also Collier, Paul, The Bottom Billion, Oxford: University Press 2007, p. 39 as well as Karl, Paradox of Plenty, p. 5.
281 Yates, Douglas A., The Rentier State in Africa, Trenton NJ: Africa World Press, pp. 27-36.
282 Yates, Douglas A., The Rentier State in Africa, p. 24.

in the hands of the foreign investors, just as the lion share of the profit flows to the home countries of the investors.[283] One of the characteristics of an enclave economy is that its negotiations are shrouded in secrecy. In other words, its accountability and transparency are cloudy.

In the case of the petroleum industry, the technology and capitals for production are in the hands of the transnational oil companies (TNOCs) and their products are directed mainly to meet the demands of the world market. It follows that decisions about the oil industry are made mostly outside the oil exporting countries. It is true that oil exporting countries, particularly in Africa South of the Sahara, are only one part of the a web of interests and relationships in the African oil booms, however the major actors determining the outcomes of this boom are foreign transnational oil companies, international finance institutions like the World Bank and International Monetary Fund, export credit agencies, and Northern governments. While African governments ultimately decide how revenues are allocated inside their borders, the policies, action and development strategies of these international players are essential, if not decisive, elements for determining what revenues actually accrue to governments, how these revenues are managed, and how they are spent. Taken together or individually, they are more powerful than any single African government.[284] In other words, governments of oil exporting countries, including Nigeria, do not have absolute control or power over how the oil economy works. And since oil exporting countries depend mainly on a single resource they "are especially vulnerable to export-earning instability, which in turn has negative consequences for the rate of growth, levels of investment, and inflation"[285].

In the case of Nigeria, the Nigerian state is represented in the oil industry by the Nigerian National Petroleum Corporation (NNPC) who runs a number of Joint Ventures (JV) with Transnational Oil Companies (TNOCs) on behalf of the Federal Government of Nigeria. The modalities of the operations of NNPC and other partners in the JVs will be treated in the next section of this chapter under corruption.

The high rate of unemployment in the Niger Delta region in spite of the presence of several transnational oil corporations, the refineries and related industries in the region, seem to find explanation in the fact that the oil industry is a capital-intensive sector and that is an enclave. Because the petroleum industry is more capital intensive than any other economic activity and involves very extensive knowledge, skills and technology, only the biggest players, either multinationals or states, are able to exploit this resource. In most cases, particularly in Africa,

---

283 Nohlen, Dieter (Hg.), Lexikon der Dritten Welt, Hamburg: Rowolt 2000, p. 227. Cf also. Nuscheler, Franz, Entwicklungspolitik , Bonn: Dietz [6]2005, p. 623.

284 Gary &Karl, Bottom of the Barrel, p. 17.

285 Karl, Paradox of Plenty, p. 47.

the multinationals owned by the industrialized countries dominate the oil industry. Moreover, this industry is characterized by low employment generation and a skewed wage structure. Unlike comparable sectors in agricultural exporters, the oil sector employs only between 1 and 2 percent of the workforce[286]. For instance, *Shell Petroleum*, which is the biggest of the oil companies in Nigeria, can only employ 12,000 persons (skilled and unskilled). One may say that 12,000 is a lot, but when compared with a population of about 30 million Niger Deltans and 150 million Nigerians, then the figure is very little.

The workforce is very few, highly technical and well structured. Wages are particularly high in the oil industry; as such those who end up being employed are expatriates and highly skilled labour that may not necessarily be indigenes of oil producing communities. This situation often results to conflicts or tensions in oil producing regions. In this regard, Schuldt and Acosta are of the view that in comparison to other branches of the economy, mining and oil exploration do absorb directly or indirectly only little work force, even when they are well paid. It is capital intensive, it depends on a lot of pre-imports, personnel both in the management and the skilled experts are engaged from abroad, essential materials and technologies that are used are almost exclusively imported from abroad. With that, the domestic economic profit, which corresponds to the value generated within a country, tends to be zero. This leads to social tensions in the regions where natural resources are exploited, because usually few people can only find job or employment in the mining and oil companies.[287]

Consequently, as the industry's wage scale surpasses that of other domestic sectors, it exerts an upward pull on the rest of the economy. The resulting wage followership produces a labour aristocracy, on the one hand, and underemployment among the unskilled, on the other. In effect, oil-led development results in a foreign-controlled, high-wage economy characterized by some unions and high unemployment.[288] Again, as an enclave, the oil sector hardly has much positive effect on the local economy. This is because most of the high wages earned by the skilled labour force are taken out of the region where oil is exploited.

4.2.3 Fluctuating Oil Revenue and Debt Accumulation

Not only is petroleum volatile by nature but also its price and market are equally volatile and fluctuating. This makes budgeting difficult as well as the management of such revenues just as the rate of expenditure of the revenues from oil by

---

286 Karl, Paradox of Plenty, p. 47.
287 Schuldt & Acosta, Ölrenten und Unterentwicklung, p. 69.
288 Karl, Paradox of Plenty, p. 48.

oil exporting countries can be outrageously high during the period of oil boom. For instance, for almost the whole of 2008 the price of crude oil was almost $150 per barrel; in July 2009, it hovered between $50 and $60. This sudden rise and fall in oil prices makes proper or effective budgeting difficult. As Collier noted, "volatile revenues are obviously difficult to manage. During a price boom, government ministries, scenting the money available, put in outrageous bids for more spending."[289] The sudden income leap from oil entices the governments' appetite to spend on grandiose plans and ideas, expanding their ministries and window-dressing their images nationally and internationally by way of embarking on white elephant projects in the cities to create a façade that all is well while the rural areas are languishing in penury and neglect.

4.2.4 Neglect of Human Capital Development and other Branches of Economy

One of the effects of resource curse is the neglect of the education sector or the lacking development of human capital of the resource rich countries. Raw stuff exporting countries tend to neglect the education of their citizens because they do not see the immediate need for it.

Under Dutch Disease we have seen how the sudden influx of foreign exchange during oil boom could lead to overvalued local currency. Not just that overvalued foreign exchange does encourage imports, but more attention is paid to the foreign exchange generating sector and other areas of urgent political interests to the government. This is done to the detriment of the other sectors of the economy. Non-oil productive activities, like manufacturing and agriculture, are adversely affected by the petroleum sector. For example, rubber plantations that were a common sight in the Niger Delta region and which used to provide employment opportunities for many rural workforces as well as produce raw materials for the manufacturing of tires have been abandoned by the government since the era of oil boom in the 1970s. Similarly, palm oil plantations, for which the Niger Delta region is known and that engaged many hands of the rural population for the production of palm oil both for local market and export, have been neglected.

Small and medium scale enterprises (SMEs) are equally not given sufficient attention by the government. As a result many local manufacturers are not just able to compete favorably with imported products in terms of prices and quality. They cannot also meet the needs of the domestic market.

---

289   Collier, The Bottom Billion, p. 40.

These other sectors of the economy used to provide more stable and sustainable revenue streams to the government, and government was obliged to justify the taxes from the people by providing corresponding services to the public. However, with continued reliance on oil revenues, non-oil taxes as well as their sources, that is, their sector of origin, appear unimportant to government. Government does not appear to be under any obligation of transparency and accountability to the citizens over revenues from petroleum, because such revenues were not collected from the people. And the government can afford to do what it wants and not attend to the needs or aspirations of the people.

4.2.5 Political Instability and armed conflicts

Another effect of resource curse in countries rich in natural resources is political instability and armed conflicts. This phenomenon is more obvious in the developing countries. Reason for this is that, it is only a very handful of elites that are profiting from the exploration and export of such raw materials like petroleum, while the majority of the population remain poor. In effect, the abundance of natural resources is contributing very little to the improvement in the overall wellbeing of the people instead; it contributes to widening the gap between the rich and poor. It equally increases the potentials for conflicts. This is because access to the revenue from the export of the natural resources serves both as source of economic and political power. No wonder then that many countries rich in natural resources are often politically unstable and constantly experience armed conflicts.

The political instability in Nigeria since independence in 1960 to 1999 can safely be attributed partly to the struggle of the elites both civilian and military to gain access to and control of the oil revenue. The Nigerian civil war from 1967 to 1970 was not unconnected with the abundance of natural resources in the Niger Delta. The availability of crude oil in Iraq plays a significant role in the Iraq war. The abundance of Diamond in Liberia and Sierra Leone serves as one of the major causes of the prolonged civil wars in both countries. Income from the abundance of the natural resources in Gold, Diamond, Crude oil, etc., is a major source of financing the decades of civil wars and armed struggles in Angola and the Democratic Republic of Congo. Though the various conflicts in Sudan are being attributed to religious and ethnic tensions, the unequal distribution of the revenue from the exports of crude oil plays a significant role. The so called "blood diamond" can be considered as part of the resource curse.

The legal and regulatory laws to ensure the control of the mineral resources put in place by the state (3.5) often work to the advantage of the elites to the detriment of the generality of the people. For example the Petroleum Act and the

Land Use act in Nigeria often work to the advantage of the elites that occupy political power or operate the state structures. They often serve as sources of conflicts in the Niger Delta region. We have pointed out under violent conflicts (3.6) that most conflicts are connected to the availability of oil and gas in the region.

Worth noting is the fact that the series of military coups and counter coups were attempts by different military officers to gain access to the oil revenue.

4.2.6 Environmental Damage and Poverty

A further consequence of abundance of natural resources is damage to the environment where such resources are being mined or explored. This is more peculiar to developing countries, where either there are no effective environmental laws or that the governments of such countries are too weak to compel the oil multinationals to comply by the rules. As Collier noted, the more oil wells there are, more the extent of environmental damage in the countries that constitute the bottom billion.[290] The adverse effect of environmental damage is the destruction of the vegetation and pollution of water which are basic sources of economic activities and thus means of livelihood for the local inhabitants. As long as the state does not provide alternative means of livelihood, the local people remain in poverty.

In the case of Nigeria or rather the Niger Delta, we have pointed out earlier (Cf. 3.3), that the environmental degradation was encouraged by the fact that there were no regulatory measures until the Federal Environmental Protection Agency was established 1988 whereas oil exploration began 1956. By the time the laws were enacted early 90s a lot of damage had been done to the environment, thus the basis of the means of livelihood for the majority of the people in the Niger Delta. Since the environment has badly polluted through oil exploration, and there are no sufficient viable alternatives for the people, they are bound to elk out there existence in poverty and penury.

There is a shortage of evidence to show that the federal government is compelling the oil multinationals to clean up the polluted environment. As a matter of fact, Ken Sarowiwa who championed the demand for environment clean up, compensation to and just participation of the Ogonis in the revenue from oil was judicially hanged by the military of government of Late General Sani Abacha in November 1995.

---

290   Collier, Paul, The Bottom Billion p. 31.

4. 2.7 Rentier Economy

A rentier is a social agent who does not actively participate in the production process yet shares in the fruits of the product. In normal economic process, wages are paid for labour, interest for capital employed, and profits for the successful management of risk. There are some elements of sacrifice and efforts involved in these factor incomes. A rentier makes no value-added effort in generating the income. The purest rentier is but a parasite feeding on the productive activities of others. In the case of petroleum, only nature is sacrificed.[291]

Rentier mentality is the attitude that grows out of the desire or pursuit of collecting rents, rather than being engaged in productive activities. It is a psychological condition that is prevalent in a rentier state running a rentier economy. Rent-seeking mentality is typical in oil-exporting countries. Because it is the governments that collects and distributes oil rents and thus controls the economy, both political and economic powers rest with the state. It follows that only links with the state can guarantee access to the oil rents. Rent-seeking is a widespread behaviour aimed at capturing petrodollars through unproductive and even corrupt means. In oil-exporting countries like Nigeria, all actors (whether public or private, domestic or foreign) have overwhelming incentives to seek links with the state in order to make money. Rent-seeking mentality is further promoted by the practices of the government, such that contracts are awarded by the government as an expression of gratitude to their supporters or loyalists rather than as a reflection of economic rationale. Civil servants see their principal duty as being available in their offices during working hours, businessmen abandon industry and enter into real estate speculation or other special situation so associated with a booming oil sector, the best and brightest abandon business and seek out lucrative government employment.

Discussing the petro-states in comparative perspective Karl points out that rent-seeking and corruption have rendered some petro-states like Nigeria dysfunctional. In Nigeria, the level of corruption is comparable to the epidemic proportions that states like Venezuela, Iran, and to a lesser (or perhaps more hidden) extent Algeria reached. It became the most visible expression of how the state was targeted and rendered dysfunctional by "pirate capitalists", politicians, and other rent seekers, who were especially venal because they believed they had little time to benefit from their links to the state.[292]

As a rentier state, running a rentier economy, all rents or revenues are centrally collected and deposited in the federation accounts. The oil revenue flows

---

291   Yates, The Rentier State in Africa, 17.
292   Karl, Paradox of Plenty, p. 208.

into the state largely through the Nigerian National Oil Company (NNPC). The amounts deposited in the federation account are shared by the three levels of government on a constitutional formula. This means that both political and economic powers lay in the hands of the state – federal, state and local governments. Since most other sectors of the economy have been neglected by the state, anyone seeking access to the economy must turn his search light on the state. And the state decides who gains access to the economy. Naturally the state favours those who are willing to do its political bidding. Since it is only the state that can finance capital projects, issue licenses, is the major employer of labour etc., only connections with the ruling class and high-ranking public officials can ensure access to all these. What all these boil down to is that access to political power means access to economic power. And so, the big game in town in Nigeria is to capture the oil money, whatever it takes to do so. This rent-seeking mentality has crept into the Nigerian society over time. To gain access to political power one must bribe his way, and it is not usually at any cheap amount of money. After attaining the political power at whatever level of government, it is only natural for one to recover his investment with surplus gain. The rent-seeking mentality has given rise to the mismanagement of public funds to the extent that Nigeria is almost synonymous with corruption.

No wonder then, that only little of the money paid by the federal government to the state and local governments from the oil revenues is actually spent on genuine development projects. Furthermore, there appears to be virtually no control or proper audit over spending by local and state authorities.[293]

4.3 Nigeria as Exporter of Petroleum

The petroleum sector plays a vital role in Nigeria's economy. For example, in 2005 oil revenues accounted for 99 percent of all Nigeria export revenues, 88 percent of government income, and 50 percent of Nigeria's GDP, amounting to over $50 billion.[294] Nigeria joined the OPEC in 1971 having qualified as a country whose main economic income is revenue accruable from oil export, which is the prerequisite for joining OPEC. Understanding oil exporters as those countries in which the high share of oil production in gross domestic product (GDP) and of oil exports in total exports place the petroleum sector at the centre of economic

---

293 Gary & Karl, Bottom of the Barrel, 26-27.
294 Lubeck, Paul M., et al: Convergent Interests. U.S. Energy Security and the security of Nigerian Democracy, International Policy Report 2007, http://www.cipoline.org/NIGERIA FINAL .pdf. Visited on 01.03.2008. Hereafter to be referred to as International Policy Report 2007.

accumulation, and following the World Bank's guiding thresholds of approximately 10 percent of GDP and 40 percent of total merchandise exports[295], Nigeria is qualified to be referred to as a petroleum exporting country. As an oil exporting country, Nigeria shares similar experiences with other oil exporting countries in the Third World.

- Generally, dependency on oil exports poses some development problems to the oil-exporting countries, among which are: Oil booms raise expectations and increase appetites for spending;
- Governments dramatically increase public spending based on unrealistic revenue projections;
- Booms decrease the quality of public spending and encourage rent-seeking;
- The volatility of oil prices hinders growth, distribution and poverty alleviation;
- Booms encourage the loss of fiscal control and inflation, further hampering growth, equity and the alleviation of poverty;
- Foreign debt grows faster in oil-exporting countries, mortgaging the future;
- Non-oil productive activities, like manufacturing and agriculture, are adversely affected by the oil sector in a phenomenon called the "Dutch Disease";
- Petrodollars replace more stable and sustainable revenue streams, exacerbating the problems of development, transparency and accountability.[296]

Government actors are prone to corruption and mismanagement of the oil revenue giving rise to a situation of resource curse on some oil exporting countries. A situation of resource curse is typified by unusually high poverty, poor health care, and widespread malnutrition, high rates of child mortality, low life expectancy, and poor educational performance. The existence of these features in the Niger Delta tends to justify the theory of resource curse to explain the reason for the poverty and underdevelopment in the region.

4.4 Corruption in Nigeria

There are various perceptions of corruption depending on the perspective from which one views it. However, a general understanding of corruption among social scientists has been provided by a Harvard social scientist, Joseph S. Nye. Nye says corruption is "behavior which deviates from normal duties of a public role

---

295   Karl, Terry Lynn, Paradox of Plenty – Oil Booms and Petro-States, Berkeley: University of California Press 1997, p. 17.
296   Gary, Ian, et al, Bottom of the Barrel – Africa's Oil Boom and the Poor, Catholic Relief Service, 2003, pp. 21-23.

because of private-regarding (family, close private clique), pecuniary or status gains; or violates rules against the exercise of certain types of private-regarding influence. This includes such behaviors as bribery (use of reward to pervert the judgment of a person in a position of trust); nepotism (bestowal of patronage by reason of ascriptive relationship rather than merit); and misappropriation (illegal appropriation of public resources for private-regarding uses)"[297]. Similarly, corruption can be defined as the deliberate and conscious pervasion of an official process, to fulfill a personal advantage. It is obtaining material enrichment or opportunities for oneself and/or for others through the use of public office or personal connection in ways other than those publicly acknowledged through the rules and procedures of office.[298] The World Bank and the non-governmental organization Transparency International (TI) define corruption as "the abuse of public office for private gain". This includes situations when public officials accept, solicit, or extort bribes, when private actors offer bribes to subvert or circumvent public policies for competitive advantage and profit. According to the World Bank, patronage or nepotism by government officials, theft of state assets, or the illegal diversion of state revenues are all forms of corruption.[299]

The World Bank distinguishes between two forms of corruption: state capture and administrative corruption. State capture is conceived to be the actions of individuals, groups, or firms in both the public and private sectors to influence the formation of laws, regulations, decrees and other government policies (that is, the basic rules of the game) to their own advantage by means of the illicit and non-transparent provision of private benefits to public officials. Administrative corruption involves changing or altering the implementation of existing laws, rules, and regulations to provide advantages to either state or non-state actors as a result of the illicit and non-transparent provision of private gain to public officials. In this case, state officials can simply misdirect public funds under their control for their own or their family's direct financial benefit.[300]

Topmost on the litany of woes besetting Nigeria is corruption. In an opinion poll conducted by the Guardian Newspapers in 2000, Nigerians picked corruption, unemployment and bad leadership as the worst problems hindering the country's development. A total of 761 respondents or 70 per cent of the 1,080

---

297 Nye, J.S, Corruption and Political Development: A Cost Benefit Analysis. *In*: Heidenheimer, A.J et al. (eds.) Political Corruption. A Handbook, New Brunswick: Transaction 1989, pp. 963-983.

298 Akani, Christian (ed.) Corruption in Nigeria – The Niger Delta Experience, Enugu: Fourth Dimension Publishing Co. 2002, p. 36.

299 The World Bank, Helping Countries Combat Corruption: The role of the World Bank, Washington DC: The World Bank 1997, p. 8. See also Transparency International, Frequently Asked Questions About the Corruption Perceptions Index: press release, 28 August 2002.

300 The World Bank, Anticorruption in Transition. A Contribution to the Policy Debate, Washington DC: The World Bank 2000, pp. 1-2.

respondents picked corruption as one of the worst problems hindering the nation's advancement.[301] It is a common knowledge that corruption has become part and parcel of Nigerian society. It is the greatest obstacle to sustainable development. Several scholars have written on it. For instance, Joseph Richard has coined the term prenbendalism[302] to describe the undercurrent of the political economy of Nigeria as patron-client, which is a form of corruption. For Richard, it is the sense of entitlement that many people in Nigeria feel they have to the revenues of the Nigerian state. Elected officials, government workers, and members of the ethnic and religious groups to which they belong feel they have a right to a share of government revenues.[303]

Similarly, Daniel O. Edevbaro of the University of Helsinki, has carried out a detailed study on the political economy of corruption and underdevelopment in Nigeria. He points out that corruption which has led to the underdevelopment of the country is fuelled by a system in which political power is also the principal source of wealth. Combined with the continued economic centrality of state power, this has engendered a vicious circle of poverty and underdevelopment.[304]

It is a fact that corruption has permeated every segment of Nigerian society. It is not limited to the ruling or political class, but cuts across all public and private sectors as well as among some development donors and practitioners.[305] It is not within the scope of this study to repeat all the studies already done on the problem of corruption in Nigeria but rather to point out to what extent the level of corruption in Nigeria has become a hindrance to poverty eradication and human development in the Niger Delta. In other words, we intend to demonstrate that corruption and mismanagement of oil revenues by the Nigerian government has robbed the majority of people the benefit of development, particularly in the Niger Delta.

Our thesis is that corruption in Nigeria is targeted at getting a share of the oil rent using the structure or institution of the state as means. As the World Bank indicates above, the state capture and administrative corruption are aimed at getting access to the oil revenue for the purpose of personal enrichment.

---

301 Igbuzor, Otive, Strategies for Winning the Anti-corruption war in Nigeria, Abuja: ActionAid Nigeria 2008, p. 4. Cf. also The Guardian Newspapers, Monday 6 November 2000 p. 19.

302 The adjective stems from the verb Prebend, "the right of a member of a chapter to his share in the revenues of the cathedral; also the share to which he is entitled; in general, any portion of the cathedral revenues set aside for the support of the clergy attached to it (semi-prebends) even for those who are not members of the chapter. They are regarded as benefices and governed by the same law. See The Catholic Encyclopedia, vol. xii, New York: Robert Appton Company 1911, p. 371.

303 Richard, Joseph A, Democracy and Prebendal Politics in Nigeria: the rise and fall of the Second Republic, Cambridge: University Press 1987, pp. 55-90.

304 Edevbaro, Daniel Osakponmwen, The Political Economy of Corruption and Underdevelopment in Nigeria, Helsinki: Yliopistopaino 1998, p. 7.

305 Smith, Daniel Jordan, A Culture of Corruption – Everyday Deception and Popular Discontent in Nigeria, Oxford: Princeton University Press 2007.

4.4.1 Corruption in the Petroleum Industry

The fact that the petroleum industry is ridden with corruption became a common knowledge in the 1980s as the Nigerian public was informed that N2.8 billion had been misappropriated from the coffers of the NNPC. The government of the then President Shehu Shagari set up the Crude Oil Sales Tribunal of Inquiry headed by Justice Ayo Irikefe. Up till today, neither Justice Irikefe nor anyone has been able to ascertain where the missing N2.8 billion from the NNPC account went. However, the efforts of the tribunal did educate the public, for the first time, on how messy the operations of the NNPC were and how much money was going down the wrong channels.

Since the first public knowledge of the phenomenal of corruption in the petroleum industry, there has been a series of reports of incidences of corruption and sharp practices in the sector involving NNPC officials and the TNOCs. For example, the Nigerian House of Representatives has recently accused the NNPC of not having a properly approved budget like any other government ministries. The accusation was based on the position of the House that what the NNPC considers a budget was nothing but a circular paper passed between its management and the presidency. This situation certainly creates room for fraud and corruption.[306] Similarly, in a memorandum to the House of Representatives Public Hearing on Non-Remittance of Revenue by Ministries, Departments and Agencies (MDAs) into Federation Account, the Accountant General of the Federation Alhaji Ibrahim Dankwabo listed eight sources of corruption in the public sector. He rated four of them to be worrisome in the following order of importance: Insufficient information on activities of the Nigerian National Petroleum Corporation (NNPC) and oil revenues, leakages in tax revenues, differential accounting methods by the Federal Inland Revenue Service (FIRS) and the Central Bank of Nigeria (CBN), leakages in Nigeria Customs Services (NCS) revenues and Federal Government and independent sources. It was further alleged that revenues running into trillions of Naira from the excess crude proceeds, signature bonus, sales of government properties, cost of collection from revenue agencies, waivers and concessions, Nigeria Liquefied Gas (NLNG) dividends, privatization proceeds, education tax proceeds and other dividends and Internally-Generated Revenue (IGR) between 2004 and 2007 were not remitted into the Federation Account.[307]

What all these point to is that, to understand the level of corruption in Nigeria, we need to begin from the mainstay of Nigeria's economy, the oil industry.

---

306 The Nigerian Tribune, 5 August 2009.
307 Oloja, Martin, "Accountant-General lists points of corruption in government", see Guardian Newspaper, Monday, 14 July, 2008.

To appreciate the level and extent of corruption in the oil industry and be able to proffer solutions, there is the need to know which government institutions or structures are involved with whom and what in the industry. Of importance also is the need to point out areas where corruption prevails most in the industry.

4.4.1.1 Government Institutions and their Roles in the Petroleum Industry

The government institutions that manage the affairs of Nigeria's oil industry are the NNPC, the Ministry of Petroleum, Department of Petroleum Resources (DPR), Presidency and Federal Executive Council (FEC). These institutions function respectively as follows:

- **NNPC**: as Nigeria's national oil company, NNPC controls a large range of upstream and downstream activities. With over nine thousand staff, its functions include the operation of 12 subsidiaries, among them refineries, petrochemical plants and oil-trading companies. The most significant subsidiary is the National Petroleum Investment Management Services (NAPIMS), which acts as the industry's concessionaire, entering into contracts with oil companies on behalf of government. Because of the size of its personnel, budget, and mandate, and its high share of industry expertise, NNPC is the lead government actor in the oil sector.

- **The Ministry of Petroleum** (sometime known as the Ministry of Energy) technically oversees and leads oil sector policy-making. From 1999 to 2007 the President served as the Minister of Petroleum. Though a junior-level minister served as Minister of State for Petroleum, his scope of influence and unilateral authority was limited. This practice continued until the beginning of 2009 when the late President Yar'Adua appointed Dr. Rilwanu Lukman as Minister of Petroleum.

- **The Department of Petroleum Resources (DPR)** is the industry's regulator. Until 1988, DPR existed as a unit within NNPC, creating the untenable situation of the regulator being subordinate to the industry's largest player. While they now operate separately under the Ministry of Petroleum, the NNPC retained some regulatory functions. The DPR's mandate includes the allocation of oil blocks, the collection of royalties, the enforcement of sector regulations (safety, environment, gas flaring, etc.), and other technical oversight functions.

- **The President and his top advisors** together with the top leadership of the NNPC form the inner circle of oil sector decision-making. Until recently, the President doubled as Minister of Petroleum, and played a direct and decisive role in oil sector operations. To assist in this endeavour, Presidents Obasanjo and Yar'Adua both appointed two senior advisors on petroleum matters who exercised a great deal of authority while acting on behalf of the President.[308]

The harmonious collaboration of these actors in the execution of their functions is a subject of criticisms that border on the weak DPR capacity, NNPC interference into regulatory and policy-making functions, lack of NNPC oversight and accountability, and weak incentives for efficiency and performance generally.

Nigeria's oil industry operates under six large Joint Venture (JV) arrangements between transnational oil companies (TNOCs) and the NNPC. Under the JV, NNPC and its TNOC partners are to jointly develop oil prospecting licenses or oil mining leases (OMLs) and facilities. Each partner in the JV contributes to the costs and shares the benefits or losses of the operations in accordance with its proportionate equity interest in the venture. But NNPC has consistently struggled to pay its share of operating costs forcing it to enter into a string of loan arrangements with its company partners.[309]

In the 1990s Nigeria opted to offer the Production Sharing Contracts (PSCs) to the TNOCs for offshore blocks in order to stimulate deepwater exploration, diversify the sector's corporate participants, and avoid the problematic of cash-call system. Under the PSC arrangement, the operator incurs all risks as it puts up the funds for exploration and production activities. If and when production begins, the oil is divided into "cost oil" and "profit oil". Cost oil goes to the operator so they can recover their investments. Profit oil is split between the operator and the NNPC at a proportion set in the contract. In addition the operator pays petroleum profit tax (PPT) on its share of profit oil as well as royalties based on production. The disadvantage of PSCs is that it gives lower average take to government than Joint Ventures.

Five main areas of activities of these regulating institutions provide fertile grounds for corruption. These are:

- **Awarding upstream licenses**

The common practice is that governments of most oil-rich countries directly allocate the highly valuable licenses to explore and produce oil. Without well-regulated award procedures, such transactions offer possible opportunities for corruption. The Nigeria's Petroleum Act gives the Minister of Petroleum full authority over the allocation of licenses for the exploration, prospecting and

308 Gillies, Alexandra, Reforming Corruption out of Nigerian Oil? Anti-Corruption Resource Centre, http://www.U4.no, no.2, February 2009.

309 Gillies, Alexandra, Reforming Corruption out of Nigerian Oil? Anti-Corruption Resource Centre, http://www.U4.no, no.2, February 2009. Cf. Catholic Secretariat of Nigeria, Nigeria The Travesty of Oil and Gas Wealth, pp. 80-84.

mining of oil. There were no legally mandated processes or oversight mechanisms for the allocation of oil blocks until most recently. This is no doubt an open invitation to corrupt practices in the industry. For instance, during the military rule, most licenses were awarded on a discretionary basis by the head of state. It was alleged that General Abdulsalam allocated some oil blocks to senior military officers shortly before he left office in 1999. Upon assuming office President Obasanjo revoked eleven of the oil blocks. In what appears to be an attempt to bring some sanity into oil industry, the Obasanjo government publicly advertised the available oil blocks and selection criteria, and disclosed the various bids received. However, each of the major bid rounds conducted by DPR in 2000, 2005, 2006, and 2007 suffered serious shortcomings arising from various manipulations.[310] In 2008, probes into the bid rounds by the Presidency and the by the House of Representatives uncovered these manipulations and resulted in the suspension of DPR's director and the revocation of several oil blocks. Throughout his presidency Obasanjo appointed himself as the Minister of Petroleum.[311]

- **Awarding contracts**

Awarding large-scale contracts mainly to oil service companies is a common practice in the oil sector. In principle, it is the operator company which awards these contracts. However, the Nigeria government retains a high degree of control over such transactions. Recent events have shown that the contracting procedures are not corruption-proof. For instance, in the prosecution under the U.S. Foreign Corrupt Practices Act (FCPA), Albert Jackson Stanley of Kellogg, Brown and Root, a US oil service company, pled guilty to paying around US$180 million in bribes to NNPC, the Petroleum Ministry, and other government officials. This was to ensure four contracts, together worth over US$6 billion, to build liquefied natural gas facilities. In addition to receiving bribes, government officials have other ways of corruptly enriching themselves in the course of awarding contracts.[312]

---

310 Companies were forced into partnerships without explanation, signature bonus deadlines were unevenly enforced, and bid round qualification standards inconsistently applied, all to the advantage of certain companies.

311 Gillies, Alexandra, Reforming Corruption out of Nigerian Oil? Anti-Corruption Resource Centre, http://www.U4.no, no.2, February 2009.

312 Government officials can also benefit from procedures that favour companies in which they have a financial stake. For instance, senior political leaders reportedly manipulated tenders to benefit Intels Nigeria Ltd, a large logistics company, for their private gain. Alternatively, officials can give preference to companies owned by their allies, and then seek repayment through other business deals or political favours.

- **Bottlenecks and inefficiencies**

Oil and oil service companies frequently confront costly delays and inefficiencies in their dealings with Nigerian state institutions. Though these do not constitute corruption per se, but such delays create the motive and opportunity for paying bribes to speed up procedures. For instance, contracts and other expenditures above a low threshold ($ 1 million) require NNPC approval process consisting of National Petroleum Investment Management Services (NAPIMS), the NNPC group Executive Council, and the NNPC Board. Larger awards also require Federal Executive Council approval. The average time for the review of contracts is 24 months, while the global industry average is 6 to 9 months. This bottleneck ensures that top NNPC officials remain the gatekeeper of the industry. Protecting this arrangement often contradicts profit maximization within the national oil company. As a result, its functions remain inefficient, politicized, and susceptible to capture by individual interests.

- **Oil bunkering**

Bunkering is the theft of crude oil directly from pipelines, flow stations, and export facilities. It is generally believed that around 100,000 barrel per day (bpd) is lost via bunkering in Nigeria, a quantity equal to the entire oil production of Cameroun. Other estimates are put around 600,000 bpd. It is also widely perceived that both government and oil company representatives are complicit in bunkering activities. Groups of well-armed young men typically execute the pipeline sabotage, but their activities are overseen by powerful figures. Other ways of bunkering like the loading of more crude than is reported onto export vessels, would certainly require some level of official complicity. The costs of bunkering are enormous. The nefarious activities of oil thieves translates into a loss of about 20 percent of the expected crude oil production output, on a daily basis. This reduction in the amount of crude Nigeria exports cuts down the revenues which should have accrued to the state. It was estimated as far back as 2001, that Nigeria was losing up to three billion Naira – N3bn annually to illegal oil bunkering carried out both on- and off-shore.[313] The security risks and damage to equipment associated with bunkering dissuade investment in onshore exploration and production. More perversely, bunkering provides a steady stream of funding for the militancy movements and corrupt syndicates responsible for destabilizing the Delta region. Buying arms, paying militant forces, and bribing officials become easier with readily available cash.

---

313 See The Daily Independent (Lagos), Nigeria: Illegal Oil Bunkering As Economic Sabotage, 28 Jul 2009. http://allafrica.com/stories/200907281037.hml. Visited on 20.8.2009.

- **The exportation of crude oil and importation of refined products**

Annually, the NNPC issues "lifting" or export contracts to the international oil trading companies, several NNPC-affiliated companies, and a few foreign governments. The traders buy the crude oil from the NNPC at market price and sell it on to refineries and other buyers worldwide. In the same way, the NNPC also grant licenses to import-refined petroleum products such as petrol, kerosene and diesel. These export and import transactions yield high levels of tangible returns, and the lack of transparency surrounding them creates considerable opportunities for corruption. Following a pre-qualification process for the licenses, it is not clear how winners are selected or how much the contracts are worth.

It is therefore not a surprise that the four refineries in Nigeria produce only around half of their combined potential capacity of 438,000 bpd. At present Nigeria imports the majority of the refined petroleum products used by its population. Petroleum and kerosene prices are subsidized by the government. The subsidy and weak market regulation provide enormous opportunities for corruption. For instance, distributors import refined products at the international market price, and sell them on the Nigerian market at the subsidized price. An NNPC subsidiary reimburses these companies for the difference. These payments are often delayed for months, creating incentives for the companies to induce government payments. The subsidy also allows for other high-profit rackets. It is often alleged that distributors collect the subsidy reimbursement on imported products, or buy them from Nigerian refineries at the subsidized price. They then re-import the same products so as to receive the subsidy refund again or sell them for much higher prices on the black market or abroad.

From the foregoing, corruption in the oil industry whether involving public sector actors or enabled by their weakness, reduces the Nigerian oil industry's earning potential by misallocating funds and contracts, rewarding inefficiency and permitting the theft of oil. In other words, corrupt practices in the oil sector deprive the state of enormous revenues that could be available for development work. It appears to us that the problem of corruption in the oil sector is due to the defect in the structure or institutions responsible for the management of the sector. It follows that a structural reform or solution is needed for the proper management of the oil industry. We shall return to this point in the last part of this work.

The corruption in the oil sector notwithstanding, the question remains how the state manages the oil revenues that are eventually paid into its coffers for the benefit of the people or otherwise. In other words, the corruption that is prevalent in the oil sector is reflected also in the management of the oil revenue by the state, the ruling class and the rentier elites. This is evident on the federal, state and local government levels.

131

4.4.1.2 The Oil Revenue

All revenues generated in the country including revenue from oil and gas is paid into a Federation Account. Following a revenue sharing formula, the revenues are shared among the three tiers of government as follows:

- Federal government: 52.68 percent
- States: 26.72 percent
- Local governments: 20.60 percent[314]
- 13 percent of oil revenue goes to the 9 oil-producing states.

Each of the tiers of government is expected to carry out its constitutional responsibilities that fall within its respective constituency or jurisdiction with its own share of the revenue. With the federal government at the centre including the Federal Capital Territory – Abuja, Nigeria has 36 states and 774 local government councils. Closest to the people are the local councils followed by the states. The extent to which these tiers of government are meeting their constitutional responsibilities toward the people with the oil revenue at their disposal will form the content of the next section.

4.4.2 The State's Corruption and Mismanagement of Oil Revenue

The implication of revenue allocation is that access to the revenue depends mainly on access to political power at whatever level of government and its respective ministries and agencies. Access to contracts and other economically viable transactions also depends on the connections or relationships with political office holders.

In part one, chapter one, we gave an overview of the history of Nigeria. One of the reasons given for executing coups in the past has always been corruption and embezzlement of public funds by a previous regime, be it military or civilian. The rate and extent of mismanagement, embezzlement and outright stealing of public fund by political office holders, the army, the police, customs, high-ranking civil servants with the connivance of the business class and technocrats, elites and contractors leaves no one in doubt that the Nigerian state has been turned into an instrument of corruption.[315]

---

314   Yushuau, Shuaib, Understanding the Revenue allocation formula, see http://www.yashuaib.com/revenuetable2.htm. Visted on 11.4.2009.
315   Akani Corruption in Nigeria, pp. 29-51.

It has been documented by the Office of Drug and Crime at the United Nations that about US \$400 billion was stolen from Nigeria and stashed away in foreign banks by past corrupt leaders before the return to democratic rule in 1999. According to the ex-Chairman of the Economic and Financial Crimes Commission (EFCC), Mallam Nuhu Ribadu, Nigeria's previous leaders stole about 64 trillion Naira (about US \$507 billion) from public coffers. When benchmarked against the 2008 proposed budget of N2.456 trillion Naira, this amount translates into 26 years budget.[316]

Since 1995, Transparency International (TI), a Berlin-based nonprofit, nongovernmental organization established for the main purpose of combating corruption primarily in international business but also at national levels, has been publishing the annual results of Corruption Perception Index (CPI). CPI score relates to perception of the degree of corruption as seen by business people, academics and risk analysts and ranges between 10 (highly clean) and 0 (highly corrupt)[317]. The survey is carried out in most countries in the world. Of the 54 countries surveyed in 1996 and 52 countries in 1997, Nigeria was perceived as the most corrupt in two successive years. In 1997 survey, Nigeria was followed by Pakistan and Kenya. Cameroon was the third African country in the top ten most corrupt lists. The country with the least perceived corruption was New Zealand. Denmark was rated second and Sweden came third; there was no African country in the top twenty least-corrupt nations list. The only other African country that was listed in the 1997 survey was South Africa which ranked 20th on the most corrupt list[318].

Speaking at the 10th anniversary of Transparency International in Berlin, 07 November 2003, the ex-President Olusegun Obasanjo noted that until 1999, Nigeria had practically institutionalized corruption as the foundation of existence. Hence institutions of society easily decayed to unprecedented proportions as opportunities were privatized by the powerful.[319] He pointed out further that at the root of the corruption quagmire in Nigeria is the failure and virtual collapse of governance, the contamination of democratic values, the erosion of accountability procedures, and the prevalence of bad leadership.

---

316 Igbuzor, Strategies for Winning the Anti-corruption war in Nigeria, 4.

317 Corruption Perception Index: http://www.transparency.org/policy_results/surveys_indices/ CPI/2002). Accessed on 7.9.2008.

318 Gire, James T., A Psychological analysis of Corruption in Nigeria, http://www.jsd-africa.com/ Jsda/summer1999/articlespdf/ARC. Accessed on 6.9.2008.

319 Obasanjo, Olusegun, "Nigeria: From Pond of Corruption to Island of Integrity", Lecture delivered at the 10th Anniversary Celebration of Transparency International, Berlin on 7 November 2003, cf. http://www.dawudo.com/obas35.htm. Visited on 14.8.2009.

In 2005, Nigeria, with 1.9 took the position 152 out of 158 countries surveyed. A category it shared with Cote d'Ivoire and Equatorial Guinea. In 2007 Nigeria scored 2.2 and thus ranked 147 out of 179 countries surveyed. The consequences of this rating for Nigeria as a country are enormous. Not only that it portrays Nigeria and Nigerians in bad image as highly corrupt with fraudulent practices which scares away intending tourists and foreign investors in Nigeria's economy, over and above all, it confirms that corruption is one of the root causes of the poverty and underdevelopment that are prevalent in Nigeria, particularly among the rural populace.

It should be noted that corruption cuts across the three levels of governance in Nigeria: Federal, State and Local governments. That is why the oil revenues in state coffers have not translated into development in Niger Delta region. The findings of Human Rights Watch on the human rights impact of Local Government Corruption and Mismanagement in Rivers State, Nigeria is very instructive in this regard.[320] The study reveals that huge amounts of money have been flowing into states and local governments since 1999 but these have not translated into the development of the people in the Niger delta region, because of corrupt practices by politicians and those who run the affairs of the states and local councils. One may conclude that the poverty and underdevelopment in the Niger Delta region is not totally as a result of shortage of fund or resources as such, rather what is lacking is the political will to put the available resources at the service of the people.

4.4.3 Public Procurement as Instrument of Corruption

We have noted that corruption in the oil sector is reflected in the governance of the country at all levels but particularly at the local government level. It appears that those who have no access directly to the oil sector corruption wait for the oil revenue to come into government treasury, where they easily gain access. Using the state structure of governance, politicians, elites, business class and technocrats take advantage of their privilege of office to steal the oil revenue that would have been used for the development of the people in the Niger Delta. These rent-seekers or rentiers are found of making use of public procurement as means of corruption to siphon public fund.

Public procurement is one of the most lucrative avenues of corruption in many countries. It is more severe in Nigeria. According to Ngozi Okonjo-Iweala,

---

320 Human Rights Watch, Nigeria. Chop Fine, The Human Rights Impact of Local Government of Corruption and Mismanagement in Rivers State, Nigeria19,2A (January 2007).

the Finance Minister in Nigeria and currently a Managing Director at the World Bank, prior to 1999 Nigeria government had lost an average of US$300 million each year from corrupt practices in public procurement alone. This took the form of:

- Inflation of contract costs
- Award of contracts for non-existent projects
- Over-invoicing
- Diversion of public funds to foreign banks
- And low project quality because of inexperienced contractor.[321]

Though the government has introduced the due process mechanism in the procurement procedure, which has saved US$1.5 billion for government since 2001, corruption related to the oil revenue is still on-going in government circles, particularly in the states and local governments of the Niger Delta region. The Human Rights Watch's study on the corruption in the local governments of Rivers State shows that the dynamics and mechanisms of corruption going on in the local government level take the form of awarding contracts to friends and relatives for the construction of multi-billion Naira projects like new secretariat buildings and hotels etc., while little attention is being given to primary health care and primary education.

Other forms include the irregularity and non-compliance with government budgets giving rise to reckless spending by the chairmen of local governments, security votes to chairmen which often exceed the total capital budgets for either health or education, making returns to political "godfathers", regular payment to ghost workers, and awarding of contracts to members of the legislative council to avoid impeachment or in order to get approval for budgets.[322] These corrupt practices endure because procedures established by state and federal laws, as well as local government bylaws that are meant to keep the contracting process both transparent and honest are routinely ignored. When most local government chairmen and officials exploit all the forms of corruption every month, little or nothing is left from the oil revenue from the federation account to the local government to carry out any development project. This brings us to the conclusion that corruption is one of the major causes of poverty and underdevelopment in the Niger Delta region.

---

321 Ngozi Okonjo-Iweala, Managing Natural Resources Revenue: Lessons from Nigeria's Experience.
322 Human Rights Watch, Nigeria: Chop Fine, pp. 28-35.

4.5 Conclusion

The situation of poverty and underdevelopment in the Niger Delta region came about due to the socio-economic problems associated with Nigeria's dependency on oil revenue coming from the region. Such problems are the consequences of Dutch Decease (4.2.1), the enclave nature of the economy (4.2.2), the fluctuating oil revenue and the growing foreign debt burden accumulation by the state (4.2.3), and neglect of the development of other sectors of the economy (4.2.4). These prevailing development problems are typical of rentier states like Nigeria that are running rentier economy. The condition of poverty and underdevelopment in the oil-producing region of Niger Delta can be described as a paradox of plenty and a resource curse. All these phenomena are made possible by the wide spread corruption and mismanagement of the oil revenue both by the principal actors in oil industry as well as by state actors. Corruption and mismanagement are made possible because of weak and ineffective control institutions or structures that should prevent their occurrences. Weak and ineffective structures or institutions are symptomatic of bad governance. We therefore wish to conclude that to be able to fight poverty and underdevelopment in the Niger Delta region, there is the need for firm and effective socio-economic structures. This can be guaranteed by good governance via democracy.

5. Political Analysis of Interest Groups in the Niger Delta

In the previous chapter we made a socio-economic analysis of the causes of poverty and underdevelopment in the Niger Delta. This chapter seeks to analyze the interests of the major stakeholders in the oil industry. The stakeholders are grouped into two. The first group comprises the international stakeholders made up of the governments of the United States of America (U.S.A), Western Europe, China and India as well as the transnational oil companies (TNOCs). In the second group are the national stakeholders who comprise the Nigerian governments (federal, state, and local). Others are: military, minority elites (businessmen, retired civil servants, traditional leaders and political leaders), youth militias, NGOs and Unions.

Our argument is that the politically influential stakeholders, both international and national, have always pursued their own interests and agenda with little or no considerations for the needs and concerns of Nigerian people, especially those in the Niger Delta. This is part of the reasons why the situation of poverty and underdevelopment prevails in the region.

In the first place, the international stakeholders are mainly interested in securing a stable and constant source of energy to meet the need of their industrialized economy. This they have found in the Niger Delta. Secondly, the national interest groups or stakeholders, particularly the Nigerian governments, require a source of stable revenues in foreign exchange to enable them meet both their domestic and international obligations. This too they have found in the Niger Delta. While we do not quarrel with the fact that the stakeholders pursue their interests, we contend that the strategies adopted in pursuance of their interests, have not been taking sufficient cognizance of the needs and development of the people. And therefore, they are partly responsible for the state of poverty and underdevelopment in the Niger Delta.

5.1 International Stakeholders' Interests

5.1.1 U.S.A.

Since the 1960s the U.S.A has been a major importer of Nigerian oil coming from the Niger Delta. In the early 1970s the U.S.A became the largest single buyer of Nigerian oil. In 1989 Nigerian oil exports to the USA stood at 52.6 per cent of the country's total oil export. In 1997, the USA still remained the main export market for Nigerian oil with a share of 48 per cent.[323] According to the Energy Information Administration (EIA) of the U.S. Department of Energy (DoE), Nigerian oil production averaged 1.94 million barrels per day (bbl/d) in 2008, although the EIA estimates that Nigeria's effective oil production was 2.7 million bbl/d. Of this, 990.000 bbl/d were exported to the United States. The country thus imported 44 percent of Nigeria's oil exports, making it the fifth largest foreign oil supplier to the United States. These figures of oil sales reveal that the U.S government is keenly interested in oil supply from Nigeria to meet the demands of its energy thirsty industrialized economy and be able to maintain the American way of life. There are also other bilateral trade relations between both countries. If energy supply from Nigeria was important to America before the September 11, 2001, it became more urgent after the September 11 episode. This is further compounded by the crisis in the Middle East and the recent arrival of the emerging economies of China and India to search for stable sources of energy. It has been observed that in the wake of the attacks and the Gulf War, Nigeria and West African oil producers have emerged as "the new Gulf oil states"[324] and therefore have been declared a priority for the national security of the U.S.A.

To ensure constant energy supply from Nigeria, the general policy of the U.S government has been to maintain a harmonious, patronage relationship with any head of state in power, provided he guarantees stability and security of energy at all cost, even when the grievances of the Niger Delta people are not adequately addressed. We have earlier addressed the problem of conflicts and violence in the region. The prevailing violence and insurgencies in the Niger Delta pose a great challenge to the stability and security of the source of energy supply to U.S. In addressing this challenge, the U.S government is adopting new strategies to secure

---

323 Frynas, Jedrzej Georg, Oil in Nigeria, Conflict and Litigation between Oil Companies and Village Communities, Münster: Lit Verlag 2000, p. 18.

324 Douglas, Oronto et al., FPIF Special Report: Alienation and Militancy in the Niger Delta. Response to CSIS on Petroleum, Politics, and Democracy in Nigeria, Foreign Policy in Focus (FPIF), www.fpif.org/papers/nigeria 2003.htmc. Visited on 13.11.2007.

the energy supply from the Niger Delta. Whether the new strategies would stem violence and ensure energy supply at all cost, time will tell. We shall return to this shortly.

5.1.2 Western Europe

The industrialized economies of Western Europe are no less energy-thirsty than that of U.S.A. In fact, since the 1960s Western Europe has been the export markets for Nigeria's petroleum, coming from the Niger Delta. In 1973 for instance, 55 per cent of Nigerian oil went to Western Europe alone. In 1997 their consumption of Nigerian oil dropped to 37 per cent due to the U.S.A's demand for oil, taking up to 48 per cent. According to Frynas, Germany has been the largest Western European importer of Nigerian oil, closely followed by France. Britain, Nigeria's former colonial power, accounted for only 0.2% of Nigeria's oil exports[325].

Like the U.S government, the governments of Western Europe have concentrated more on their needs for energy supply from Niger Delta. Anna Khakee of FRIDE,[326] in 2008 released a Policy Brief (No 1, June 2008) from European Development Co-operation (EDC 2020) titled "Energy and Development: Lessons from Nigeria". In the policy brief she points out how Nigeria's conflict over energy has affected development and how the European Union has attempted to tackle the development – energy linkage. She highlights the main elements of Nigeria's 'oil curse' and how EU policies have been split between support for a stable, democratic and economically advancing Nigeria on the one hand, and for secure energy supplies on the other hand. She warns that "without major changes to its policies, the EU is unlikely to be making a positive impact to energy-development-governance linkages in Nigeria in 2020."[327] Furthermore, she points out that the EU policies have been directed at supporting democracy and governance-related projects, funding of EFCC and helping to track down proceeds of looting and corruption ending up in the banks of EU states (though not all EU states are cooperating in this effort). However, since 2005 the U.S and U.K have set up the Gulf of Guinea Energy Security Strategy (GGESS) intended to counter criminality and insecurity in the oil-producing communities in the Niger Delta region. Not only have other EU countries like France and Nederland joined them, the priority of GGESS has been to secure energy supply at all cost including giving military support to Nigerian government. Khakee notes that: "EU countries' aid

---

325   Frynas, Oil In Nigeria, p. 18.
326   A European Think Tank for Global Action.
327   Khakee, Anna, Energy and Development. Lessons from Nigeria, see http://www.edc2020.eu/
       fileadmin/Textdateien/EDC2020_PolicyBrief. Visited on 6.9.2009.

profile in Nigeria is weak. Only the United Kingdom and Germany have bilateral aid programmes of any substance in the country. A more concerted development effort is needed from other European actors"[328].

As for the relationship between development in the Niger Delta and oil industry, Khakee points out that it is only recently that European policy-makers discovered that it is impossible to separate the issue of development in Delta communities from the oil industry, and that no solution can be found without the involvement of all stakeholders, including the oil majors. Even as efforts are been made at positive development in the region by some EU states, the EU dependency on oil supply and protection of their oil companies appear to be hampering such efforts. Again, the violence and insurgencies ranging in the Niger Delta are threatening the security of energy supply from the region and making governments of Western Europe to consider other strategies.

5.1.3 China

With its 1.3 billion people, China is the world's most populous and fastest developing country and its second largest oil importer or market after U.S.A. In 2005 China's GDP reached $2.3 trillion, up by 9.9 percent. This rapid economic growth poses energy challenges. The rapid economic growth has boosted oil and gas consumption remarkably. To meet its energy need, China has strengthened its international cooperation and diversified supplies by pursing the principle of "non-interference in others' internal affairs". China is tapping into energy resources in countries that do not have sound oil and gas infrastructure and helping them establish their own energy industries. Believing that this will bring about a win-win situation where both are able to share the benefits. China currently imports a quarter of its total oil imports from Africa, largely from Nigeria, Angola, Chad and Sudan. In 2006 Nigeria and China signed deal to offer China four oil exploration licenses in Nigeria at the cost of US$2.3 billion, in return for a commitment to invest US$ 4 billion in Nigerian infrastructure.[329] Currently China is working in 35 oil fields in Nigeria. In addition China is willing to sell arms to Nigeria for use in the troubled Niger Delta.[330]

There is no doubt that China's policy of "non-interference in others' internal affairs" in the pursuit of its energy interest in the oil industry, as well as its lavish attention, coupled with support for prestige projects and development assistance

328   Khakee, Energy and Development. Lessons from Nigeria.
329   Xuecheng, Liu, China's energy security and its grand strategy, http:www.stanleyfoundation. org/publications/pup/pub06 Chinasenergy.pdf. Visited on 27.9.2009.
330   Alden, Chris, China in Africa, London: Zed Books 2008, pp. 42-44.

(in the form of low interest loan and outright grants) to potential recipient countries is attractive and beneficial to Nigerian government. But all these have little or no benefit to the needs of the people in the Niger Delta.

5.1.4 India

India and Nigeria have cordial and friendly relations, marked by mutual respect and understanding. There are no contentious issues between the two countries. Since India officially opened its embassy in Nigeria in 1958, the bilateral trade relations between the two countries have been steady. Other areas of cooperation include defense, mining, and manufacturing.

In 2005 India made a significant entry into the Nigerian oil industry. India's interest in Nigeria's oil sector has three components: term contract for crude oil purchase, participation in the upstream sector and refineries. In 2005, there had been several significant developments in India-Nigeria hydrocarbon cooperation. An Inter-Ministerial Task Force of the Government of India visited Nigeria in November 2005.[331] At the conclusion of discussions, a memorandum of understanding (MoU) was signed between ONGC-Mittal Energy Ltd (OMEL) of India and the Nigerian government for a US$ 6 bn "oil-for-infrastructure" deal. This amounted to 650.000 BPD per year over 25 years. On its part, India would assist Nigeria in the establishment of a 2000 Mega Watts (MW) thermal power plant, a refinery and upgrade its railway.

In May 2006 OMEL was awarded two oil blocks. Some other Indian companies like ESSAR and STERLING had been allocated oil blocks in May 2007. In the upstream sector, ONGC Videsh (OVL) won a 15% stake in Block 11 of the Joint Development Zone (JDZ) of Nigeria and Sao Tome Principe (May 2005). Separately, OVL is making efforts to acquire some other oil blocks in Nigeria. Traditionally, Nigeria has been a major supplier of crude oil to India. In May 2005, Indian Oil Corporation (IOC) and NNPC agreed on a contract for NNPC to supply 40,000 BPD to IOC. However, by the end of 2007 the contract was increased to 60,000bpd. As for refineries, the IOC was still discussing setting up one in Edo state.[332]

While the "oil-for-infrastructure" strategy of India in pursuing its interest in the oil industry is commendable, at least to the government, it does not take

---

331   The visit of the Inter-Ministerial Task Force was preceded by the visit of a similar team from Nigeria led by its Minister of State for petroleum Dr. Edmund Daukoru to India in October 2005.

332   High Commission of India, Abuja. http://www.indianhcabuja.com and http://www.hicomindlagos.com/docs/Nigeria-Fact-Sheet.htm. Visited on 27.9.2009.

cognizance of the real needs of the oil producing communities. It is doubtful whether the MoU included such things as basic infrastructure like schools, health facilities, roads and manufacturing that could provide employment for the youth in the region. The local people can only hope that perhaps when the 2000 MW power plant is fully implemented, they might have access to electricity. But that is yet to happen.

5.1.5 Transnational Oil Corporations

In Nigeria, most oil is lifted onshore, from about 250 fields dotted across the Delta. But Nigeria's total oil sector now represents a much larger domestic industrial infrastructure with more than six hundred oil fields, 5,284 on-and off-shore wells, 7,000 kilometers of pipelines, ten export terminals, 275 flow stations, ten gas plants, four refineries (Warri, Port Harcourt I and II, and Kaduna), and a massive Liquefied Natural Gas (LNG) project (in Bonny and Brass)[333]. With these installations the TNOCs are able to carry out their upstream (drilling and pumping of oil) and downstream (refinement, transportation and marketing of oil) activities. These represent some of the investment of the major multinational oil companies in Nigeria's Niger Delta region. In addition there are the human capital, administrative logistics and oil-related services which make up part of the investment of the various oil producing companies in the region.

From these infrastructures the TNOCs are not only making profits for themselves and their home governments but they have generated over $400 billion in oil revenues to the Nigerian government over the last 35 years.[334] For instance, in its 2007 report *Shell* claimed that it remitted $1.6 billion revenue to Nigerian government from oil and gas, in form of taxes and royalties from *Shell*-run operations.[335]

Owing to the volume of their investment, their profit margins, the whopping revenue the oil companies generate for the Nigerian state and most importantly the need to ensure constant energy supply to their home countries, the TNOCs have become a dominant factor in Nigeria. Their influence on the domestic affairs of their host countries is described by Karl as follows:

> Because of the enormous capital and technological resources necessary to exploit minerals, foreign oil companies became dominant internal actors in all oil exporters ... They are able

333   Lubeck Paul M. et al., Convergent Interests, p. 5. See also Müller, Axel et al., Misereor Themen, „Erdöl: Reichtum, der arm macht – Der Erdölboom im Golf von Guinea", Aachen: Misereor 2007, p. 27.
334   Lubeck, Paul M. et al., Convergent Interests, p. 7.
335   The Shell sustainability report 2007 – Nigeria Cf. http://sustainabilityreport.shell.com/2007 responsibleoperationstoday/nigeria.html. Accessed on 17.1.2009.

to subvert the political process by forming partnerships with local elites and other domestic allies or by relying on their home governments for support ... the complexities of the international market, the continuing need for foreign investment and technology, and their links to other powerful actors means that these companies still retain significant power even after nationalization.[336]

Almost all the global oil majors – *Shell, ExxonMobil, Chevron Texaco, British Petroleum,* and *Agip*, etc. are prominent in Nigeria's oil sector: each operating various joint venture (JV) arrangement with the state-owned Nigerian National Petroleum Company (NNPC) as principal partner on behalf of the federal government. This dominance by major multinationals is evident by the small number of private indigenous oil companies who together account for about 5% of the investment in the sector.[337] Most outstanding among them is *Shell*. With just only 5 per cent of the investment in the oil sector belonging to Nigerian citizens and 95 per cent being owned by foreign companies, it is hard for Nigerians to lay claim to the control or ownership of the oil resources. Moreover, even the 5 per cent is mostly dominated by people who are not from the Niger Delta.

The influences of the TNOCs often compel government to act or not to act according to their dictates. In pursuance of their interests, their influences are played out in the Nigerian scenario thus:

> As the principal goose laying the golden egg, multinational oil companies are in a particularly vantage position to enjoy a close symbiotic and working relationship with the government. This sometimes 'unholy' alliance operates at the official and unofficial levels, but it boils down to essentially the same thing in terms of their multiplier effects of fostering a mutually rewarding political and economic relationship between state and multinational oil companies to the exclusion of oil communities.[338]

The environmental pollutions caused by oil exploration and exploitation as well as oil spills from the oil companies are tolerated by the government because the government is too weak to resist the influence of the TNOCs. In cases of conflicts the government tends to protect the interests of the TNOCs against the fundamental concerns of the local people.

It must be added, though, that following the tragic event of the hanging Ken Saro-Wiwa and the eight Ogoni compatriots by the late General Abacha-led military government for their protests against *Shell*'s operations in the Niger Delta in 1995, multilateral oil companies have launched various "community outreach" projects, funding education, health care, and basic infrastructure development in the some of the communities in the region. Unfortunately, the effects of such efforts in a few selected communities have not been able to heal the festered

336 Karl, The Paradox of Plenty, p. 55.
337 Catholic Secretariat of Nigeria, Nigeria. The Travesty of Oil and Gas Wealth, p. 16.
338 Catholic Secretariat of Nigeria, Nigeria. The Travesty of Oil and Gas Wealth, p. 25.

wounds already inflicted by poverty and underdevelopment on the generality of the people. And the location of these projects in some selected communities has been a cause of inter-communal conflicts. Scholars are of the view that the contentious Petroleum Act and the Land Use Act, that is, the legal security of the oil by the government did not come to be without the influences of the oil majors.

5.2 National Stakeholders' Interests

We have argued above that the governments of the USA, Western Europe, China and Indian as well as the transnational oil corporations are pursuing their legitimate interests in the oil sector of Nigerian economy with strategies that have little or no concern for the needs and well-being of the local population in the Niger Delta. Similarly, some of the national stakeholders are pursuing their interests in the region with strategies that have little or half-hearted interest in the needs of the local people while others appear to be genuinely committed to seeing human well-being and development flourish in the region. Unfortunately, those who have the political and economic power to transform the region for better do not seem to have the political will to so do and those who claim to be genuinely committed to seeing development in the region have no political power. The failure of governments' past development efforts in region attests to our claim. Some of the strategies (arms struggle, vandalism or destruction of oil installations, hostage taking, kidnapping, disruption of oil production etc.) that are being used by those who claim to be genuinely committed to development of the region are counterproductive. As long as this situation persists, there will continue to be poverty and underdevelopment in the region.

5.2.1 Nigerian Governments

5.2.1.1 Federal Government

Like any sovereign state, the federal government's interest in Niger Delta is to secure a constant source of revenue and energy supply. And since the federal government is also the custodian of the treasury, it holds both economic and political powers. Other interests include maintaining the unity of the country, ensuring security of lives and property of the citizenry and ensuring the overall development of the country. No one contests these interests. But we contend that the approaches or strategies being adopted by the state in prosecuting these interests over the years have taken little or no cognizance of the well-being, quality of life

144

and the needs of the people in the Niger Delta. This is one of the reasons why poverty and underdevelopment still prevail in the region. A concrete example is the contentious revenue allocation.

Up to the end of the Civil War in 1970, the federal government operated the revenue derivation formula of sharing revenue between the regions as follows: federal government received 55% while 45% went to the regions where such revenues were derived from. The implication was that the more revenue from a region the more it got from the Federation Account. This meant more revenue to the oil-producing region. From 1976 to 1979 it was 20% to the oi-producing region. From 1982 to 1992 only 1.5% of oil revenue went to the region. It was raised to 3% between 1993 and 1998. The percentage increased to 13% as included in the 1999 Constitution of Federal Republic of Nigeria. It means that from the seventies to 1999 less and less revenue flowed to the oil-producing region and therefore there could not be much development in the region.[339]

As Oronto et al. noted, since 1970, the country's political, economic and policy elites have established an authoritarian power structure to enable them to centralize control of strategic resources, including the country's substantial oil deposits. Such avarice has not only banished the great majority of ordinary Nigerians from the policymaking process, but it has also led the power elites to pursue social and economic strategies that are shortsighted, self-serving and not driven by the needs of the people. The consequences have been material scarcity, deepening frustration and social unrest in the Niger Delta and elsewhere.[340]

The federal government has both the political and economic powers to translate the human and natural resources in the region to a development standard where poverty and underdevelopment would become a history, if only it has the political will to do so. However, based on political expediency, budget constraints and power considerations, the governments decide the kind of intervention they want in the Niger Delta. The approaches of legal and regulatory control of the oil sector (3.5), repressions and intimidations by the state (3.6.1), revenue allocation instead of revenue derivation and setting up of development commissions (3.7) have not really addressed the needs and quality of life of the people in the Niger Delta region. Not to forget is the fact that of the three interventions by the government, only the first two are permanent while the third has been inconsistent due to political instability, shortage of fund and corruption.

---

339   Niger Delta Human Development Report 2006, pp. 13-15.
340   Douglas et al., (FPIF Special Report): Alienation and Militancy in the Niger Delta: A Response to CSIS on Petroleum, Politics, and Democracy in Nigeria. www.fpif.org /papers/Nigeria 2003 html. Visited on 13.11.2007.

For instance is the case of OMPADEC (3.7.1). Like other commissions be-fore it, it has shown that the federal government merely selected those who con-stituted the commission to represent its interests; and those selected saw their appointment as reward for their loyalty to the federal government. As noted elsewhere, perhaps the greatest weakness of OMPADEC was that the people of oil-producing communities were totally excluded from its decision-making process. This was further compounded by corruption and its lack of accountability to the people of the oil-producing communities. The lack of transparency and divide-and-rule tactics of its operations soon marked out OMPADEC as part of the infrastructure of federal hegemony in the Niger Delta.The barrage of critiques leveled against the commission and why it finally failed showed that the then federal military governments were not really committed to fighting poverty and underdevelopment in the Niger Delta region. Those who were appointed to serve at the commission saw it as an opportunity for them to gain access to the oil revenues.

Though on the other hand additional states and local governments have been created in the region, the primary beneficiaries are the rentier elites; these are in most cases loyalists of the federal government. It is not enough to create states and local governments in the region merely with the view to bring government closer to the people, the local people must be seen to be actively participating in the political activities in the region. The local people are not to just be spectators in oil industry as it is now (a situation that has led some people into illegal oil deals) but active stakeholders. It is hoped that the pending Petroleum Industry Bill (PIB), would address this anomaly when it is passed by the National Assembly and signed into law by the President. It is hoped also that the pending deregula-tion of the downstream sector of the oil industry will afford the local people and the oil-producing communities the opportunity of participation in the oil business.

On September 10, 2008, late President Yar'Adua announced the creation of the Ministry of Niger Delta Affairs. He said that the new ministry would have a Minister in charge of development of the Niger Delta area, and a Minister of State in charge of youth empowerment. The existing Niger Delta Development Commission (NDDC) was to become a parastatal under the ministry. Yar'Adua further explained that the ministry would coordinate efforts to tackle the challenges of infrastructural development, environment protection and youth empowerment in the Niger Delta. In December 2008, he appointed Obong Ufot Ekaette, as the substantive Minister and Mr. Godswill Orubebe as the Minister of State of the Niger Delta Affaires.[341] This is a laudable step by the government towards solving the Niger Delta development problems, however, critics are of the view that if all

---

341   The Guardian Newspaper, Niger Delta Ministry: One year later, 19 January 2010.

the already existing Ministries in the country have not been able to bring about the desired development to the people generally, what miracle will the new Ministry work to effect development in the Niger Delta? If NDDC which was created for the same purpose in 2001 has been facing similar problems which previous commissions had suffered what guarantee do we have that the new Ministry will not face the same problems? It is over a year now that the Ministry has been created, the Niger Delta region is yet to record any positive sign of development embarked upon by the Ministry.

5.2.1.2 State Government

Since the 1960s, the people of the Niger Delta have been agitating for creation of states and local government that would give them autonomy and freedom from domination by the majority tribes of Yoruba, Hausa-Fulani and Igbo. It was hoped among other things that state creation exercise would afford the region more access to the oil revenue. Over the years, additional states and local governments have been created. But, as Obi[342] et al. have noted, if the elites and people hoped to have direct access to the oil revenue, through the creation of states, they have been disappointed. This is because the economic and political strategies of the federal government in the forms of revenue allocation in place of revenue derivation and unitary system of government instead of federalism do not allow the elites direct access to the resources. Aspirants and occupants of the state structures are seen by the federal government as exercising political and economic powers on its behalf and not on behalf of the people. For instance, the security forces (police, army, etc.) are centrally commanded by the federal government just as it determines what percent of the federal revenues goes to the states and local governments. However, once revenue allocations get to the state, the state government is responsible for the development of the state with such revenue and generally the state is semi autonomous of the federal government in terms of how it disburses its finances.

The 1999 Nigerian Constitution guarantees at least 13% of oil revenue to be remitted from the federation account to the oil-producing states of the Niger Delta. This is in addition to their statutory allocation. The nine states in the region are expected to carry out development projects and programs that should alleviate if not totally eradicate poverty and underdevelopment in the region. Apart from a few states that have created a special commission to actualize the use of their share of the 13% in the form of OSOPADEC and DESOPADEC, it is hard to point out what other states of the region are doing with the billions of

---

342   Obi, The Changing Forms of Identity Politics in Nigeria under Economic Adjustment, 25-31.

Naira flowing to the region every month since 1999. Instead, what prevails are corruption and embezzlement of the funds by state officials including political office holders, as we have discussed in the previous chapter. In other words, the interests of most state governors in the Niger Delta region are far from meeting the needs and concerns of the local people. Instead, they seem to be more interested in mega projects in the big cities which would afford them the opportunities to steal money.[343]

5.2.1.3 Local Government

Of the three tiers of government, the local government is the closest to the people. The constitutional responsibilities of the local government include "construction and maintenance of roads, streets, streets lightings, drains and other public highways, parks, gardens open spaces or such public facilities as may be prescribed from time to time by the House of Assembly of a State". The Nigerian Constitution states further that "The functions of a local government council shall include participation of such council in the Government of a State as respects the following matters: (a) the provision and maintenance of primary, adult and vocational education; (b) the development of agriculture and natural resources, other than the exploitation of minerals; (c) the provision and maintenance of health services; and (d) such other functions as may be conferred on a local government council by the House of Assembly of the State".[344] . To be able to carry out these obligations, 20 per cent of the federal allocation is shared to 774 local government councils in the country. Each local government is expected to supplement its share with internally generated revenue.

Critics have pointed out that it is generally difficult for LGCs to meet all their constitutional responsibilities with just 20% shared among 774 LGCs. This difficulty is further compounded by the practice by some states to deduct some amount from such funds whenever it gets to the states from the federation accounts. However, that is not say that the councils cannot on their own embark on some tangible development programs if the will to do so is there.

During election campaigns politicians claim that their primary interest is to development the local government areas; and while taking the oath of office, political office holders like local government chairmen, councilors and others promise to carry out these constitutional responsibilities. To be able to carry out these assignments effectively, every local government in Nigeria is required to

---

343 Human Right Watch, Nigeria: Chop fine, pp. 28-35.
344 Oluwole, Smith Imran, The Constitution of the Federal Republic of Nigeria Annotated, Lagos: Ecowatch Publications 1999, pp. 406-408.

produce an annual budget. The approach or strategy they adopt in carrying out these duties is through budgetary allocations to the various items like re-current expenditure in form of staff salary; others are health, education, transportation, roads etc.

Studies carried out in some oil-producing local government areas have revealed that the budgetary allocations to staff salary, Chairman's travel expenses and security votes take a lion share of their annual budget. Hence, very little is left to carry out responsibilities in the health, education, roads and provision of other social infrastructure in the local the government area. Whatever little contracts are to be awarded for the provision of certain basic infrastructure are awarded to councilors as a way of pacifying or "settling" them so as not to impeach the Chairman who they believe is taking a bigger share of the revenue than themselves. In most cases such contracts are poorly done, if at all they are carried out.[345]

This implies that those who are saddled with the responsibility of governance and provision of basic social infrastructure on the local government level are more interested in servicing their own interests and paying little attention to the basic needs of the people. More importantly, the local governments depend mainly on the budgetary allocation from the federal government. Little efforts are being made to raise locally generated revenue to complement federal allocation. It is difficult to expect development on the local government level as long as this kind of situation prevails.

5.2.2 Technocrats and the Business Class

The technocrats are experts or specialists in the oil industry who serve as engineers or who assist the government to formulate policies for the governance of the country generally but in oil sector in particular. Those among them that have formulated policies and advised the governments on the Niger Delta development problems over the years have either ill-advised the government (perhaps to please the government in order to keep their job) or did not present the government with real situation or reality of the Niger Delta development problems.

The set of the business class that are directly involved with oil industry are those that are engaged in the downstream sector of the industry, that is, those involved with refinery and marketing of petroleum products, precisely the oil marketers who are engaged in importing and selling government subsidized finished products like petrol, diesel and kerosene. Their interest lies in the fact that they enjoy the monopoly of the market as suppliers of finished products.

---

345   HRW, Human Right Watch, Nigeria: Chop fine, pp. 28-35.

They always resist every attempt of the government to deregulate the down-stream sector and the withdrawal of government subsidies from petroleum products for fear that deregulation of the sector would bring more competitors and that they would lose their practice of double profit.[346] Their insistency on the maintaining the status quo means that government would continue to subsidize oil products while the 4 refineries in Nigeria are working below their average capacity. This cannot be informed by their love for the generality of the people. The continued subsidy of petroleum products provides excuse for the government to starve the development commission (NDDC) and the newly created Niger Delta ministry of fund needed to develop the Niger Delta. However, one can only hope that the pending Petroleum Industry Bill (PIB) with the National Assembly would resolve a lot of the bottleneck problems in the oil sector whenever it is passed by the Assembly and signed into by the President.

5.2.3 Military Heritage

It is almost impossible to discuss the issue of development in Nigeria without reference to the military. This is because since Nigeria's independence in 1960, particularly with the first successful military coup in 1966, the military has occupied the central stage of governance for almost three decades. The long period of military regime has militarized the Nigerian society.

As earlier pointed out, the military regime covered the period between 1966 to 1979 and 1983 to 1999. During these periods, the military did not only have access to oil revenue, they also presided over the oil boom of 1972 and 1973. It was the military regime that reduced the revenue going to the oil producing areas of the Niger Delta from 50% to 1.5% then 3%, thereby retarding the development of the region.

We have discussed in part one, chapter one of this work the series of military coups in Nigeria. The various coups were attempts by different military interest groups to have access to the oil revenue. The major bones of contention in the Niger Delta issue, the Petroleum Act and the Land Use Act, are the products of military arrangement to ensure legal control of the oil industry.

The various development commissions formed by the military regimes could be considered to be military maneuvers aimed at controlling and manipulating the region to their own advantage. That the commissions failed is a proof that they were not people-centred, instead they served military interest. Current reports of the activities of the Joint Military Task Force (JTF) in the Niger Delta

---

346 See corruption in the oil industry (1.3.1).

reveal unabated human rights abuses, intimidation and oppression of defenseless civilians by the armed forces operating in the region. It is regrettable that the JTF lost some of their officers in the course of engaging the armed militias. But we are of the view that if the military regimes in the past had heeded the voice of reason, by attending to the development problems of the people, the situation in the region would not have degenerated to the extent of soldiers engaging armed civilians. In fact, there would have been no cause for militancy in the region.

Over and above all, the long period of military rule had weakened, by suppressing, almost all private or public structures and institutions in the Nigerian society that would have resisted and challenged all forms of corrupt practices and excess of the military rulers. For instance, despite all international support and sympathy for MOSOP and Ken Saro-Wiwa, the military regime of late General Sani Abacha still went ahead to hang him and the eight other compatriots for demanding justice and fairness in the use of the resources and care of the environment in the Niger Delta. As we shall see, one of reasons for youth militias is the counter-reaction on the part of the youth to the long years of oppression and intimation by the military.

5.2.4 Minority Elites

The term minority refers to tribes or nationalities that are not among the three dominant tribes of Yoruba, Ibo and Hausa/Fulani who are considered to be the majority in the political landscape of Nigeria. By elites we mean a small group of people or stratum that exerts influence, authority or decisive power in any society[347] and in our case, in the Niger Delta region. Osaghae et el have identified two sets of actors in the self-determination struggles in the Niger Delta namely, the elders/elites and the youths. Those who constitute the elites, their roles and their interests can be described as follows:

> The elders/elites are the businessmen, retired civil servants, traditional leaders and political leaders in the Niger-delta. They dominate the political, economic and traditional power structures of the region. Their prominence flows from their role as intermediaries between the ordinary people of the region and the state/multinational corporations exploiting the oil reserves of the region. Through their role as intermediaries they are able to build-up great prestige and wealth with which they have established region-wide client networks.[348]

The overall interests of the elders/elites are captured as follows:

---

347 Webster's Third New International Dictionary, vol. 1, Chicago: Encyclopaedia Britanica, Inc. 1986, p. 736.

348 Osaghae, Eghosa et al., Youth Militias, Self –determination and Resource Control Struggles in the Niger-Delta Region of Nigeria, 2007, see http://www.ascleiden.nl/pdf/cdpnigeriaRevised Osaghae%5B1%5D2.pdf. Visited on 2.7.2008.

1. A restructuring of the Nigerian state and its federalism in such ways that guarantee self-determination, political autonomy and fiscal control, true federalism, community control over development strategies, protection of land, dignity, culture, freedom, environment and natural resources of the Niger Delta people, and the right of states and communities to resource control.
2. A broad-based development program to transform the region.
3. A political autonomy that guarantees political participation, representation and community participation in resource management.
4. Implementation of a minimum of 50% derivation.
5. A halt to the development of new oil and gas pending the complete clean up of the environment.
6. Achievement of self determination and resource control to be addressed through a sovereign National Conference of ethnic nationalities.[349]

Since the 1990s these demands have been codified as bills of rights, charters, resolutions or declarations directed at the federal government and the oil multi-nationals. The first and the most famous of these was the Ogoni Bill of Rights (OBR) drawn by up the Ogoni people in 1990. Many other movements led by their elites have since followed the OBR example.[350] In addition to these charters and bills, resolutions from important meetings of these movements constituted another platform for making demands, serving notice and delivering ultimatum to the federal government and oil companies.

Based on the federal government's experiences with Isaac Adaka Boro led Niger Delta Volunteer Force (NDVF) that attempted cessation from Nigeria in 1966 and the Biafra in the same year, which eventually led to 30 months of civil war, the federal government seems to perceive such demands from ethnic minorities as political confrontation and provocation. This probably explains why the federal government has been responding with military force to nip the agitations at the bud and offer development commissions as a way of accommodating the elites and the elders into the rentier space of the oil revenue.

Traditionally, the elites have adopted a peaceful, non-violent approach that involves the use of negotiation and bargaining with key stakeholders, principally the state and the multi-national corporations operating in the region. To achieve their quest for more political participation and access to resources for the develop-

---

349 Osaghae et al., Youth Militias.
350 Obi, The Changing Forms of Identity Politics, 74. Some of these include: the Charter of demands by the Movement for the Payment of Reparations to Ogbia (MORETO), the Ogba Charter, the Isoko Youth Charter, the Resolutions of the Urhobo Economic Summit, the Communiqué of Itsekiri Patriots General Conference, the Aklaka Declaration of the Egi people; and the Kaiama declaration and "Operation Climate Change" of the Ijaw Youth Council (IYC).

ment of the region, the elites have negotiated for the creation of more states and local governments in the Niger Delta region.

The elites have made some political progress in their intermediary role. They have succeeded in getting more political structures created in the region, like more states and local governments. But such structures are yet to address the yearning of the people, that is, their development problems. As Osaghae et al. noted:

> They have generally advocated as solution to Niger-delta problems, separate or own states and local governments. Even though elite's agitations produced results in the form of creation of more states, from two (Rivers and Cross Rivers) in 1967 to four (Bayelsa, Rivers, Akwa Ibom and Cross Rivers) in 1995 and five (Bayelsa, Rivers, Akwa Ibom, Cross Rivers and Delta), such solution has not achieved the satisfactory results envisaged because of the erosion of the fiscal and jurisdictional powers and weakened governance capacities of the state governments relative to those wielded by the former regions.[351]

The political and economic influences of the elites easily pave the way for them to either occupy the political offices or determine who occupied such positions as soon as states and local governments were created in the region. For as soon as revenue allocations from the Federation Account come to the state and local government, they stop at the desk of the elites who occupy the political offices and these hardly percolate down to the grass-root in form of development programs or projects that should tackle poverty and underdevelopment. As noted earlier, the elites control the state and local governments' mechanisms, such that they end up being the main beneficiaries of this approach.

The point we attempt to make here is that even when elites claim to be fighting for the interests of their oil-producing minority communities, they usually end up being the main beneficiaries of such agitations and not the local communities. As we earlier pointed out while discussing the intra-communal conflicts, the practice of the elites trying to short-change the communities had been a major cause of conflicts and violence that have also been a hindrance to development. The fact that the approach of the elites and elders has not addressed the problem of poverty and underdevelopment in the region since Nigeria's independence partly informed the decision of the youth to take up arms and the leadership role in the region, as we shall discuss under youth militias shortly.

---

351   Osaghae et al., Youth Militias.

5.2.5 Non-Governmental Organizations

Since the 1990s the NGOs have started to emerge forcefully in the region. The interests of the NGOs in the region can best be seen in the roles they are playing in the areas of their influences and approaches. The earlier group of NGOs in the region engaged mainly in human and environmental rights intervention. The approach of these groups has been that of defense of human and environmental rights within the context of the Delta. Their approach includes: educating the people about their rights, empowering them to fight for their rights, informing Nigerians and the international community about the violations of rights in the Delta, and exposing the perpetrators of these violations. Others include, documenting the role of the state and oil multinationals in the violation of rights, identifying the victims, and ramifications of such violations, providing basic assistance to empower the people economically, politically and socially, and documenting the deleterious impact of the oil industry on the fragile Delta ecosystem. They are also involved in networking with local groups, donors and international NGOs interested in promoting human rights in the Niger Delta[352]. Examples of these NGOs are: Civil Liberty Organization (CLO), the Environmental Rights Action/Friends of the Earth Nigeria, ANEEJ, Trocaire, etc. The publications of these groups in the form of books, newsletters, press releases, faxes and message posted on the Internet and international campaigns have continue to inform the international community on the poor state of human rights in the Niger Delta region.

Their approach and activities have gained them acceptance among the oil-producing communities and the civil society organizations. The state and the oil companies have also reluctantly recognized them as a formidable force or stakeholders in the Niger Delta affairs. If poverty and underdevelopment and thus human development issues have not been so prominent in the Niger Delta problems until recently, it is because NGOs who are development-oriented only arrived at the scene since the dawn of democracy in Nigeria in 1999. Most development-oriented NGOs which are now active in the region would probably trace their arrival to 2000 upwards.

The Catholic Church is among the NGOs which have always engaged in development work in the region through provision of schools, health facilities and meeting the pastoral – spiritual needs of the people. Since the 1990s the local Church has been trying to get involved with the Niger Delta problems through the Justice Development and Peace Commission (JDPC), but owing to weak capacity of most of the personnel and funding of the various Diocesan JDPC

---

352   Obi, Changing Forms of Identity Politics in Nigeria, p. 74.

commissions in the region, the Church has not been able to assert much politically serious influence in the Niger Delta region.

5.2.6 Youth Militias

Scholars of Niger Delta studies like Eghosa Osaghae, A. Ikelegbe, O. Olarinmoye and S. Okhonmina[353] have done a detail study on the origin, nature, ideology, mode of operations etc. of youth militias in the Niger Delta. Suffice it to point out briefly who the militias are, their interests, and how the approaches they adopted in pursuing their interest are affecting the development of the region.

The emergence of the youth militias was informed by the general feeling or opinion among the youth that the elders' approach to the development of the region is too slow and has not brought about the desired development. The elders' approach has always been negotiations and dialogues with the governments and the oil companies in the region over the years. Moreover, some of the elders were accused of compromising the development of the region for their own private gains. Eghosa Osaghae et al. pointing out the difference between the youth militias, the elders and elites, say that:

> They (youths) believe that the system as it exists is not beneficial to the poor and ordinary people as a whole and desire a change. They perceive that the objectives of the elites are highly parochial and not necessarily in the interest of the people. They thus do not seek to advance their cause via the traditional access to elite influence; rather, they embrace militant, activist and extremist political tactics that seek to challenge the system itself and its governing rules.[354]

Added to all this is the fact of state repression and brutal attack of state security forces on the defenseless civilians whenever they demonstrated to express their grievances against the effects of the operations of the oil multinationals. These factors prompted some of the youth to take up arms in self-defense against aggressions from the state and the oil multinationals' private security agencies.

Stating what can be described as the interests of the youth militias, Osaghae et al. have pointed out that there is a convergence of interests of the militias and those of the Niger Delta elites and elders. As articulated at different times, the major interests are as stated above (2.2.4). There are several youth militia groups but prominent among them are the Movement for the Emancipation of the Niger Delta (MEND) and the Niger Delta Volunteer Force (NDVF).

---

353 Osaghae et al., Youth Militias.
354 Osaghae et al., Youth Militias.

In the meantime, other activities of the youth militias include hostage-taking of oil companies' workers and other prominent Nigerians, oil bunkering, vandalizing oil facilities, etc., all with the aim of forcing the government and oil companies to be committed to the development of the region. The activities of the youth militias have escalated to series of violence resulting to destruction of lives and properties. Unfortunately, many criminals have taken the opportunity of the youth militias to carry out their nefarious activities, in the forms of armed robbery, terrorizing civilians and engaging security forces on regularly basis in the region. This poses a problem for the government. It is now quite difficult to differentiate between genuine youth militias fighting for the development of the region and armed robbers who are purely criminals. Ironically, some politicians and multinational oil companies engage the services of the some militia groups to prosecute their political agenda by using them to intimidate their opponents and as armed security for oil installations. In the process, there has arisen a situation of bitter rivalry between various armed youth militias, which further aggravated more violence in the region.

The effects of this approach of the youth militias in pursuing their interest in the region are so many. On the one hand, the youth militias have proved to the government and the oil companies, though odd it may sound, that they (the state and oil multinationals) do not have the monopoly of arms or weapons to intimidate civilians at will. On the other hand, their activities have affected oil production and thus the reduction in government revenue intake as well as interrupting the security and constancy of energy supply to the international community. Over and above all, the atmosphere of violence, tensions, insecurity of life and property is not conducive for engaging in development work and thus fighting the poverty and underdevelopment in the region.

On a heartwarming note, it is delighting to know that the government of late President Musa Yar'Adua has granted amnesty to the youth militias on the condition that they surrendered their arms.[355] The rationale behind the government's amnesty deal, it is claimed, is to separate the youth militias from armed criminals. Critics of this arrangement are of the view that the militias are merely fighting for their rights and therefore the term amnesty does not apply to them, as they have not been adjudged to be criminals. However, majority of the youth militias has taken the advantage and subsequently laid down their arms. One can only hope that the government will make good its promise to embark on rapid development of the region and provide alternative means of livelihood for the youths that have surrendered their arms and other youths in the region as wells as in the other parts of the country.

---

355   The surrender of arms was to take place on or before the 4th of October 2009.

5.2.7 Unions and Civil Society Organizations

The unions and civil society organizations (CSOs) are non-governmental organizations that are actively involved in the development drive of the region. It is the delayed and failed response of the state and oil multinationals to meet the demands of the people that have given rise to the emergence of the civil society organizations in the region. With the emergence of Movement for the Survival of Ogoni People (MOSOP) in the 1990s led by the environmental activist late Ken Saro-Wiwa, several other ethnic and regional CSOs have arisen to protest and challenge the unjust structures of the state that have neglected the region for decades and the continuous degradation of the environment by the multinational oil companies, a situation that has made the people in the region feel like economic colony of Nigerian state and the international oil companies. In his study of the civil society in the region Ikelegbe has pointed out that:

> [t]he grievances, demand and anger in the region have given rise to the flourishing of civil society. While in the 1970s and 1980s, the communities disparately and un-co-ordinatedly articulated grievances to the MNOCs and blocked access routes to oil installations as protests, civil society emerged in the 1990s as a mobilization platform of popular struggle against the state and MNOCs. The entrance of civil society has created a communal, ethnic and regional formation of resistance with considerable coordination, and has raised the quality, intensity and extent of articulation, aggregation and expression of demands to that of a regional struggle for equity and justice.[356]

There are various types of CSOs in the region. Firstly, the communal and ethnic groups comprising the apex associations, which represent and speak on behalf of communities and ethnic groups which in turn are made up of local leaders, elders and elites. Secondly, there are associations that mobilize members either from the generality or from specialized categories. This groups are pan-ethnic, Niger Delta or even national organizations which articulate Niger Delta problems and interests. The youth associations are in this category. Thirdly, there are the civil and environmental rights groups[357].

The methods of the CSOs have generally been that of advocacy, agitation and the challenge of state and MNOCs policies and practices. These are in form of raising public awareness of the Niger Delta development problems and pressure on the state and MNOCs through press statements, interviews, and conferences communiqués, placing of statements in newspapers, commentaries and publicized

---

356 Ikelegbe, Augustine, Civil Society, Oil and Conflict in the Niger Delta Region of Nigeria: Ramifications of Civil Society for Regional Resource Struggle. *In*: The Journal of Modern African Studies 39,3 (September 2001) pp. 437- 469.

357 Ikelegbe, Civil Society, Oil and Conflict in the Niger Delta Region of Nigeria, pp. 442-456.

meetings. Other methods include calling for dialogue and the search for meetings to consult, discuss and negotiate solutions to demands and grievances.

The civil and environmental rights groups have been particularly engaged in the monitoring and challenging of the state use of force, deployment of troops and human abuses in the region. Other strategies of the CSOs include litigation and peaceful demonstrations. It has been documented that it is the failure of the state and MNOCs to grant audience to the youth groups of the CSOs and brutal rebuff from state security agents which have provoked the youth groups to take to violence. Again, in an atmosphere of violence, there can be no development. On a positive note, the continuous agitations and protests of the CSOs have made them become a force, a structure to be reckoned with as a stakeholder in the Niger Delta issue.

5.3 Conclusion

From our treatment of the constellations of interests groups in the Niger Delta region, it is clear that the interests of major stakeholders, the international and national, are not principally focused on the needs and concerns of the ordinary people in the region. It is our view that before real development can take place, consideration for the needs and concerns of the people have to be at the centre of all engagements by the major stakeholders in the region.

Part III: ethical orientation

In the preceding parts of this work, we have treated the human development problems in the Niger Delta as characterized by the state of poverty and underdevelopment in the region. We have also analyzed the socio-economic as well as the political factors responsible for the problems. This part of the work focuses on the needed ethical orientation that should inform and guide development efforts necessary for alleviating the problems of poverty and underdevelopment in the region in question. In the first chapter we shall examine the Capability Approach to development as a socio-philosophical and ethical framework or approach to human development developed by Amartya Sen and presented in his book *Development as Freedom*. The second chapter will examine the impulses from the Catholic Social Teaching, giving special attention to the development model presented by Pope Paul VI in *Populorum Progressio* and updated by Pope John Paul II in *Sollicitudo rei Socialis*. The third chapter represents the situation in the Niger Delta in the light of chapters 1 and 2. We shall proffer a development agenda for region based on the ethical orientation to conclude this part.

6. Sen's Capability Approach

6.1 Introduction

Among the most recent approaches that have gained popularity and acceptance among scholars of various disciplines and development practitioners is the capability approach. The capability approach is a broad normative framework for the evaluation and assessment of individual well-being and social arrangements, the design of policies, and proposals about social change in society.[358] Its uses can be found in a wide range of fields, most prominently in development studies, welfare economics, social policy and political philosophy. It serves the purpose of evaluating the many aspects of people's well-being, such as inequality, poverty, the well-being of the individuals or the average well-being of the members of a group. Apart from its multiple uses, the capability approach has also provided the theoretical foundations of the human development paradigm.[359] It is an approach originally developed by the 1998 Nobel Prize winner in economics, Amartya Sen and later expanded by Martha Nussbaum and other scholars. For the purpose of this study, we shall focus on capability approach as developed and applied to Human Development by Amartya Sen.

6.2 Sen's Biography

Amartya Kumar Sen was born in 1933 in India. As his parents and grandparents were academicians he grew up and lived most of the time in university campuses. One may say that he had the advantage of an elitist educational background. He describes with a sense of mild humour his curriculum vitae as follows:

---

358 Robeyns, Ingrid The Capability Approach. A Theoretical Survey, The Journal of Human Development, March 2005.

359 Fukuda-Parr, Sakiko &. Shiva, Kumar A. K (eds.), Readings in Human Development, Concepts, Measures and Policies for a Development Paradigm, New York: Oxford University Press 2003, p. xv.

161

I studied at Presidency College in Calcutta and then at Trinity College in Cambridge, and I have taught at universities in both these cities, and also at Delhi University, the London School of Economics, Oxford University, and Harvard University, and on a visiting basis, at M.I.T., Stanford, Berkeley, and Cornell. I have not had any serious non-academic job[360].

Two experiences he had as a teenager later greatly influenced his future academic interests. The first was his experience of famine in Bengal 1943 and the second was the sectarian conflicts in India in the 1940s to each of the experiences he says:

> The memory of the Bengal famine of 1943, in which between two and three million people had died, and which I had watched from Santiniketan, was still quite fresh in my mind. I had been struck by its thoroughly class-dependent character. (I knew no one in my school or among my friends and relations whose family had experienced the slightest problem during the entire famine; it was not a famine that afflicted even the lower middle classes – only people much further down the economic ladder, such as landless rural labourers.[361]

This probably motivated him to start working on the causation and prevention of famines from the, mid-1970s the result of which came out as a book on *Poverty and Famine* in 1981.

The second experience was the communal killings fomented by sectarian politics that engulfed India through much of the 1940s. The divisive politics of that time had led to massive identity shift. He recalls some of that mindless violence he observed:

> "One afternoon in Dhaka, a man came through the gate screaming pitifully and bleeding profusely. The wounded person, who had been knifed on the back, was a Muslim daily labourer, called Kader Mia. He had come for some work in a neighbouring house – for a tiny reward – and had been knifed on the street by some communal thugs in our largely Hindu area. As he was being taken to the hospital by my father, he went on saying that his wife had told him not to go into a hostile area during the communal riots. But he had to go out in search of work and earning because his family had nothing to eat. The penalty of the economic unfreedom turned out to be death, which occurred later on in the hospital. The experience was devastating for me, and suddenly made me aware of the dangers of narrowly defined identities, and also of the divisiveness that can lie buried in communitarian politics. It also alerted me to the remarkable fact that economic unfreedom, in the form of extreme poverty, can make a person a helpless prey in the violation of other kinds of freedom: Kader Mia need not have come to a hostile area in search of income in those troubled times if his family could have managed without it"[362].

360   Sen Amartya – Autobiography, http://nobelprize.org/cgi-bin/ Cf. www.geocities.com/gfh_axds _as/com/sen-autobio.html?200715. Accessed on 13.12.2007.
361   Sen Amartya – Autobiography, http://nobelprize.org/cgi-bin/ Cf. www.geocities.com/gfh_axds _as/com/sen-autobio.html?200715. Accessed on 13.12.2007.
362   Amartya Sen – Autobiography http://nobelprize.org/cgi-bin/. See also Sen, Amartya, Development as Freedom, Oxford: University Press 1999, p. 8. This may explain the crucial importance

He is a Fellow of the British Academy and of the Econometric Society, as well as a Foreign Honorary member of the American Academy of Arts and Sciences. He has received honorary doctorates (more than forty) from major universities in North America, Europe and Asia. Sen has received various honours, including the "Bharat Ratna" (the highest honour awarded by the President of India). Among the awards he has received are the Frank E. Seidman Distinguished Award in Political Economy, the Senator Giovanni Agnelli International Prize in Ethics, the Alan Shawn Feinstein World Hunger Award, the Jean Mayer Global Citizenship Award, and the Nobel Prize in Economics.

Of significance to this work is his capability approach to development as a means or instrument to free people from poverty and underdevelopment. The basic ideas of the capability approach as found in his book *Development as Freedom* will be partly applied to the development problems of the Niger Delta Region in Nigeria. This book will come more into focus in the course of this study.

6.3 Sen's Concept of Development

It is pertinent to begin by focusing on Sen's understanding of development, as it will enable us understand his capability approach. He leaves no one in doubt about his notion of development as expressed first in the famous book, *Development as Freedom*: "Development can be seen...as a process of expanding the real freedoms that people enjoy."[363] This understanding is premised on the conviction that people are the real wealth of nations. He is of the view that, the basic purpose of development is to enlarge human freedoms. The process of development should enlarge human freedom by expanding the choices that people have to live full and creative lives. Sen believes that people are both the beneficiaries of development and the agents of the progress and change that bring it about. According to the Human Development Report, this approach to development – human development – has been advocated by UNDP ever since the first in 1990[364].

Sen's reflections on development can best be situated within the context of his critique of the neoliberal notion of economic progress indicated by the growth rate of per capita income as measurement of development. Orthodox view on development is based primarily on an economic focus on growth in gross national product (GNP or GDP) per capita, the monetary measurement of

he attached to instrumental freedoms in the capabilities approach. These comprise political freedom, economic opportunities, social facilities, transparency guarantees and protective security.
363   Amartya Sen, Development as Freedom, 3.
364   Human Development Report 2004, p. 127.

the total of goods produced and services rendered, food security in terms of food availability, and poverty in terms of income deprivation. Emphasis is usually placed on economic efficiency, with no explicit role being given to fundamental freedoms, individual agency and human rights. There is no doubt that the level of real income is important for the consumption and living standard of people, but Sen argues that real income or gross national product (GNP) says little or nothing about the right to long life, the possibility of escapable morbidity, about gainful employment and life in a peaceful non-violent society. He says for example, "growth of GNP or of individual incomes can, of course, be very important as means to expanding the freedoms enjoyed by the members of the society. But freedoms depend also on other determinants, such as social and economic arrangements (for example, facilities for education and health care) as well as political and civil rights (for example, liberty to participate in public discussion and scrutiny)."[365] Sen is of the view that industrialization or technological or social modernization can contribute to human freedoms; but they are means to human freedom and not the ends in themselves. He points out what development should be: "Development requires the removal of major sources of unfreedom: poverty as well as tyranny, poor economic opportunities as well as systematic social deprivation, neglect of public facilities as well as intolerance or overactivity of repressive states."[366] These major sources of unfreedom are obstacles to development.

His critique of neoliberal notion of economic growth is based on the fact that a country can be very rich in conventional economic terms (i.e., in terms of the value of commodities produced per capita) and still be very poor in the achieved quality of human life.[367] Moreover, it is to be noted that despite unprecedented increases in overall opulence, the contemporary world denies elementary freedoms to vast numbers, perhaps even the majority of people. The need to direct development towards expanding human freedom is premised on the fact that:

Sometimes the lack of substantive freedoms relates directly to economic poverty, which robs people of the freedom to satisfy hunger, or to achieve sufficient nutrition, or to obtain remedies for treatable illnesses, or the opportunity to be adequately clothed or sheltered, or to enjoy clean water or sanitary facilities. In other cases, the unfreedom links closely to the lack of public facilities and social care, such as the absence of epidemiological programs, or of organized arrangements for health care or educational facilities, or of effective institutions for the maintenance of local peace and order. In still other cases, the violation of freedom results directly from a denial of political and civil liberties by authoritarian regimes and from

365 Sen, Development as Freedom, p. 3.
366 Sen, Development as Freedom, p. 3.
367 Sen, Amartya, Development as Capability Expansion. *In*: Fukuda-Parr, Sakiko and Shiva, Kumar A.K., Readings in Human Development, Concepts, Measure and Policies for Development Paradigm, New Delhi: Oxford University Press 2003, pp. 3-4. For example, South Africa, with five or six times the GNP per capita of Sri Lanka or China has a much lower longevity rate.

imposed restrictions on the freedom to participate in the social, political and economic life of the community.[368]

All these forms of unfreedom are results of human action and social arrangement. Removing these major sources and conditions of unfreedom, as stated above, is the goal of development. It is in this sense that the expansion of freedom is viewed as both the primary end and the principal means of development.[369]

Because people are both the beneficiaries and end of development, they must be its centre. Therefore, there is the need to evaluate social change and government policies in terms of the richness of human life resulting from them. In other words, policies are to be assessed or evaluated in terms of their effects in enriching human life in the society. The goal of development politics is not primarily the promotion of fundamental rights and not the increase of economic utility or economic growth rather it is freedom.

Sen argues that the ends and means of development call for placing the perspective of freedom at the center of the stage. The people have to be seen, in this perspective, as being actively involved, given the opportunity to shape their own destiny, and not just as passive recipients of the fruits of cunning development programs. The state and the society have extensive roles in strengthening and safeguarding human capabilities. This is a supportive role, rather than one of ready-made delivery.[370] Simply put, the end of development must be the human being.

6.4 The Essentials of Capability Approach

Capability is a state of being able to be and do what one considers valuable and freely chooses in a given society. What one considers valuable and freely chooses to be and do is reflected in his/her well-being. The choices available to one depend on the arrangements put in place by the society. It is the normative framework for the evaluation of individual well-being and social arrangements that is referred to as capability approach. It is the normative framework for the design of policies and proposals about social change. The main characteristic of capability approach is its focus on what people are effectively able to do and to be, that is, on their capabilities.[371] Broadly speaking, capability approach refers

---

368 Sen, Development as Freedom, p. 4.
369 Sen, Development as Freedom, p. xii.
370 Sen, Development as Freedom, p. 53.
371 Robeyns, Ingrid, The Capability Approach: An Interdisciplinary Introduction, University of Amsterdam, Department of Political Science and Amsterdam School of Social Sciences Research, 9 December 2003, p. 5.

to the conceptual model, where capabilities (usually referred to in plural) are the real opportunities to achieve valuable states of being and doing. The core emphasis of capability approach is the freedom of choice that people have. In relation to development, progress or development or poverty reduction occurs when people have greater freedoms.[372]

The key idea of the capability approach is that social arrangements should aim to expand people's capabilities – their freedom to promote or achieve valuable beings and doings. An essential test of progress, development or poverty reduction, is whether people have greater freedoms. According to Sen: "A person's capability to achieve functionings (beings and doings) that he or she has reason to value provides a general approach to the evaluation of social arrangements, and this yields a particular way of viewing the assessments of equality and inequality"[373]

With capability approach Sen wants to identify the conditions and factors which essentially contribute to (or hinder) the ability of people to live a worthwhile life. Identifying such conditions and factors in a given country or region would reveal existing deficits and allow the formulation of appropriate policies as remedy:

> The capability approach to a person's advantage is concerned with evaluating it in terms of his actual ability to achieve various valuable functionings as a part of living. The corresponding approach to social advantage, for aggregative appraisal as well as for the choice of institutions and policy, takes the set of individual capabilities as constituting an indispensable and central part of the relevant informational base of such evaluation. [374]

The capability approach asks whether people are healthy, and whether the resources necessary for this capability, such as clean water, access to medical care, protection from infections and diseases, and basic knowledge on health issues, are present. It asks whether people are well-nourished, and whether the conditions for this capability, such as sufficient food supplies and food entitlements, are met. It asks whether people have access to a high quality education, to real political participation, to community activities which support them to cope with struggles in daily life and which foster real friendships, to religions that console them which can give them peace of mind.[375]

Basically, Sen's capability approach to development entails the following elements: Entitlement (goods which are commodities and services), Function-

372 Alkire, Sabina Using Capability Approach: Prospective and evaluative analysis, see www.capabilityapproach.com/pubs/Alkire%Pdf. Accessed on 19.3.2009.
373 Sen, Amartya, Inequality Reexamined, Cambridge: University Press 1992, p. 5.
374 Sen, Amartya, Capability and Well-Being. In: Nussbaum, M. & Sen, A.(eds.), Quality of life, pp. 30-53.
375 Robeyns, The capability approach, p. 7.

ings, Freedoms and Capability, Agency and Well-being. The logic is that human beings require commodities to enhance their well-being, which depends on the totality of doings and beings called functionings. In order to convert commodities into functionings there is the need for the capability to do so. This in turn requires the freedom of choice to combine the various commodities into functionings. We shall proceed to examine in some details what constitute each of these elements and how they all work together to enhance human development.

6.4.1 Entitlements

Human beings require material and immaterial resources of various forms in order to live well. How one relates to the commodities i.e, goods and services over which a person has the command and ownership, like income, property, food, etc., is what Sen calls entitlement.[376] With this understanding of commodities, Sen emphasizes that economic growth and the expansion of goods and services are necessary for human development. A person's entitlement set is a way of characterizing his or her overall command over things, taking note of all relevant rights and obligations. Whereas rights are generally characterized as relationships that hold between distinct agents (e.g between one person and another person or one person and the state), a person's entitlements are the totality of things he can have by virtue of his rights. According to Sen, ownership of commodities is not enough, more important is how the owner commands their use for his/her well-being:

> Commodities are seen in terms of their characteristics. The characteristics are the various desirable properties of the commodities in question. Securing amounts of these commodities gives the person command over the corresponding characteristics. For example, the possession of food gives the owner access to the properties of the food, which can be used to satisfy hunger, to yield nutrition, to give eating pleasure and to provide support for social meetings.[377]

To possess commodities is one thing, to be able to make use of them for one's own well-being is another. Commodities are not ends in themselves; they are merely means to an end which are human's beings and doings.

6.4.2 Functionings

Sen's understanding of functionings relates to the things a person may value doing or being. These are the valuable activities and states that are contributing

---

376   Sen, Development as Freedom, p. 162.
377   Sen, Commodities and Capabilities, p. 6.

to people's well-being, such as a healthy body, being safe, being calm, having a warm friendship, an educated mind, a good job. Sen says, "the concept of functionings ... reflects the various things a person may value doing or being. The valued functionings may vary from elementary ones, such as being adequately nourished and being free from avoidable diseases, mortality, undertaking usual movements etc., to many complex functionings such as achieving self-respect, taking part in the life of the community and appearing in public without shame."[378] Sen explains that a functioning is a possible achievement of a person: what he or she is able to do or to be. It reflects, as it were, a part of the 'state' of that person. It has to be distinguished from the commodities which are used to achieve those functionings. For example, bicycling has to be distinguished from possessing a bike. It has to be distinguished also from the happiness generated by the functioning, for example, actually cycling around must not be identified with the pleasure obtained from that act.

A functioning is thus different both from (1) having goods (and the corresponding characteristics), to which it is posterior, and (2) having utility (in the form of happiness resulting from that functioning), to which it is, in an important way, prior.[379] Sen argues that, the conversion of commodity-characteristics into personal achievements of functionings depends on a variety of factors – personal and social. In the case of nutritional achievement it depends on such personal conversion factors as (1) metabolic rates, (2) body size, (3) age, (4) sex (and, if a woman, whether pregnant or lactating), (5) activity levels, (6) medical conditions (including the presence or absence of parasites), (7) access to medical services and the ability to use them, (8) nutritional knowledge and education, and (9) climate conditions. In the case of achievements involving social behavior and entertaining friends and relatives, the functioning will depend on such influences as (1) the nature of the social conventions in force in the society in which the person lives (public policies), (2) the position of the person in the family and in the society (societal hierarchy), (3) the presence or absence of festivities such as marriages, seasonal festivals and other occasions such as funerals (social norms), (4) the physical distance from the homes of friends and relatives, and so on.[380] For example, a disabled person in a wheelchair needs a lift if he or she wants to be able to use public transport, such as trains or buses, which able-bodied passengers do not need. Thus, disability is a conversion factor which makes it harder for a disabled person to 'convert' a bundle of resources into the functioning of being mobile: even if he or she has the same income as an able-bodied person, he or she will not be able to travel with public transport as long as there are no lifts in the buses.

378   Sen, Development as Capability Expansion, p. 5. Cf. also Sen, Development as Freedom, p. 75.
379   Sen, Commodities and Capabilities, p. 7.
380   Sen, Commodities and Capabilities, pp. 17-18.

Another important set of factors that plays a role in the conversion from characteristics of the good to the individual functioning is the environmental conversion factors (e.g. climate, geographical location). For example, if there are no paved roads (as is the case in most parts of the Niger Delta region), or if a government or the dominant societal culture imposes a social or legal norm that women are not allowed to cycle without being accompanied by a male family member, then it becomes much more difficult or even impossible to use the good (bicycle) to enable the functioning.

6.4.3 Capability

The concept of capability is the ability of people to freely choose to do and be what they have reason to value. According to Sen, capability "represents the various combinations of functionings (beings and doings) that the person can achieve. Capability is, thus, a set of vectors of functionings, reflecting the person's freedom to lead one type of life or another...to choose from possible livings."[381] For example, when Mahatma Gandhi went on hunger strike to protest British colonial rule in India, he had the means and the choice of eating to nourish himself but he chose to fast, in contrast to a destitute that is forced to starve because he has no choice or means to eat for self nourishment. Both would experience hunger as a form of functioning but each has a different capability set for the functioning.

Capabilities are a kind of opportunity freedom. Just like a person with much money in his pocket can buy many different things, a person with many capabilities could enjoy many different activities, pursue different life paths. For this reason the capability set has been compared to a budget set. So capabilities describe the potentials that one has to make use of the possibilities that are open to a person.

In order to be able to utilize his entitlements to realize the functionings a person needs to have the freedom to choose between various opportunities that are available to him. This freedom to choose depends on his knowledge of the commodities, state of health, educational level, socio-political and economic environment in which he lives. To this effect Sen says:

> What people can positively achieve is influenced by economic opportunities, political liberties, social powers, and the enabling conditions of good health, basic education, and the encouragement and cultivation of initiatives. The institutional arrangements for these opportunities are also influenced by the exercise of people's freedoms, through the liberty to participate in social choice and in the making of public decisions that impel the progress of these opportunities.[382]

---

381   Sen, Inequality Reexamined, p. 40.
382   Sen, Development as Freedom, p. 5.

169

The amount or the extent of each functioning enjoyed by a person may be represented by a real number, and when this is done, a person's actual achievement can be seen as a functioning vector. The 'capability set' would consist of the alternative functioning vectors that he or she can choose from. While the combination of a person's functionings reflects his or her actual achievements, the capability set represents the freedom to achieve: the alternative functioning combinations from which this person can choose.[383]

As we already noted, individuals need commodities i.e goods and services over which one has command (entitlement); and the amount of commodities a person has depends on his or her income or opportunities to access the commodities. This in turn depends on the kind of social arrangement concerning the distribution of income or resources in a given society or country among its citizenry. From economic perspective, it is expected that the greater the economic growth or income of a country, the better the standard of life of its citizens should be. However, Sen's empirical researches have highlighted the possibility of divergences between the expansion of economic growth and income on the one hand, and the expansion of valuable human capabilities on the other. His findings establish that economic growth and income can be poor predictors of the capability to live to a mature age, without succumbing to premature mortality, in different countries (e.g. India, China, Sri Lanka, Costa Rica, and Jamaica) and for different population groups in the U.S.A: the population in the Indian state of Kerala in relation to other states.[384] He points out that a country can be very rich in conventional economic terms (i.e., in terms of the value of commodities produced per capita) and still be very poor in the achieved quality of human life.[385]

The discrepancies or divergences are attributed to unequal access to economic resources. That is to say, the justice or injustice of the social arrangement put in place by a given state to redistribute the resources or the economic growth and income in various sectors of the society as to bring about the expansion of valuable human capabilities of the citizens. It is a question of public provisioning.[386] In contrast to John Rawls who advocates the priority of liberty including some basic political and civil rights, in considering social justice, Sen prefers that consideration be given first to intense economic needs of the people in order that economic resources be translated to the expansion of people's capability. He

383 Sen, Development as Freedom, p. 75.
384 Sen, Development as Freedom, pp. 5-6.
385 Sen, Development as Freedom, p. 47. See also Sen, Development as Capability Expansion. *In*: Readings in Human Development, pp. 3-4 as well as Kesselring, Thomas, Ethik der Entwicklungspolitik., Gerechtigkeit im Zeitalter der Globalisierung, München: C.H. Beck 2003, p. 93.
386 Sen, Development as Freedom, p. 46.

asks: "why should the status of intense economic needs which can be matters of life and death, be lower than that of personal liberties?"[387]

6.4.4 Well-being

The goal or purpose of functioning is the well-being of the person that undertakes the functionings. It is the end product of the process of conversion of commodities through the activities of the acting person. Well-being is concerned with a person's achievement: how 'well' is his or her 'being'? This in turn depends on the advantage(s) that a person has to convert his or her entitlement into well-being. Advantage refers to the real opportunities that the person has compared with others. The opportunities are not judged only by the results achieved, and therefore not just by the level of well-being achieved. It is possible for a person to have genuine advantage and still to 'muff' them, or to sacrifice one's own well-being for other goals and not to make full use of one's own freedom to achieve a high level of well-being.[388]

The well-being of a person can be seen in terms of the quality (the well-ness, as it were) of the person's being. Living may be seen as consisting of a set of interrelated 'functionings', consisting beings and doings. A person's achievement in this respect can be seen as the vector of his or her functionings.

6.4.5 Agency

Agency describes the human person in action, the acting person. Sen's use of agency is focused on individual freedom as a social commitment to solve the problem of poverty and deprivations. He considers individuals as agents and not as patients of development. Individuals are agents of development and not mere recipients of governmental handouts. An agent is someone who acts and brings about change, and whose achievements can be judged in terms of his own values and objectives, whether we assess them or not in terms of some external criteria as well.[389] He argues that individual agency is, ultimately, central to addressing all forms of deprivation. But other factors are involved: "The freedom of agency that we individually have is inescapably qualified and constrained by the social, political and economic opportunities available to us."[390] If development is about

---

387   Sen, Development as Freedom, p. 64.
388   Sen, Commodities and Capabilities, New Delhi: Oxford University Press 1999, p. 3.
389   Sen, Development as Freedom, p. 19.
390   Sen, Development as Freedom, p. xii.

expanding the capability that we have as individuals, then the role of the agency of individuals as subjects cannot be over emphasized. This is because "individuals are active agents of change, rather than as passive recipients of dispensed benefits."[391] The agency aspect of the individual is reflected in freedom, which is both the basis of the evaluation of success and failure as well as a principal determinant of individual initiative and social effectiveness. In evaluating the success or failure of any policy the acts of omission as well as of commission of the individuals involved are very important.

6.4.6 Freedoms and Achievement

One of the constituent elements of development is the freedom that people have to make decisions on the type of life they have reason to value. The role of individual freedom in development is very crucial. Sen considers the various roles of freedom as the building blocks of development. Freedom means the expansion of individual capability. What is paramount is not whether the individual utilizes the freedom he has or not, rather the fact that he has the freedom of choice. Stressing the important linkage between freedom and development, Sen says:

> The linkage between freedom and development goes, however, well beyond the constitutive connections. Freedom, it is argued, is not only the ultimate end of development, it is also crucially effective means. This acknowledgement can be based on empirical analysis of the consequences of and interconnections between freedoms of distinct kinds, and on extensive empirical evidence that indicates that freedoms of different types typically help to sustain each other. What a person has the actual capability to achieve is influenced by economic opportunities, political liberties, social facilities, and the enabling conditions of good health, basic education, and the encouragement and cultivation of initiatives. These opportunities are, to a great extent, mutually complementary, and tend to reinforce the reach and use of one another. It is because of these interconnections that free and sustainable agency emerges as a generally effectual engine of development.[392]

He points out two distinct reasons why freedom is central to the process of development. First, the evaluative reason: assessment of progress has to be done primarily in terms of whether the freedoms that people have are enhanced; second, the effectiveness reason: achievement of development is thoroughly dependent on the free agency of people.[393] Sen distinguishes between two dimensions of freedom – substantive (constitutive) and instrumental roles of freedoms. He makes an analytical differentiation of dimensions of freedom and their

---

391   Sen, Development as Freedom, p. xiii.
392   Sen, What Difference Can Ethics Make?, see www.iadb.org/etica/encuent/enc-wdc/docs/dc sen queimp-i.htm. Visited on 2.12.2010.
393   Sen, Development as Freedom, p. 4.

relationship to development, that is, their roles in the development process. They are both the goals as well as the means of enhancing capabilities.

6.4.6.1 Substantive Roles of Freedom

Substantive freedoms are the freedoms individuals have to lead the kind of lives they value and have reason to value. The success of a society is to be evaluated primarily by the substantive freedoms that the members of that society enjoy. Sen argues that "having greater freedom to do the things one has reason to value is (1) significant in itself for the person's overall freedom, and (2) important in fostering the person's opportunity to have valuable outcomes."[394] According to him, the constitutive freedoms have crucial roles in the process of expanding the freedom that people enjoy. The constitutive role of freedom relates to the importance of substantive freedom in enriching human life. The substantive freedoms include elementary capabilities like being able to avoid such deprivations as starvation, undernourishment, escapable morbidity and premature mortality, as well as the freedoms that are associated with being literate and numerate, enjoying political participation and uncensored speech and so on.[395]

Another reason for taking substantive freedom to be so crucial is that freedom is not only the basis of the evaluation of success and failure, but it is also a principal determinant of individual initiative and social effectiveness. Greater freedom enhances the ability of people to help themselves and to influence the world, and these matters are central to the process of development.[396] For example, the denial of freedom of speech or not being allowed to take part in public debates is a form of deprivation that could hinder development. Substantive or constitutive freedoms are intrinsic to human beings and therefore they are preeminently objective to development.

6.4.6.2 Instrumental Roles of Freedoms

Under instrumental role of freedom, freedom is considered as a means to achieving development and not as an end in itself. Sen says: "The instrumental role of freedom concerns the way different kinds of rights, opportunities, and entitlements contribute to the expansion of human freedom in general, and thus to promoting development. This relates not merely to the obvious connection that expansion of freedom of each kind must contribute to development since development itself can be seen as a process of enlargement of human freedom in gen-

---

394 Sen, Development as Freedom, p. 18.
395 Sen, Development as Freedom, p. 36.
396 Sen, Development as Freedom, p. 18.

eral."[397] Furthermore, that the effectiveness of freedom as an instrument lies in the fact that different kinds of freedom interrelate with one another, and freedom of one type may greatly help in advancing freedom of other types[398]. For practical purposes, Sen discussed five roles or dimensions of instrumental freedoms that may help to focus on some particular policy issues that demand special attention. These are: *political freedoms, economic facilities, social opportunities, transparency guarantees and protective security.* These instrumental roles of freedom tend to contribute to the general capability of a person to live more freely, and they also serve to complement one another. They provide the enabling environment or conditions for the realization of constitutive or substantive freedom. Each of these distinct types of rights and opportunities helps to advance the general capability of a person.

6.4.6.2.1 Political Freedom

Every human being is political in nature, and therefore everyone should have the freedom to participate actively in the political process of the society. There should be the freedom for individuals to belong to any political party they choose to belong, vote and be voted for in contesting a political office, freedom to contribute to public debates on the formulation of policies in the society, etc. For Sen, democracy as a form of government has no alternative. Political freedom is a type of right of the people. With several historical evidences, he demonstrates that under democratic rule poverty, famine and all forms of unfreedoms can be overcome.[399]

In addressing the question: what should come first – removing poverty and misery, or guaranteeing political liberty and civil rights, for which poor people have little use anyway?[400] Sen argues that the situation of poverty and misery provides more reason for the urgency of political freedom. He pleads for general extensive rights of liberty. He points out that while it is true that some authoritarian regimes like South Korea, Singapore or China have higher growth rate than many democratic countries, there is also the example of Botswana, an African country with a long tradition of democracy that is doing well. In support of democracy Sen points out that "political and civil rights give people the opportunity to draw attention forcefully to general needs, and to demand appropriate public action. Governmental response to the acute suffering of the people often depends on the pressure that is put on the government, and this is where the exercise of political

---

397   Sen, Development as Freedom, p. 37.
398   Sen, Development as Freedom, p. 37.
399   Sen, Development as Freedom, p. 38.
400   Sen, Development as Freedom, p. 147.

rights (voting, criticizing, and protesting and so on) can make a real difference. This is part of the instrumental role of democracy and political freedoms."[401]

To construct and strengthen a democratic system is for Sen an essential part of development process. This is because democracy increases the immediate opportunity of self realization for people through the process of political and social participation. It enhances the possibility of people to be heard concerning their economic needs. It creates the conditions to establish through public debate the values and priorities of a given society. However, he warns that "while we must acknowledge the importance of democratic institutions, they cannot be viewed as mechanical devices for development. Their use is conditioned by our values and priorities, and by the use we make of the available opportunities of articulation and participation. The role of organized opposition groups is particularly important in this context."[402] As a matter of fact, one of the essential elements in any democratic system is the role of opposition groups. This is because through their critique of public policies and drawing of government attention to the needs of the people, for instance, through protests, governments are put on their toes. As government responds positively to the yearnings of the electorate being represented by the oppositions groups, progress, and thus development is being realized.

6.4.6.2.2 Economic facilities

Sen defines economic facilities as the opportunities that individuals respectively enjoy to utilize economic resources for the purpose of consumption, or production, or exchange. He says the economic entitlements that a person has will depend on the resources owned or available for use as well as on conditions of exchange, such as relative prices and the working of the markets.[403] If that be the case, it means that people's freedom to participate in the economy would depend on the resources and market mechanism that is working in a given society. It follows that the state must distribute resources among the citizenry in such a way as to guarantee access to economic activities by all in the society at same time operate a conducive market mechanism for free exchange of goods and services. He has always emphasized the ability of the market mechanism to contribute to high economic growth and to overall economic progress. But this ability is secondary and it takes place only after the direct significance of the freedom to interchange words, goods, gifts, service etc, has been acknowledged. Sen agrees with Adam

---

401 Sen, Development as Freedom, pp. 150-1.
402 Sen, Development as Freedom, p. 158.
403 Sen, Development as Freedom, pp. 38-39.

Smith when he says: "freedom of exchange and transaction is itself part and parcel of the basic liberties that people have reason to value."[404] The freedom to enter markets can itself be a significant contribution to development, quite aside from whatever the market mechanism may or may not do to promote economic growth or industrialization.

Of particular importance to Sen is free entry into the labour market. He points out that the rejection of the freedom to participate in the labour market is one of the ways of keeping people in bondage and captivity. It should be noted that the struggle against a relationship of feudal dependency is part of the decisive challenges of development politics. The crucial challenges of development in many developing countries today include the need for the freeing of labour from explicit or implicit bondage that denies access to the open labour market. Similarly, the denial of access to product markets is often among the deprivations from which many small cultivators and struggling producers suffer under traditional arrangements and restrictions. The freedom to participate in economic interchange has a basic role in social living.[405] It cannot be denied that markets are elements of the development process.

While acknowledging the importance of an inclusive market mechanism that guarantees the freedom of participation to all, Sen is also of the view that state interventions and regulations can be legitimate and necessary under specific circumstances. He argues that it is hard to think that any process of substantial development can do without very extensive use of markets, but that does not preclude the role of social support, public regulation, or statecraft when they can enrich, rather than impoverish human lives. The approach used here provides a broader and more inclusive perspective on markets than is frequently invoked in either defending or chastising the market mechanism.[406]

The government of a country should engage such market system or economic system that would ensure greater increase in the income and wealth of the country and at the same time guarantee fair distribution of such increase and wealth among the population. Sen argues: "insofar as the process of economic development increases the income and wealth of a country, they are reflected in corresponding enhancement of economic entitlement of the population. It should be obvious that in the relation between national income and wealth, on the one hand, and the economic entitlements of individuals (or families), on the other, distributional considerations are important."[407]

---

404 Sen, Development as Freedom, p. 6.
405 Sen, Development as Freedom, p. 7.
406 Sen, Development as Freedom, p. 7.
407 Sen, Development as Freedom, p. 39.

6.4.6.2.3 Social Opportunities

The arrangements which a society puts in place to offer people the chances or opportunities to obtain substantive freedom are what Sen calls social opportunities. Social opportunities refer to the arrangements that society makes for education, health care and so on, which influence the individual's substantive freedom to live better. These facilities are important not only for the conduct of private lives (such as living a healthy life and avoiding preventable morbidity and premature mortality), but also for more effective participation in economic and political activities. For example, illiteracy can be a major barrier to participation in economic activities that require production according to specification or demand strict quality control. Similarly, political participation may be hindered by the inability to read newspapers or to communicate in writing with others involved in political activities.[408]

Social opportunities are imperative to the overall development or economic growth in a society. The creation of social opportunities, through such services as public education, health care, and the development of a free and energetic press, can contribute to growth on two levels: to economic development and to significant reductions in mortality rates. Reduction of mortality rates, in turn, can help to reduce birth rates, reinforcing the influence of basic education, especially female literacy and schooling on fertility behaviour. The history of the economic growth of Japan and the so-called East Asian miracle provides concrete examples of the importance of social opportunities.[409] The expansion of social opportunities has facilitated an economic growth with higher employment rate and has also created favourable conditions for the reduction of mortality rates and expansion of life expectancy.[410] As it is, social opportunities are complementary to market mechanism and to influencing political control.

In the context of developing countries in general, Sen argues that the need for public policy initiatives in creating social opportunities is crucially important. The history of the rich countries of today is a history of public action, dealing respectively with education, health care, and land reforms and so on. The extensive sharing of these social opportunities made it possible for the bulk of the people to participate directly in the process of economic expansion.[411]

---

408 Sen, Development as Freedom, p. 39.
409 Sen, Development as Freedom, p. 41.
410 Sen, Development as Freedom, p. 45.
411 Sen, Development as Freedom, p. 143.

6.4.6.2.4 Transparency Guarantees

The role of transparency guarantees in freedom has to do with mutual trust and openness among people as the basis of interaction. There is the need for clarity or unambiguousness when interacting with one another in the society. According to Sen, in social interaction, individuals deal with one another on the basis of some presumption of what they are being offered and what they can expect to get. In this sense, the society operates on some basic presumption of trust. Transparency guarantees deal with the need for openness that people can expect: the freedom to deal with one another under guarantees of disclosure and lucidity. When that trust is seriously violated, the lives of many people, both direct parties and third parties, may be adversely affected – by the lack of openness. Transparency guarantees (including the right to disclosure) can thus be an important category of instrumental freedom.[412] These guarantees have the instrumental role of preventing corruption, financial irresponsibility and underhand dealings.[413]

There is a close correlation between transparency guarantees and political freedom as well as economic facilities. As a rule, they are more expressed in a democratic system than in half-democratic or authoritarian regimes. They are more felt in market economy than in feudal system and in centrally controlled planned economies. In stressing the importance of transparency and trust Sen points out that "the development and use of trust in one another's words and promises can be a very important ingredient of market success."[414] Successful operation of an exchange economy depends on mutual trust and the use of norms, explicit and implicit. Here the roles of the judiciary and law enforcement agents as umpires are crucial provided also that they can operate according to the rule of law and not with political prejudices and social bias.

6.4.6.2.5 Protective Security

Protective security refers to the arrangement a society should put in place to cater for the weakest or helpless members of the society. So that they do not have to live a life of destitution or even die of starvation. Such people are often at the periphery of the society and thus excluded from the life of the society. Where extended family system still works, like in some part of the Third World countries, such people are at the mercy of their family members who can still afford to spare them something for survival. Others earn their livelihood as beggars on the

---

412 Sen, Development as Freedom, p. 40.
413 These are among the major menaces hindering the development of the Niger Delta region.
414 Sen, Development as Freedom, p. 262.

street, where there is no social arrangement to meet their needs. Such a situation must not be. Therefore Sen advocates for a social or protective security that would guarantee a life of dignity to all human beings in every society. He argues that:

> No matter how well an economic system operates, some people can be typically on the verge of vulnerability and can actually succumb to great deprivation as a result of material changes that adversely affect their lives. Protective security is needed to provide a social safety net for preventing the affected population from being reduced to abject misery, and in some cases even starvation and death. The domain of protective security includes fixed institutional arrangements such as unemployment benefits and statutory income supplements to the indigent as well as ad hoc arrangements such as famine relief or emergency public employment to generate income for destitute."[415]

His experience of the Bengal famine of 1943 where between two to three million people died of hunger, and which affected mainly the very poor in the lower ladder of the society, as well as the plight of the landless rural laborers may have inspired or motivated Sen to advocate for social or protective security for those who may not be able to participate in the economic system and thereby become vulnerable to deprivation and misery in the society.

The need for security guarantee is anchored on ethical considerations even while making rational choices. Rational choices must not always be made for personal advantage. For the sake of ethics, justice or interest of future generations, one should be moved with either sympathy for destitute or commitment to the course of changing the unjust structures or systems giving rise to destitution in the society. Sen argues that "if you help a destitute person because his destitution makes you very unhappy, that would be a sympathy-based action. If, however the presence of the destitute does not make you particularly unhappy, but does fill you with the determination to change a system that you think is unjust,…then this would be a commitment-based action"[416]. A commitment-based action is informed by the fact that one is convinced that it is not fair for someone to suffer from destitution. Above all, security guarantee is a way of guaranteeing participation of all in the life of community.

6.5 The State, Society and Individuals' Capabilities

After presenting the essentials of the capability approach, it is natural to ask such questions as: Who should be responsible for what? Who is responsible for the expansion of human capabilities or freedoms? Who takes responsibility for the

---

415 Sen, Development as Freedom, p. 40.
416 Sen, Development as Freedom, p. 270.

poor and the down trodden in the society? Before answering these questions, Sen states that: "It is hard to understand how a compassionate world order can include so many people afflicted by acute misery, persistent hunger and deprived and desperate lives, and why millions of innocent children have to die each year from lack of food or medical attention or social care."[417] He goes on to answer that addressing the problem of poverty and misery is the responsibility of everyone in the society and that it requires a social commitment. People themselves must have responsibility for the development and change of the world in which they live. One does not have to be either devout or non-devout to accept this basic connection. As people who live, in a broad sense, together, we cannot escape the thought that the terrible occurrences that we see around us are quintessentially our problems. They are our responsibility, whether or not they are also anyone else's.[418]

As already noted, Sen's understanding of development is that freedom takes the centre position and people are the active subjects of their own destiny. This sense of responsibility is constitutive of our humanity. He argues that our sense of responsibility need not relate only to the afflictions that our own behaviour may have caused (though that can be very important as well), but can also relate more generally to the miseries that we see around us and that lie within our power to help remedy. That responsibility is not, of course, the only consideration that can claim our attention, but to deny the relevance of the general claim would be to miss something central about our social existence. It is not so much a matter of having exact rules about how precisely we ought to behave, as of recognizing the relevance of our shared humanity in making the choices we face.[419]

Next to the general social responsibility is individual responsibility. Sen disagrees with the neoliberal's view that the individual is exclusively responsible for his own life and that dependence on others is not only ethically problematic, it is also practically defeatist in sapping individual initiative and effort, and even self-respect. He agrees with the point that there is no substitute for individual responsibility. But then, such individuals must have been enabled by the society to take that responsibility. For individuals to take responsibility, they must have the freedom to do so. The limited reach and plausibility of an exclusive reliance on personal responsibility can best be discussed only after its essential role has first been recognized. However, the substantive freedoms that we respectively enjoy to exercise our responsibilities are extremely contingent on personal, social and environmental circumstances. A child who is denied the opportunity of ele-

417 Sen, Development as Freedom, p. 282.
418 Sen, Development as Freedom, p. 282.
419 Sen, Development as Freedom, p. 283.

mentary schooling is not only deprived as a youngster, but also handicapped all through life (as a person unable to do certain basic things that rely on reading, writing and arithmetic). The adult who lacks the means of having medical treatment for an ailment from which he suffers is not only vulnerable to preventable morbidity and possibly escapable mortality, but may also be denied the freedom to do various things, for himself and for others, that he may wish to do as a responsible human being. The bonded labourer born into semi-slavery, the subjugated girl child stifled by a repressive society, the helpless landless labourer without substantial means of earning an income are all deprived not only in terms of well-being, but also in terms of the ability to lead respectable lives, which are contingent on having certain basic freedoms.[420] Responsibility requires freedom.

Concerning the responsibility of the state, the state has the duty to provide facilities and the enabling environment that would give the freedom and empower individuals to take responsibilities. It is not the case of a state "nannying" individual choices and responsibilities (the so-called nanny state), thereby denying the individual the initiative of taking responsibility, but that the state creates more opportunity for choice and substantive decisions for individuals who can then act responsibly on that basis[421]. It is like the state playing a subsidiary role of empowering the individuals. Elsewhere Sen says: "Responsible adults must be in charge of their own well-being; it is for them to decide how to use their capabilities. But the capabilities that a person does actually have (and not merely theoretically enjoys) depend on the nature of social arrangements, which can be crucial for individual freedoms. And there the state and the society cannot escape responsibility."[422]

6.6 The Roles of Institutions

In presenting what constitute human freedoms, Sen stresses the vital roles of the respective institutions that should ensure substantive and instrumental freedoms.[423] Besides the state or government, other institutions and agencies that have the functions or duties to ensure individuals freedoms and thus capability include political parties, social organizations, community-based arrangements, non-governmental organizations or agencies of various kinds, the media and other means of public understanding and communication, and the institutions

---

420   Sen, Development as Freedom, p. 284.
421   Sen, Development as Freedom, p. 284.
422   Sen, Development as Freedom, p. 288.
423   Sen, Development as Freedom, pp. 9-10.

that allow the functioning of markets and contractual relations (the judiciary).[424] Last but not the least, the church (though not mentioned by Sen, but as can be implied) as a religious institution, an expert in humanity and custodian of the spiritual realm has a duty in ensuring that individuals have the freedoms, and thus capability to effect their development.

6.7 Capability Approach and Human Development

According to Sakiko Fukuda-Parr and A.K. Shiva Kumar, human development is "an expansion of human capabilities, a widening of choices, an enhancement of freedoms and a fulfillment of human rights. Rising incomes and expanding outputs are seen as the means and not the ends of development."[425] There is a correlation between these notions of human development and Sen's understanding of development as the process of expanding the real freedom that people enjoy which is what the capability approach is all about. This correlation comes about because Sen's articulation of development as an expansion of human capabilities and human freedoms, i.e., his capability approach, constitutes the essential underpinnings of the human development paradigm which is being reported annually by the United Nations Development Program (UNDP) since its inception in 1990.[426]

In arguing to support human development as a way of capability expansion, Sen points out the East Asian economic miracle and attributes it to the fact that Meiji-era Japan invested in human development and thus the accelerated economic growth. In answering the question "what does human development do?" he says:

> The creation of social opportunities makes a direct contribution to the expansion of human capabilities and the quality of life (…). Expansion of health care, education, social security, etc., contributes directly to the quality of life and to its flourishing. There is every evidence that even with relatively low income, a country that guarantees health care and education to all can actually achieve remarkable results in terms of the length and quality of life of the entire population…The rewards of human development go, as we have seen, well beyond the direct enhancement of quality of life, and include also its impact on people's productive abilities and thus on economic growth on a widely shared basis. Literacy and numeracy help the participation of the masses in the process of economic expansion (well illustrated from Japan to Thailand)…Furthermore, there is considerable evidence that improved health care as well as nutrition also make the workforce more productive and better remunerated.[427]

---

424   Sen, Development as Freedom, p. 297.
425   Fukuda-Parr &Shiva (eds.) Readings in Human Development, p. xxi.
426   Fukuda-Parr &Shiva (eds.) Readings in Human Development, xxiii.
427   Sen, Development as Freedom, 144.

We have also pointed out earlier on that Sen was instrumental to the development of the Human Development Index (HDI) Human Poverty Index (HPI-I for developing countries), Human Poverty Index (HPI-II for advanced countries) and the Gender Empowerment Measure (GEM) as alternative measurement or indicators of human development in contrast to the conventional GNP or GDP as indicators of economic growth.

These indicators were used to assess the human development situation in the Niger Delta region by the UNDP. The outcome is the Niger Delta Human Development Reports 2006 which we have discussed in the earlier part of this work (3.2.1 and 3.2.2 indicators and incidence of poverty).

7. Impulses from Catholic Social Thought

In the preceding chapter we have presented a socio-philosophical ethical orientation based on the capability approach as developed by Amartya Sen. This second chapter intends to present the principles of reflection, criteria for judgment and ethical guidelines for actions that should accompany all development efforts, as contained in the rich tradition of the social teaching of the church. We shall examine three basic principles of personality, solidarity and subsidiarity as a first step. Secondly, we shall consider the church's teaching on the common good, Justice, environmental ethics and Human Rights. And thirdly we shall consider the church's model of development as presented by the encyclicals *Populorum Progressio* and *Sollicitudo rei Socialis*.

7.1 Principles of the Catholic Social Teaching

The social teachings of the church are based primarily on a set of principles. Not only do these principles serve as foundation, they also constitute the very heart of the Catholic social teaching.[428] These are the principles of: the dignity of the human person or personality, the subsidiarity and solidarity. These principles are expressions of the church's understanding of man in society as he encounters the message of the gospel. They form the church's principles for reflection, criteria for judgement and guidelines for action in addressing the social, political and economic issues or problems in every society. These principles complement and interconnect one another. In this regard, the Compendium says: "The principles of the social doctrine, in their entirety, constitute that primary articulation of the truth of society by which every conscience is challenged and invited to interact with every other conscience in truth, in responsibility shared fully with all people and also regarding all people."[429] Since these principles are meant to serve as organisational foundations of life in the human society, they certainly have moral relevance in addressing the development problems in the Niger Delta region of Nigeria.

---

428 Pontifical Council for Justice and Peace, Compendium of the Social Doctrine of the Church, Nairobi: Paulines Publications Africa 2004, p. 160. To be referred to as "Compendium" hereafter.
429 Compendium, 163.

7.1.1 Personality

The principle of personality or the dignity of the human person states that the human being is a person, and that all institutions are made by man. Central to the concept of person is the fact that the human being is endowed with intellect and is capable of knowledge and self-determination through his freely chosen actions. All structures of the society and that of international co-operation are traceable to human actions and therefore can also be changed by man. The principle tells us how we should treat our fellow human beings and how institutions should be organised. Every person is endowed with dignity. We should therefore treat others and influence societal as well as international structures in such a way that the dignity of all human beings remains untarnished and they are in a position to be able to develop their personality. To this effect, John XXIII gives a classical understanding of the principle of human dignity as follows:

> The permanent validity of the Catholic Church's social teaching admits of no doubt. This teaching rests on one basic principle: individual human beings are the foundation, the cause and the end of every social institution. This is necessarily so, for men are by nature social beings. This fact must be recognized, as also the fact that they are raised in the plan of providence to an order of reality which is above nature.[430]

The principle of the dignity of the human person in the social teaching of the church is based on Christian anthropology, that is, Christian view of man. The human person is created by God (Gen. 1, 27), redeemed by Jesus Christ and sanctified by the Holy Spirit. The human person possesses body and soul, a being capable of knowledge and love, and of functioning as a responsible moral agent. As Dwyer points out, from Christian perspective the dignity of the human person is biblical and thus theo-centric. It sees human dignity as flowing from the person's relationship with God and not as the result of some quality that the human being possesses independently; the person is the woman or man created by God, addressed by God, called by God, accepted by God. In both the Old and New Testaments the dignity of the person is rooted in the fact that the human being is made in the image and likeness of God (Gen 1:26-27) and is therefore capable of being God's partner in dialogue.[431] The human person is not only in partnership with God, he is also answerable to God (Gen. 2, 15). Endowed with knowledge of good and evil (Gen. 2, 17), man is capable of committing sins. The account of the Fall and the consequent expulsion from Paradise shows how man's relationship with God and his fellow humans in the society can be corrupted through sin and guilt.[432]

430   John XXIII, Mater et Magistra, 218-219.
431   Dwyer, John C., Person, Dignity of, 725.
432   Anzenbacher, Arno, Christliche Sozialethik, Paderborn: Schöningh1997, p. 20.

Despite the Fall, human dignity is so precious to God, that he sent his only be-gotten son to redeem man (John 3, 16). John Paul II describes the principle of the dignity of the human person as follows:

... the dignity of the human person is manifested in all its radiance when the person's origin and destiny are considered: created by God in his image and likeness as well as redeemed by the precious blood of Christ, the person is called to be a "child in the Son" and a living tem-ple of the spirit, destined for eternal life of blessed communion with God. For this reason every violation of the personal dignity of the human being cries out in vengeance to God and is an offence against the Creator of the individual.[433]

It follows from the foregoing, that all societal structures, institutions and policies must be at the service of promoting the dignity of every human person. Again, *Gaudium et Spes* says: "... there is a growing awareness of the exalted dignity proper to the human person, since he stands above all thing and his right and duties are universal and inviolable. Therefore, there must be made available to all men everything necessary for leading a life truly human, such as food, clothing, and shelter; the right to choose a state of life freely and to found a family, the right to education, to employment, to a good reputation, to respect, to appropriate information, to activity in accord with the upright norm of one's own conscience, to protection of privacy and rightful freedom, even in matters religious"[434]. By virtue of being human and on account of his God-given dignity, everyone is a subject of rights and obligations. The dignity of the human person assumes con-crete expression in the fundamental human rights.

7.1.2 Solidarity

The principle of solidarity says on the one hand, that we as human beings depend for our well-being on one another, that is, on the actions of others and the condi-tion of the community. On the other hand, everyone is co-responsible for the entire development of the community and the well-being of others. Therefore, each one should take cognisance of this fact in all his actions. In other words, "solidarity highlights in a particular way the intrinsic social nature of the human person, the equality of all in dignity and rights and the common path of individuals and peoples towards an ever more committed unity."[435] It is the mutual assistance that human beings owe one another in the community. It also means the assis-tance given to someone in need for the sake of humanity that binds all together.

---

433   John Paul II, *Christifideles Laici*, (Apostolic Exhortation) 37.
434   GS, 26, 1.
435   Compendium, 192.

Solidarity is the practical expression of the sociality of human nature. No one moulds his luck or success alone. Contrary to the position of the economic liberals, that the successful deserved their success and therefore have the right to enjoy the fruits of their labour undisturbed, the principle of solidarity says that when somebody achieves something in life, it is not only the result of his own efforts but also that of others: the care of the parents and educators, the services of those who have worked to ensure a peaceful society, a worthwhile environment and a functional infrastructure, the efforts of his partners in communication and cooperation. It holds then that no one is exclusively "the Smith of his luck"; his action affects the chances or opportunities of others, their imaginations of pursuing a successful life. The idea of solidarity expressing the reality of mutual interdependence of people in the society is expressed in the statement of Oswald von Nell-Breunig that "We are all sitting in one boat".

The principle solidarity has its root in both Old and New Testaments. The Old Testament is a treasure for social cases and references, for social laws and obligations towards the poor, the stranger, and the oppressed. In a particular way, the covenant made by God with Abraham and his people Israel has a social dimension. In fact, as Rauscher says, many of the elements that are today associated with solidarity were then determinants for co-existence and social structures.[436] With idea of the love of God and neighbour, Christianity has taken over completely these knowledge and reflections and developed a particularly strong personal dimension to them. We find the idea of solidarity with St. Paul when he urged Christians to "carry each other's burden; that is how to keep the law of Christ." (Gal.6,2). His teaching on the organic nature of the unity of humanity strongly expressed the same idea, he says "for as with the human body which is a unity although it has many parts – all the parts of the body, though many, still making up one single body – so it is with Christ"(I Cor. 12,12).

The term solidarity is rooted in the Latin word "solidum" meaning firm, solid, complete or whole. It means the readiness to engage oneself for a common good or for the good of the others. These are the goals which one considers to be threatened and at the same time valuable and legitimate, particularly the committed support of a struggle against dangers, above all that of injustice. It also means in a wider sense the holding together, social bond, the feeling of belonging together. In a narrower sense, it means a practical and emotional engagement or involvement for common or in most cases co-operative goals; above all, it means a struggle against injustice.[437]

---

436   Rauscher, Anton, Kirche in der Welt, 3Bd, Würzburg: Echter 1998, Pp.90-91.
437   Rauscher, Kirche in der Welt, 90-91.

As a concept solidarity originates from the Roman legal phrase "*Obligatio in solidum*" meaning "the unlimited liability of individual member within a family or other community to pay common debts"[438]. The payment of such debts or damages is done by everyone in the same measure but in accordance with the different abilities of the individuals. Out of this legal framework, solidarity broadens its meaning, and can now be described as social- political brotherhood. Solidarity describes that mutual closeness and union of several persons that are interdependent on one another so that they are able to achieve their goal only by working together.[439] Solidarity is expressed in the common saying: "one for all and all for one" or in the illustration "we are all sitting in one boat and the life of each and everyone altogether depends on whether or not the boat reaches its destination – the shore". Rauscher says "no one can exempt himself nor escape from this common fate, just as the necessary collaboration serves the good of all."[440] Since the end of the 18th century, this principle of mutual responsibility between the individual and society, where each individual vouches for the community and the community for vouches for the individual, has been generalised beyond the law of obligations' context and applied to the field of morality, society and politics.[441]

Though the concept has historical antecedents in the thought of Heinrich Pesch and Gundlach's solidarism, John Paul II gives it a new dimension and popularity that makes it synonymous with common good when he describes solidarity as an authentic moral virtue, not a "feeling of vague compassion or shallow distress at the misfortunes of so many people, both near and far. On the contrary, it is a firm and persevering determination to commit oneself to the common good. That is to say to the good of all and of each individual, because we are all really responsible for all" [442]

There are two forms of solidarity, namely pro-solidarity and con-solidarity. Pro-solidarity is the disposition and actions of the powerful, influential or the rich in favour of and to the advantage of the weak or the poor in the society. In this case it is the disposition of the state, the church, corporate organisations and wealthy and influential individuals, in short the strong towards the weak and the poor. It is the "option for the poor". Con-solidarity is the mutual support and cooperation among the weak and the poor with the aim of achieving a common goal. This is typified by the cooperative societies, labour unions, etc. It is charac-terised by the sense of self-help by people who find themselves in similar disad-

---

438 Bayertz, Kurz, Four uses of solidarity. *In*: Bayertz, Kurz (ed.), Solidarity, Dordrecht: Kluwer Academic Publisher, 1999, p. 3.
439 Rauscher, Anton, Solidarität- Begriff und Inhalt. *In*: Staat Lexikon Bde 4, s 1191-1194.
440 Rauscher, Anton, Solidarität- Begriff und Inhalt. *In*: Staat Lexikon Bde 4, s 1191-1194.
441 Bayertz, Solidarity, 3.
442 SRS, 38.

vantaged conditions and are willing to mutually assist one another to overcome their situation.[443]

To be able to translate solidarity into concrete action in the society, there is the need to know that, the principle of solidarity indicates that everyone is co-responsible for the chances and opportunities of good life of our fellowmen, particularly those with whom we have something to do directly or indirectly and for the positive development of the community. For instance, in the area of economy, one should take cognizance of the collective interests of all concerned in all of one's actions (e.g, on a reliable legal system), preserving the genuine and justified interests of others. Another is we also have the obligation to help or see to it that the life's chances and development opportunities of those with whom we have something to do are good. The duty of support for individuals turns into obligation to provide the institutions with the necessary means. Independent of the probability of a future need, the contributions of the strong should be higher than those of the weak members of the solidary community.

7.1.3 Subsidiarity

In the light of the above, different institutions have their respective roles to play in the society and therefore no unit should suppress or usurp the other. This is the basic understanding of the principle of subsidiarity which states that the lowest unit that can perform a particular function adequately, efficiently, and with benefit to the welfare of the whole should do so before a higher level becomes involved.[444] The involvement of a higher level is to support the lower unit. This is based on the conviction that people are the agents of their own development. According to Paul VI, "Man is truly human only if he is the master of his own actions and the judge of their worth, only if he is the architect of his own progress. He must act according to his God-given nature, freely accepting its potentials and its claims upon him."[445] The human person as a social being acts in collaboration with other persons in his immediate society to realise the dignity of his person. For it is impossible to promote the dignity of the person without showing concern for the family, groups, associations, local territorial realities; in short, for that aggregate of economic, social, cultural, sports-oriented, recreational, professional and political expressions to which people spontaneously give life and

---

443 Prüller-Jagenteufel, Gunter M., Solidarität – eine Option für die Opfer, Frankfurt am Main: Peter Lang 1998, pp. 93-94.

444 Coulter, Michael L. et al. (eds.), Encyclopedia of Catholic Social Thought, Social Science, and Social Policy, Vol. 2, Maryland-Toronto: The Scarecrow Press 2007, p. 1040.

445 PP, 34.

which make it possible for them to achieve effective social growth.[446] It follows that "neither the State nor any society must never substitute itself for the initiative and responsibility of individuals and of intermediate communities at the level on which they can function, nor must they take away the room necessary for their freedom."[447]

Generally, Subsidiarity is about the fact that individuals develop themselves through their own actions, efforts and self determination. The society serves the purpose of helping the individuals to pursue their well-being. It is about when and how the society should support the individual or a group of individuals. In the first place, it determines the relationship between the individual's own efforts and his societal support: groups, organisations and state institutions should support the individual only if he is not able to carry out a duty out of his capability or if doing so would lead to the negligence of other more important duties. In the second instance, is the question of who is responsible for which support to the individual. The social unit (group, organisation or state institution), among the units that are capable of fulfilling such duty and closest to the individual should take over such an assignment or duty. Thirdly, it indicates the nature of the support to be given. As far as possible, it should be a support towards self-help to the individual concerned. It is in line with the true meaning of the word *subsidium* to support. The principle of subsidiarity is traceable to Pope Pius XI's encyclical *Quadragesimo Anno* of 1931 where he says: "it is an injustice and at the same time a grave evil and disturbance of right order to assign to a greater and higher association what lesser and subordinate organizations can do. For every social activity ought of its very nature to furnish help to the members of the body social and never destroy or absorb them."[448] The principle of subsidiarity underpins the political system of federalism whereby responsibilities are assumed first to reside with local states and accrue at the national level only in compelling interstate circumstances.[449]

7.2 Common Good

Personality implies sociality. The human person is social by nature – born into a family in a society. It follows that he can only develop and find self-fulfilment in a society. It means that the person needs other persons in order to become who

---

446   Compendium, 185.
447   MM,138.
448   QA, 79.
449   Coulter et.al (eds.), Encyclopedia of Catholic Social Thought, p. 1040.

he ought to be in the society. The totality of all the goods and services that persons in the society require in order that all may find fulfilment is the common good. It is in this sense that the common good is considered to be "those social conditions necessary for the development of the whole person. Concerned with the totality of conditions faced by all individuals and groups, the common good is the web of interdependence that attempts to promote human dignity and allow all individuals to attain fulfilment more readily."[450] The common good is the sum of those conditions of social life which allow social groups and their individual members' relatively thorough and ready access to their own fulfilment (GS 26). The realization of the fact that the individual or families alone cannot on their own strength meet their needs or find fulfilment informed the formation of the political community, so that the large political community could provide the necessary goods and services needed for fulfilment. It is therefore the responsibility of the state to promote the common good that would enable people find their fulfilment. It is in this sense that the Vatican II states that:

> Men, families and the various groups which make up the civil community are aware that they cannot achieve a truly human life by their own unaided efforts. They see the need for a wider community, within which each one makes his specific contribution every day towards an ever broader realization of the common good. For this purpose they set up a political community which takes various forms. The political community exist, consequently, for the sake of the common good, in which it finds its full justification and significance, and the source of its inherent legitimacy...It is clear, therefore, that the political community and public authority are founded on human nature and hence belong to the order designed by God[451].

At the foundation of the common good are the principles of human dignity and solidarity. Individuals are therefore challenged to promote the dignity of human person in solidarity with others in working for the common good. According to the *Catechism of the Catholic Church* (CCC § 1906-1909), there are three elements that make up the common good. The first is a true respect for the dignity of the human person. Without such a foundation, society frequently tramples upon the inherent dignity of the individual in order to achieve particular objectives. Second, the common good necessitates authentic human development. This refers to the social betterment of each group and individual taking into consideration those items necessary for humans to reach fulfilment. Finally, in order for the common good to be promoted, persons ought to be afforded security and peace.

The central idea of the common good is that it is a good shared in by all. It is a shared good by all who are forming a certain community. In the words of Hollenbach, it "is immanent within the relationships that bring this community or society

---

450   Randall, Jay Woodard, Common Good. *In*: Coulter, Michael L., et al. (eds.), Encyclopedia of Catholic Social Thought, Vol. 1, pp. 213-214.
451   GS, 74.

into being."[452] For the sake of the existence of this common good, every human being, that is, every member of a particular community, has a duty to share in promoting the good of the community (understood as the well-being of the members of that community) as well as a right to benefit from that good.[453] This is why the principle of solidarity is synonymous with commitment to the common good, because the good of each member of a community cannot be separated from the good of the community as a whole. The common good of the community and the good of the members are mutually implicating.[454]

7.3 Justice

Catholic social teaching considers it a scandal to see countless number of men and women, children, adults and old in various parts of world to be under the burden of unbearable condition of misery. Such misery that is the result of poverty and underdevelopment is adjudged to be rooted in the unjust social, political and economic structures existing in the society and the world at large. In other words poverty is essentially rooted in structural injustice. To correct these structural injustices, Catholic social teaching considers the practice of justice as one of the foundations on which society must be built if it is to enjoy progress, peace and harmony.

In line with the tradition of Aristotle and Thomas Aquinas, justice is generally expressed in the phrase – *suum cuique* – to each what is due.[455] There are social relations, patterns of mutuality and structures of interdependence which bind human beings together in communities. In order to determine what is due to each, in the light of human relationships and interdependence, the social teaching of the church distinguishes three modes of justice namely: commutative justice (*iustitia commutativa*), distributive justice (*iustitia distributiva*), and social justice (*iustitia socialis*).

Commutative justice is about the claims which exist in relationships between individuals and individual or between social groups which are essentially private and non-political such as in voluntary associations. It lays claims to fidelity to agreements, contracts or promises made between persons or groups outside the

---

452 Hollenbach, David, The Common Good and Christian Ethics, Cambridge: Cambridge University Press 2002, p. 9.
453 Catholic Bishops' Conference of England and Wales, The Common Good and the Catholic Church's Social Teaching, London, 1996, § 70.
454 Hollenbach, The Common Good and Christian Ethics, p. 189.
455 Hollenbach, Modern Catholic Teaching Concerning Justice, p. 207.

political or public process. It is based on equality and genuine freedom of all persons in the agreement. According to Hollenbach,

> The obligation of commutative justice is one of fidelity to freely formed mutual bonds and of fairness in exchange. It is rooted in the fundamental equality of persons, an equality which implies that no one may ever presume an arbitrary sovereignty over another by setting aside contracts or promises which bound free beings into a relation of mutual interdependence. It implies further that if contracts or agreements are to be just, they must be genuinely free.[456]

In other words, it is about the respect for equal human dignity of each and every person in the case of contracts within social cooperation and fairness of conditions of contract and exchange between social groups.[457] In the light of the foregoing, it is against commutative justice to compel a worker, for example, to accept an insufficient wage simply because the only alternative is no wage at all. Putting the example the other way round, workers owe their employers diligent work in exchange for their wages. Employers are obliged to treat their employees as persons, paying them their fair wages in exchange for the work done and establishing conditions and patterns of work that are truly human.[458] Commutative justice is an expression of dignity and equality of the human person.

Distributive justice relates to the mutual interaction between individuals and the public societies, the state or the society as a whole. It defines the claims that individuals have to share in the public good. It places obligation on the state to distribute available resources in such a way that everyone is able to meet his basic needs required to live a life of dignity in the society. For example, the state must give to individuals what is due to them in, say, the natural resources or fertility of the earth, production of industrialized economy and social security provided by advanced systems of health care and social insurance. No individuals or groups ought to claim exclusive ownership of these goods because they belong to the general public. It may well happen that the degree of participation in the creation of these public goods may differ according to one's state and ability, e.g children, infirm or aged persons, that notwithstanding, the fact of one's membership of the human community accords the rights to share in the public good to the minimum degree compatible with human dignity.[459] In other words, in the sense of preferential option for the poor, the poor and the needy also have a right to share in the common good of the society. In the light of *Rerum Novarum*, distributive justice is the norm which states the obligation of society and the state to guarantee this participation by all in the common good.[460] It establishes the

---

456 Hollenbach, Modern Catholic Teaching Concerning Justice, p. 219.
457 Anzenbacher, Christliche Sozialethik, p. 222.
458 U.S Catholic Bishops' Conference, Economic Justice for All (Pastoral Letter), 69.
459 Hollenbach, Modern Catholic Teaching Concerning Justice, p. 220.
460 Hollenbach, Modern Catholic Teaching Concerning Justice, p. 220. Cf. also RN, 33.

equal right of all to share in all those goods and opportunities which are necessary for genuine participation in the human community.

Social justice defines the institutional action(s) necessary to bring about distributive justice. It refers to the action(s) of the state on behalf of all citizens. According to Hollenbach, "It refers to the obligations of all citizens to aid in the creation of patterns of societal organization and activity which are essential both for the protection of minimal human rights and for the creation of mutuality and participation by all in social life … it is based on that form of human interdependence which occurs through the state."[461] Social justice is a political virtue that places obligation on the state to ensure that all are active and productive participants in the life of society (social, political and economic) and that society has a duty to enable them to participate in this way. As Heimbach-Steins noted, "social justice means that people are obliged to participate actively and productively in the life of the society, and that the society is duty bound to create for them the opportunity for such participation."[462] Social justice, a requirement related to the social question which today is worldwide in scope, concerns the social, political and economic aspects and, above all, the structural dimension of problems and their respective solutions.[463]

Understanding justice as participation of all in the life of the community, the U.S.A Bishops' Conference offers justice as means of overcoming marginalization and powerlessness in the society. It is argued, in the letter "economic justice for all", that

> Basic justice demands the establishment of minimum levels of participation in the life of the human community for all persons. The ultimate injustice is for a person or group to be treated actively or abandoned passively as if they were nonmembers of the human race. To treat people this way is effectively to say that they simply do not count as human beings.[464]

Commenting on the U.S.A Bishops' letter – Economic Justice for all, Hengsbach defines justice as "the minimum amount of mutual love, sympathy and respect that human beings own one another."[465] He points out further that there is a connection between the use of the concept of justice in the letter and that the use of justice by John Rawls in his theory of justice as fairness. For Rawls, a just societal structure is built on two principles, one which assigns rights and obligations and the other that relates to the distribution of social and economic goods. The first principle defines for everyone equal right of equal fundamental freedoms. The

---

461 Hollenbach, Modern Catholic Teaching Concerning Justice, p. 220.
462 Heimbach-Steins, Marianne, Beteiligungsgerechtigkeit. In: Stimmen der Zeit, 217 (1999) 149.
463 LE, 2: AAS 73 (1981), 580-583.
464 U.S Catholic Bishops' Conference, Economic Justice for All, 77, see http://www.osjspm.org/economic_justice_for_all.aspx. Visited on 12.11.2009.
465 Hengsbach, Gegen Unmenschlichkeit in der Wirtschaft, 268.

second principle permits economic and social inequalities arising from different natural and milieu conditioned starting opportunity, on the condition that the differences are in favour of the disadvantaged; the least favoured have equally veto rights in relation to the extent or degree of social and economic differences. Besides, societal positions that are equipped with power and responsibility must be open to all. The principle of basic freedom has priority or preference over the principle difference. The abuse of basic freedom cannot be compensated through economic and social advantages.[466]

Common to all these modes of justice is the notion of equality. As Hollenbach noted, equal claims to mutual freedom and fidelity to contracts in the case of commutative justice, equal right to mutual participation in the public goods in the case distributive justice, and equal obligation to aid in the creation of social and political structures for participation and mutuality in the case of social justice.[467] In the realization of social justice or participatory justice, distributive justice is inevitable. It is when an individual member of the society has been empowered or enabled with the necessary means (material and immaterial) through distributive justice that social justice places obligation on the individual to participate actively and productively in the formation of societal structures particularly as subject in the realization of solidarity and subsidiarity.

In the light of three dimensions or forms of justice, one can conclude that justice demands equality and fairness in all private transactions, wages, and property ownership. It demands equal opportunity for all to participate in the public goods generated by society as a whole, such as social security, health care, and education. It demands that all persons share in material well-being at least to a level which meets all basic human needs, such as those for food, clothing, shelter, association, etc. And finally it demands that all persons are under obligation to participate in the creation of those public institutions which are necessary for the realization of these other claims of justice. Participation in economic life of the society means gainful employment for all who are capable and willing. Political participation demands that all are actively involved in the democratic process of opinion formation and the building up of respective political institutions in the society.

7.4 Human Rights

The fact that the dignity of the human person is inherent in all human beings implies that the human person is a subject of rights and obligations. As subject of

---

466 Hengsbach, Friedhelm, Gegen Unmenschlichkeit in der Wirtschaft, Freiburg: Herder 1987, p. 267.
467 Hollenbach, Modern Catholic Teaching Concerning Justice, p. 221.

rights, the human being has rights that are fundamental to his/her being human and must be respected without making distinctions between race, sex, colour, nationality and religion. In other words, the human rights are expressions of the dignity of the human person. Characteristics of the human rights are that they are universal, inalienable and inviolable, as well as indivisible and inseparable from the human person. They can neither be negated nor be destroyed. Human rights are concrete expressions of human dignity.

The preamble to the December 10, 1948 Universal Declaration of Human Rights by the United Nations states that the "recognition of the inherent dignity and of the equal and inalienable rights of all members of the human family is the foundation of freedom, justice and peace in the world .... [and that] the United Nations have in the Charter reaffirmed their faith in fundamental Human Rights, in the dignity and worth of the human person and in the equal rights of men and women and have determined to promote social progress and better standards of life in larger freedom"[468]. The preamble sets out the affirmation of the fundamental human rights and the consequences that follow, that is, the promotion of social progress and better standards of life for all.

7.4.1 The Church and Human Rights

Generally human rights serve the purpose of safeguarding the freedom of person(s). It is a set of regulation or system to protect the individual or group of persons against any form of assaults from fellow human beings, societal institutions and the state. Human rights are a means to protect the dignity of the human person. As Fritzsche noted: "... Most fundamental, it is one way to deal with a person's relation to public authority – and indeed to the rest of society. If one has a human right, one is entitled to make a fundamental claim that an authority, or some other part of society, do – or refrain from doing something that affects significantly one's human dignity. Human rights most fully understood involve not static property, something possessed, but rather a social and behavioral process. Human rights constitute a fundamental means to the end of basic human dignity".[469]

The Church has always shown concern about human rights. She does this in relation to the protection of the dignity of the human person that is created in the image of God, redeemed by Jesus Christ and sanctified by the Holy Spirit. A

468   Tarcisio, Agostoni, Every Citizen's Handbook – Building a Peaceful Society, Nairobi: Paulines Publications Africa 2000, p. 386.
469   Fritzsche K. Peter, Menschenrechte, Eine Einfürhrung mit Dokumenten, Ferdinand Schöningh, Paderborn, 2004, pp. 15-16 Cf. David P. Forseythe: The Internationalization Human Rights, Lexington 1991, p. 1.

concise teaching of the church on human rights is made clear in the Compedium of the social teaching of the church.[470] The Vat. II council states that "the movement towards the identification and proclamation of human rights is one of the most significant attempts to respond effectively to the inescapable demands of human dignity."[471] The Church considers the human rights as the opportunity which modern times offer to recognize human dignity inscribed by God in everyone. It is in this regard that the church recognizes the positive value of the Universal Declaration of Human Rights, adopted by the United Nations on 10 December 1948. Pope John Paul II describes it as "a true milestone on the path of humanity's moral progress."[472] To give credence to the importance of human rights, the church sees its promotion and realization for individuals and nations, within the context of rights and duties, as one of the prerequisites for peace on earth.[473] Similarly within the context of the common good the Vat. II council affirms the fundamental rights of individual and people.[474]

The human rights flow directly as practical implication and protection of the dignity of the human person created in the image and likeness of God. For this reason, Catholic social teaching considers it as part of the evangelizing mission of the church to promote and defend the human rights (CA 54). Beginning with the defense of the rights of workers with the encyclical *Rerum Novarum* of 1891(RN 51) the social teaching of the church has recognized the importance of human rights to the human society. In *Pacem in Terris* 1963 Pope John XXIII not only praises the United Nations' Universal Declaration on Human Rights, he reiterates the importance of each of the rights and gives them theological backing. He states that:

> They are not given to the human person by any earthly authority: Any human society, if it is to be well-ordered and productive, must lay down as a foundation this principle, namely that every human being is a person, that is his nature is endowed with intelligence and free will. Indeed, precisely because he is a person he has rights and obligations flowing directly and simultaneously from his very nature. And as these rights and obligations are universal and inviolable so they cannot in any way be surrendered (PT,9).

The Pastoral Constitution *Gaudium et Spes* situates human rights in context of fundamental theology precisely creation and Christology (soteriology) and draws the implication for human equality, non-discrimination, and social justice.[475]

---

470 Compendium of the social doctrine of the Church, pp. 82-87.

471 Dignitatis Humanae, 1: AAS 58 (1966), 929-930.

472 John Paul II, Address to the 34th General Assembly of the United Nations (2 October 1979) 7: AAS 71 (1979), 1147-1148.

473 John XXIII, Encyclical Letter Pacem in Terris: AAS55 (1963), 259-264.

474 GS, 26.

475 GS, 29.

Affirming and explaining the characteristics of human rights, the *Compendium of the Social Doctrine of the Church* states that these rights are "Universal, inviolable, inalienable. Universal because they are present in all human beings, without exception of time, place or subject. Inviolable insofar as they are inherent in the human person and in human dignity and because it would be vain to proclaim rights, if at the same time everything were not done to ensure the duty of respecting them by all people, everywhere, and for all people. Inalienable insofar as no one can legitimately deprive another person, whoever they may be, of these rights, since this would do violence to their nature"[476].

For John Paul II, human rights as declared by the United Nations and understood and taught by the Catholic Church have the welfare of man as the goal. And therefore, not only must human rights be respected, but commitment to the welfare of man must also be the motivating factor propelling any program in the society. Anything to the contrary cannot be acceptable. He says for instance: "If, in spite of these premises, human rights are being violated in various ways, if in practice we see before us concentration camps, violence, torture, terrorism, and discrimination in many forms, this must be the consequence of the other premises, undermining and often almost annihilating the effectiveness of the humanistic premises of these modern programmes and systems. This necessarily imposes the duty to submit these programmes to continual revision from the point of view of the objective and inviolable rights of man."[477] The *Catechism of the Catholic Church* (CCC) affirms the intrinsic relationship between human dignity and human rights by teaching that the respect for human right is also respect for human dignity which is given him by God.[478] With reference to the liberating and evangelizing mission of the Church in the modern time, Paul VI sees human rights as constitutive of the church's mission of liberation and evangelization.[479]

7.4.2 Third Generation Human Rights

The jurist Karel Vasak, one-time president of the International Institute of Human Rights in Strasbourg, initiated in 1979 the division of human rights into three generation following the three slogans of the French Revolution: *Liberte, Egalite and Fraternite*[480]. First generation human rights deal essentially with

---

476 Compendium, 85.
477 RH, 17.
478 Catechism of the Catholic Church, Liguori: Ligouri Publications, 1994, 1930.
479 EN, 39.
480 Karel Vasak, "Human Rights: A Thirty-Year Struggle: the Sustained Efforts to give Force of law to the Universal Declaration of Human Rights", *UNESCO Courier* 30:11, Paris: United Nations

liberty. They are fundamentally civil and political in nature and serve to protect the individual from excesses of the state. These rights include: freedom of speech, the right to a fair trial, and freedom of religion. (see Articles 3 – 21 of Universal Declaration on Human Rights 1948.) Second generation human rights are related to equality. They are social, economic, and cultural in nature. They ensure that different members of the citizenry have equal conditions and treatment. They also grant people the right to work and to be employed, thus securing the ability of the individual to support a family. The state is obliged to provide for the people under its jurisdiction all that is needed to fulfill these rights. (Cf. Article 22 – 27). The third generation human rights focuses essentially on fraternity and, in generic terms, can be seen as solidarity rights. They cover group and collective rights: the right to self-determination, to economic and social development, to sovereignty over natural resources, right to healthy environment, to communicate, and to participate in the common heritage of mankind.[481] The third generation rights are also known as the solidarity rights.

Konrad Hilpert[482] has rightly asserted that the state of poverty and underdevelopment of millions of world's population particularly in the developing countries is a violation of human rights. This violation is the injustice that maintains the gradient between countries and the interdependences to the extent that people are not able to meet their basic necessities of life like food, healthcare, shelter, clothing, education etc, in spite of their intensive efforts. This poses an ethical challenge to the international community. In what appears to be a response to this assertion, Armin Barthel[483] has pointed out that the international community is aware of this ethical challenge and it is confronting it headlong by insisting through its various declarations, covenants, summits and conferences that development is a human right. The right to development is to be located under the Third Generation of Human Rights

According to Barthel, the clamor to consider development as human right began in the 1960s. The idea was initiated in the papal encyclical *Populorum Progressio* of 1967 where it stated: "The duty of promoting human solidarity also falls upon the shoulders of nations. It is a very important duty of the advanced nations to help the developing nations."[484] This is because development is not

Educational, Scientific, and Cultural Organization, November 1977 Cf. http://en.wikipedia.org/wiki/Three_generations_of_human_rights.

481   http://www.economicexpert.com/a/Three:generations:of:human:rights.htm visited on 24.4.2010.

482   Hilpert, Konrad, Die Menschenrechte – Geschichte Theologie Aktualität, Düsseldorf: Patmos Verlag 1991, pp. 288-296.

483   Barthel, Armin, Die Menschenrechte der Dritten Generation, Aachen. Horedot (Alano Edition) 1991.

484   PP, 48.

only an aspiration but a right (PP 22). Similarly, at the International Conference on Human Rights held in Tehran, Islamic Republic of Iran, from 22 April to 13 May 1968, the belief was expressed "that the enjoyment of economic and social rights is inherently linked with any meaningful and profound interconnection between the realization of human rights and economic development." It recognized "the collective responsibility of the international community to ensure the attainment of the minimum standard of living necessary for the enjoyment of human rights and fundamental freedoms by all persons throughout the world"[485]. Furthermore, Article 12 of the 1968 Tehran Declaration states that:

> The widening gap between the economically developed and developing countries impedes the realization of human rights in the international community. The failure of the Development Decade to reach its modest objectives makes it all the more imperative for every nation, according to its capacities, to make the maximum possible effort to close this gap.[486]

The declaration justifies its calling on the international community to close the gap of economic disparity between nations by stating in Article 13 that: "Since human rights and fundamental freedoms are indivisible, the full realization of civil and political rights without the enjoyment of economic, social and cultural rights is impossible"[487].

The United Nations further demonstrates its commitment to seeing that everyone has the right to development when in 1986 it made the Declaration on the Right to Development and was adopted by the United Nations General Assembly resolution 41/128.

The Declaration on the Right to Development defines such rights as "an inalienable human right by virtue of which every human person and all peoples are entitled to participate in, contribute to, and enjoy economic, social, cultural and political development, in which all human rights and fundamental freedoms can be fully realized." (Article 1) According to the Declaration, individuals and peoples have the right to:

- Full sovereignty over natural resources
- Self-determination
- Popular participation in development
- Equality of opportunity
- The creation of favourable conditions for the enjoyment of other civil, political, economic, social and cultural rights.[488]

---

485   http://www2.ohchr.org/english/issues/development/right/index.htm. Accessed on 20.04.2010.
486   Barthel, Die Menschenrechte der Dritten Generation, 57.
487   Barthel, Die Menschenrechte der Dritten Generation, p. 58.
488   Declaration on the right to development, http://www.un.org/documents/ga/res/41/a41r128.htm. Visited on 28.4.2010.

As with all other human rights, the right to development is proper to the human person who is the central subject and beneficiary. The fact that the General Assembly of the United Nations has passed a solution on and made this declaration, both individual states and the international community are obliged to ensure equal and adequate access to essential resources and to promote fair development policies and effective international cooperation respectively.

Since the Paul VI proposed the idea of development as human rights to be promoted in the spirit of universal solidarity (PP 43-53), subsequent social teachings of the church have continue to emphasize importance of realizing the right to development by individuals and nations. For example, the Roman Bishops' Synod of 1971 insists in the document, "Justice in the World", that people have the rights to development and that "the right to development must be seen as a dynamic interpenetration of all those fundamental human rights upon which the aspirations of individuals and nations are based."[489] In the same vein, John Paul II teaches in *Sollicitudo rei Socialis* that "people and nations have a right to their own development" (SRS 32). In keeping with the teaching tradition of his predecessors Benedict XVI, in *Caritas in Veritate*, also affirms that development is not simply an economic process: it is a call to respond to God's love.[490]

In sum, both the church and the international community are agreed on three points. Firstly, that all men and women, children and aged have rights to development in accordance with their human dignity. Secondly, that the condition of extreme or absolute poverty and underdevelopment makes the attainment of human rights to development difficult, if not impossible. Thirdly, that the international community is duty-bound to ensure development for all. Individuals and nations must be committed to development as a human right. No one or nations should be left behind in development.

7.5 Universal Destination of Earth's Goods and the Ecological Question

In providing an ethically justified guideline for development, the church points out that consideration must be given to the universal destination of the goods of the earth. While at the same time, particular attention must be given to the environment not just as instrument of manipulation to meet man's material needs but

---

489   Synod of Bishops, Justice in the World, pp. 13-16.
490   CV, 23, 78-79.

also its transcendental dimension to serve the totality of the dignity of the human person.

One of the implications of the principle of common good (7.2) is the universal destination of the goods of the earth. The church teaches, that "God destined the earth and all it contains for all men and all peoples so that all created thing would be shared fairly by all mankind under the guidance of the justice tempered by charity"[491]. This is based on the creation account of Gen. 1: 28-29). According to the Compedium of the social teaching of the church, "God gave the earth to the whole of human race for the sustenance of all its members, without excluding or favouring anyone."[492] This implies that each person has the right to the use of the goods of the earth to meet his well-being necessary for his full development. In order that everyone may claim his in born right to the use of the goods of the earth, there is the need for regulated interventions that are the result of national and international agreements, and a juridical order that adjudicates and specifies the exercise of this right. Furthermore, it is to be noted that "the universal destination of goods requires a common effort to obtain for every person and for all peoples the conditions necessary for integral development, so that everyone can contribute to making a more humane world, in which each individual can give and receive, and in which the progress of some will not longer be an obstacle to the development of other, nor a pretext for their enslavement."[493]

In attempts to use the goods of the earth to meet the needs of man, man has developed science and technologies for industrialization and exploitation of natural resources thus the environment. While the sciences and technologies themselves are not bad, their use is posing serious dangers to man and the environment. These are in the form of pollutions (water, air and soil) and greenhouse effects that is depleting the ozone layer thus resulting to climate change. This has come to be known as the ecological crisis. The church attributes this crisis between man and environment to "man's pretension of exercising unconditional dominion over things, heedless of any moral considerations which, on the contrary, must distinguish all activity."[494] At the root of the crisis is man's perception of the environment as mere instrument to be manipulated through science and technology thereby placing emphasis on doing and having rather than to being, and this causes serious forms of human alienation.[495] It is also the failure to recognize the transcendence in nature, particularly of the human person and

491 GS, 69.
492 Compendium, p. 93.
493 Compendium, p. 95.
494 Compendium, p. 249.
495 Compendium, p. 250 Cf. SRS, 28.

the creation itself. Therefore the solution to the crisis is to put the dignity of the human person at the central stage of development and the use of the environment. The church is of the view that "if humanity today succeeds in combining the new scientific capacities with a strong ethical dimension, it will certainly be able to promote the environment as a home and a resource for man and for all men, and will be able to eliminate the causes of pollution and to guarantee adequate conditions of hygiene and health for small groups as well as for vast human settlements. Technology that pollutes can also cleanse, production that amasses can also distribute justly, on condition that the ethic of respect for life and human dignity, for the rights of today's generations and those to come, prevails."[496]

7.6 Development Model: *Populorum Progressio* and *Sollicitudo rei Socialis*

The Catholic Church's concern for development is based on her understanding of what development should be in the human society. Development is not just about economic growth; it is about the totality of the human person (immanent and transcendental – body and soul) in the society. The social teaching of the church on development based on her tradition is presented by Paul VI in the encyclicals *Populorum Progressio* and up dated by John Paul II in *Sollicitudo rei Socialis*. We shall present the church's model of the development according these encyclicals briefly.

7.6.1 The Model of Integral Human Development

The encyclical *Populorum Progressio* (1967) has been rightly described as the magna carter of the church's teaching on development. This is because in it Paul VI offered the first systematic attempt by the Magisterium to participate in the global debate on development[497]. Against the background of the prevailing modernization theory in the 1960s that presented a model of development, Paul VI considers development primarily as a process that involves series of transitions "from less human conditions to those which are more human" (PP 20). Devel-

---

496 Compendium, p. 251.
497 Cartagenas, Aloysius Lopez, Catholic Development Ethics. Forty Years After Populorum Progressio: Cross-Cultural Revisions and the Prospects of Global Solidarity *In*: Hapag *A Journal of Interdisciplinary Theological Research* 5, 1-2 (2008) 35-85 This section relies mainly on this article.

opment is, for those "without the minimum essentials of life" the passage from their "lack of material necessities" to the "possession of necessities, victory over social scourges, the growth of knowledge, and the acquisition of culture". When this stage of development is attained, people are empowered to move to an "increased esteem for the dignity of others, cooperation for the common good, will for peace" which, in turn, enhances them to appreciate supreme values such as God and faith in him.[498] Paul VI noted that the success of every stage of development depends on whether or not people meet their basic needs.

Paul VI is of the view that for development to be authentic and integral "it has to promote the good of every human person and of the whole human person" (PP 14). On the one hand, he affirms that "the desire for necessities is legitimate, and work undertaken to obtain them is a duty." On the other hand, he warns that this desire can harden into personal and collective greed which can undermine the value of solidarity, while the pursuit for possessions can lead to personal and collective avarice which could lead to a stifling materialism (PP 18-19). Furthermore, it is permissible "to seek to do more, to know more and have more", but it must be only in view of the "full human enhancement" of persons and groups (PP 6), "without one (person or group) making progress at the expense of another" (PP 44).

Contrary to the position of modernization theorists that propose the Western model of development as the ideal for developing nations or less well-off people to catch up with, Paul VI in *Populorum Progressio* is of the view that a model of development that is overly engrossed in worldly affairs and primarily aimed at the conquest of material prosperity is not worth imitating. Instead, "developing nations...must be able to assess critically, and eliminate those deceptive goods which would only bring about the lowering of the human ideal, and to accept those values that are sound and beneficial, in order to develop them alongside their own, in accordance with their own genius."[499] For Paul VI the aim of development must be a "complete humanism," one that is "open to the values of the spirit and to God [and] is conscious of a vocation which gives human life its true meaning" (PP 42).

After presenting a model of development, the Paul VI goes on to analyze the causes of global poverty and underdevelopment. He accused colonialism of being the root cause of global poverty. He points out that colonial politics cultivated the elites, as a "small restricted group" enjoying "more in the exercise of power" while the remainder of the population is "deprived of all possibility of personal initiative and responsibility" (PP 9). Economically, colonialism be-

---

498   PP, 21, 6.
499   PP, 41.

queathed mono-cultural economy to its colonies, an economy "bound up for instance with the production of one kind of crop whose market prices are subject to sudden and considerable variation" (PP 7). Socially, colonialism destroyed the natural cohesion of ethnic units such as family or tribe, thus paving the way for a serious "conflict of generations" (PP 10). Culturally, colonial civilization tended to devalue "ancestral institutions and convictions" and "reject along with the traditions of the past all their human richness" (PP 10).

Moreover, Paul VI attributes the imbalance and unequal development of nations to neo-colonialism to explain why "rich peoples enjoy rapid growth whereas the poor develop slowly" and why "some produce a surplus of foodstuffs, others cruelly lack them" (PP 8). This is evident at the international level "in the form of political pressures and economic suzerainty disguising as financial aid or technical assistance" that aims "at maintaining or acquiring complete dominance" (PP 52). In the area of trade, "the trade between developed and underdeveloped economies" where "conditions are too disparate and degrees of genuine freedom available too unequal" (PP 61) and "inequalities of economic power are excessive" (PP 58).

Paul VI is of the view that these "glaring injustices that cry out to the heaven" (PP 32) are caused by the liberal capitalist system. The system "which considers profit as the key motive for economic progress, competition as the supreme law of economics, and private ownership of the means of production as an absolute right that has no limits and carries no corresponding social obligation" (PP 26). The Pope is convinced that "individual initiative alone and the mere free play of competition could never assure successful development" (PP 33). For this reason he calls for universal solidarity as the means of bringing about integral human development (PP 43-80, especially Nr. 72).

7.6.2 Authentic Human Development

In keeping with the purpose of the encyclical *Sollicitudo rei Socialis* (1987), which was to commemorate the 20th anniversary of *Populorum Progressio*, John Paul II takes up the topic of development as his central theme. In doing so, he appraised the development model in PP, went beyond it and presented a distinguished and multidimensional view of the same model of development. For John Paul II, for development to be adjudged authentic, certain criteria must be fulfilled.[500] First, development must be "human centered", in other words, it must contribute to the realization of the vocation of persons as creative, responsible,

---

500   Cartagenas, Catholic Development Ethics, p. 42.

loving individuals within a social context (SRS 9, 28). Second, as a human task, development must include cultural, transcendent and religious dimensions of man and society, because every phase of economic or cultural advancement is "a moment in the story that began at creation" (SRS 30). In this sense, maldevelopment or underdevelopment must, as matter of urgency, be reversed because these amount to violations of God's creative plan.

Third, development is a right, and like other human rights, it must be respected and fulfilled (SRS 33). It follows that the "respect and promotion of human rights is its necessary condition and guarantee" (SRS 44). Fourth, development should foster and protect the right to culture as guarantee to the growth of people's innate potentials. In other words development must be intellectual and cultural to guarantee literacy and basic education. "The self –affirmation of each citizen, through access to wider culture and a free flow of information" form the basis of authentic development (PP 35, SRS 44). This is because the fundamental problems connected with development are ethical and cultural in character, for it involves resisting the erosion of the best in one's moral heritage and ethnic characteristics either due to domination or the clash of values in the development process (SRS 8).

Fifth, in authentic development it is "either all the nations of the world participate, or it will not be true development" at all (SRS 17). Anything to the contrary would mean that the unity of the human race would be compromised (SRS 14). Sixth, development must embrace environmental concern, in order for it to be sustainable both for present and future generations. In other words, authentic development entails "the responsible use of the elements of nature," and ecological consciousness, which is the "respect for beings which constitute the natural world" in view of their "mutual connection", "integrity" and "cycles" (SRS 26, 34). Seventh, development must promote democratic and participatory political institutions that would liberate people from all unjust structures and oppressive systems. Development must promote just political institutions to replace corrupt, dictatorial and authoritarian regimes (SRS 44, 5). John Paul II argues further that human beings are totally free only when they are completely themselves, in the fullness of their rights and duties. The same can be said about the society as a whole (SRS, 44-46).

Like his predecessor, John Paul II indicted current world trade, monetary and finance systems as part of the "structures of sin" responsible for the poverty and underdevelopment in the world and therefore called for their reform (SRS 43, 16, 36). He offered a development strategy anchored on new fronts of solidarity as an "alternative to excessive dependence" on richer and more powerful countries (SRS 45). This entails con-solidarity which is "solidarity of the poor among themselves, (pro-solidarity) that is, solidarity with the poor to which the rich are called, solidarity among workers and with workers."[501]

Based on the position of Paul VI and John Paul II in the encyclicals under consideration, we are made bold to speak of integral and authentic model of development as the version of the social teaching of the church on development.

7.7 Comparing Sen's Capability Approach with the Impulses from Catholic Social Thought

We have presented Sen's concept and capability approach to development, we have also treated the impulse from Catholic social thought and in particular the development model according *Populorum Progressio* and *Sollicitudo rei Socialis*. The present section seeks to compare both positions on development; and in doing so we shall point out areas of similarity and differences, with the intention of showing where both complement each other. We shall not be able to give in details all the areas of similarity and differences but a few examples will be cited to make our point clear. We shall look at such areas as poverty, development, freedom, human agency, common good and Institutions (democracy or governance) – participation.

To begin with, Deneulin[502] points out the understanding of poverty by both and what development must do about it. For instance, Sen conceives poverty as lack of freedom, as an unfreedom, and development can be regarded as the removal of the various types of unfreedoms that leave people with little choice and little opportunity of exercising their reasoned agency[503]. In other words, development should liberate people from whatever debars them from living a worthwhile life that they have reason to value. Similarly, Catholic social teaching in *Populorum Progressio* and *Sollicitudo rei Socialis*, consider poverty as a lack of freedom, as "less than human conditions", "lack of material necessities", low esteem for the dignity of others, as lack of appreciation for the common good, etc. Development is also viewed as a process that involves series of transitions "from less human conditions to those which are more human" (PP 20). Development is, for those "without the minimum essentials of life" the passage from their "lack of material necessities" to the "possession of necessities, victory over social scourges, the growth of knowledge, and the acquisition of culture". When

501 LC, 89.
502 Deneulin, Severine, Poverty. Amartya Sen Compared to Catholic Social Thinking, Hügel Institute, Cambridge. http://www.theology-centre.org/Leuven 28_04.doc. Visited on 26.5.2008.
503 Sen, Development as Freedom, xii.

this stage of development is attained, people are empowered to move to an "increased esteem for the dignity of others, cooperation for the common good, will for peace" which, in turn, enables them to appreciate supreme values such as God and faith in him.[504] For both Sen and Catholic social teaching (CST) human freedom is constitutive of development and poverty prevents people from reaching their full human freedom. For example, a clever female teenager in a village in the creeks of Bayelsa State in the Niger Delta region dreams of going to university to become a medical doctor, but her freedom to live such a life is hindered by the poverty of her family who cannot pay for her going to school and by the inability of the government for offer free education for all.

Though both Sen and CST accord importance to freedom, each views it from a different perspective. Sen's capability approach focuses on individual freedom of choices and CST emphasizes freedom for the common good. Sen considers freedom as capability of individual(s) to make choices, reflecting the person's freedom to lead one type of life or another, to choose from possible livings. CST sees individual freedom which development should bring about as finding fulfillment in the common good.

Deneulin opines that because Capability Approach is focused on individual freedom or choices, it has little to offer for guiding collective choices. She argues further, that collective choices such as the government's actions to provide its population with the conditions for them to live long and healthy lives through the provision of public health services, cannot be assessed at the level of each individual's freedom to choose that particular functioning but will have to be assessed at the level of each individual's achievements and not each individual's freedoms. Certain areas of human life like education and health cannot be left to people's choices. Deneulin thinks that there is the need to take cognizance of the fact that public actions will often have to be guided by the concern of making people function in one way or another rather than by the concern for giving them the opportunities to function should they choose to do so. She cites the example of environmental problems, stating that when dealing with them, it is more relevant that policies ensure that people do live in a non-polluted environment, rather than make them able to do so, should they choose or not.[505]

According to Demeulin, Sen's capabilities approach seems to represent ethical individualism (emphasis on individual's freedom and wellbeing as yardstick for judging development or social institutions), by insisting that social institutions are to be investigated as per the role they play in individual freedom.[506]. He

---

504   PP, 21, 6; SRS, 44-46.
505   Deneulin, Poverty: Amartya Sen Compared to Catholic Social Thinking, p. 3.
506   Sen, Development as Freedom, pp. xii-xiii.

argues that "human freedoms are seen in the form of individual capabilities to do things that a person has reason to value[507], but individuals are "quintessentially social creatures" and therefore the freedom that each individual enjoys is inescapably qualified and constrained by the social, political and economic opportunities that are available to us" through societal institutions or structures necessary for human flourishing. Sen seems to be aware of this criticism; he opines that for some critics to identify capability approach as methodological individualism would be a significant mistake. This is because capability approach does not detach individual thought, choice and action from the society in which they exist. He argues that "the capability approach not only does not assume such detachment, its concern with people's ability to live the kind of lives they have reason to value brings in social influences both in terms of what they value (for example, taking part in the life of the community) and what influences operate on their values (for example, the relevance of public reasoning in individual assessment.)"[508]

In contrast to Sen's capability approach, Catholic social teaching sees freedom for cooperation in the common good, which is the sum total of social structures or resources that are necessary for human flourishing. We have treated common good in some details earlier. Suffice it to say that personal fulfillment or the pursuit of one's own well-being requires participating in the goods that transcend individuals, which is the common good. As Demeulin noted, while Sen's Capability Approach focuses on individuals, and then looks at institutional arrangements to promote the well-being of individuals, a common good approach to development focuses on the institutions themselves, as well as on individuals, because it is precisely within these institutions that individuals are formed and nurtured.[509]

Political participation is another area of similarity between Sen's Capability Approach and CST. Emphasizing the role of human agency in development Sen believes that "the ability of the people to help themselves and to influence the world"[510] is essential to the capability approach. He argues that people should not be seen as passive spoon-fed patients of social welfare institutions, but they have to be seen as being actively involved in shaping their own destiny. For Sen, democratic-decision making and public debate are *conditio sine qua non* for development. There is the need for democratic freedom. It is democratic freedom that can enable people to specify and decide the capabilities that are worthwhile

507   Sen, Development as Freedom, p. 56.
508   Sen Amartya, The Idea of Justice, London, Penguin, 2010, pp. 244-247.
509   Deneulin, Poverty: Amartya Sen Compared to Catholic Social Thinking, p 7. Cf. also Hollenbach, David. The Common Good and Christian Ethics, Cambridge: University Press 2002, p. 81.
510   Sen, Development as Freedom, p. 18.

to be promoted. He gives the example of the choice between modernity and material prosperity for a people saying: "If a traditional way of life has to be sacrificed to escape grinding poverty or minuscule longevity, then it is the people directly involved who must have the opportunity to participate in deciding what should be chosen"[511]. What Sen says on the need for people's political democratic freedom or ability to participate in the life of the community holds as well for the economy and social life of the society.

Catholic social teaching on subsidiarity and social justice or participatory justice bears similarity to Sen's notion on participation as an essential element of Capability Approach to development. Of importance too in CST is human agency in development. In the words of Paul VI, "Man is truly human only if he is the master of his own actions and the judge of their own worth, only if he is the architect of his own progress. He must act according to his God-given nature, freely accepting its potentials and its claims upon him."[512] In the understanding of CST, development must promote democratic and participatory political institutions that would liberate people from all unjust structures and oppressive systems. It must promote just political institutions and structures to replace corrupt, dictatorial and authoritarian regimes (SRS, 44, 5).

Another area of convergence is the role of institutions. Both Sen's Capability Approach and CST accord importance to social structures or institutions as inevitable for human flourishing. However, as already noted, Sen's Capability Approach views institutions from the standpoint of how they contribute to enhancing individuals well-being and freedom. For CST, social structures are synonymous with common good. Individuals are to participate in it because the common good cannot be separated from the individual needs. CST considers that the social, political and economic structures of the society exist for the common good. It is within the common good that individuals find their fulfillment through cooperation and participation. The more people participate in the common good the better for everyone in the society.

Another area of similarity is the need to have concerns and care for the poor in the society. Under the protective security role of freedom (6.4.6.2.5), Capability Approach talks about the importance of the moral sentiments of 'sympathy' and 'commitment' to ensure that all participate in the life of the community, so that the extreme poor do not suffer starvation. Similarly CST calls for solidarity which goes beyond sympathy or sentiment. This solidarity also calls for commitment to the common good. SRS says solidarity is not just a vague feeling of compassion but "a firm and persevering determination to commit oneself to the

---

511   Sen, Development as Freedom, p. 31.
512   PP, 34.

common good: that is, the good of all and each because we are all responsible for all" (SRS § 38).

Comparing both Sen's Capability Approach with CST on development, reveals that while Sen considers the individual's freedom as the ultimate goal of development and that participation in the life of the community is an important form of expression of individual agency, CST does not deny the role of individual freedom and agency but adds that individual freedom finds meaning and fulfillment by sharing or participation in the common good, which the structures of the society represent. The point of difference seems to be on Capability Approach's focus on autonomy and individual freedom and CST insistence on the role of the common good in development.

The difference stems from the perspective from which each of them views the human person and the human society. While Sen sees the human person and human society from the point of view of empirical social philosophy, CST considers the human person and human society from the point of view Christian anthropology. This is a perspective that is both transcendental and immanent.

This difference needs not be a hindrance to collaboration or cooperation in the work of addressing human deprivation, a goal of development which is common to both approaches. The *conditio humana* beckons on both approaches to cooperate and collaborate in the work of making the world a better place for all to live in peace and freedom. The human condition in the Niger Delta region is an invitation to heed this clarion call.

8. A Niger Delta Development Agenda

8.1 Introduction

We have discussed the problems facing the development of the Niger Delta region. A socio-economic and political analysis has been made. Ethical orientations needed to bring about an overall sustainable development have been presented. It is only imperative to proffer an ethically oriented development agenda for the region. As our analysis reveals, the problems are the results of deficient or dysfunctional socio-economic and political structures. Therefore an ethically tenable development agenda must gear towards establishing just functional or efficient socio-economic and political structures that would ensure political participation, build functional infrastructures (social and physical), guarantee economic participation and promote transparency as well as eradication of corruption.

8.2 Political Participation

In the light of participatory and commutative justice, integral and authentic development, the political marginalization giving rise to political unfreedom (3.6) in the region, must be addressed by a system that would guarantee political participation of the generality of people. Political participation implies that the people have freedom to take part in structuring and directing any comprehensive social systems to which they belong. This includes the freedom publicly to express ethical criticisms of political institutions and decisions, freedom of assembly, and freedom to participate on equal terms in the competition for political offices and in the struggle over political decisions.[513] Under the magic pentagon of development (2.5.3.4) we pointed out that people must be involved in decision making process via consultation as well as execution of decisions. Since the local government is the closest to the people, local governance must be responsive to the needs of the people. There is the need to promote or strengthen democracy at the grassroots level via education of the people on their fundamental human rights

---

513 Pogge Thomas, World Poverty and Human Rights, Cambridge, Polity 2010, pp. 54-5.

and duties, electoral process and election monitoring, better interaction between the electorate and the elected, project monitoring and follow-ups. In other words, "democratic decentralization should devolve decision-making to the communities" (NDHDR). There must be an end to the era of "order from above". There must be civic education and capacity building programmes that would empower socially marginalized groups and individuals, strengthen social and infrastructural institutions and develop the capacity of existing local groups to take active part in political goings on in the region. This is also in line with the principle of subsidiarity.

Nohlen and Nuscheler have rightly argued that "development takes place when people and communities act as subjects and are not treated as objects; when they claim their autonomy, self-reliance and self-confidence, when they plan and execute projects. Development means to be and to change, and not to have."[514] Political participation of the people can truly flourish in an atmosphere of freedom and peace. The oppression and suppression of people by the law enforcement agents in the Niger Delta region not only pose a hindrance to political participation, it is also an outright violation of people's fundamental rights to freedom of speech. It follows that all forms of oppression and suppression must stop. We neither support nor approve any act of hooliganism and criminality, we however demand that law enforcement agents uphold the rule of law and respect people's fundamental human rights while carry out their legitimate duties of the state.

8.3 Infrastructural Development

In the light of Sen's social opportunity, the CST's integral and authentic development, the deficient or dysfunctional infrastructures in the region must be built up. In doing so, preference must be given to smaller projects in the rural areas that are simple, measureable, achievable and time-bound (SMAT). Attention must be given to such small projects that would improve the living standard of the people. Such projects could be local roads, health facilities, and educational facilities like schools, electricity, portable water, health care facility and other essential social services. Not only could these projects be initiated and completed within a very short time, their implementation could easily be monitored by the local people. We do not object to mega projects like railways or coastal roads but we have our doubts on them because not only that they take years before completion, they also give room for corruption and mismanagement of funds. The poor performances of past development commissions in the region give credence to

---

514   Nohlen & Nuscheler, Was heißt Entwicklung?, 71. Cf. IFAD-Dossier, 17/1980.

our doubts. In providing infrastructure "resources should be targeted towards enhancing access to opportunities, goods, services and facilities for all stakeholders,
and developing capacities to overcome obstacles and engage in activities necessary for sustainable livelihood."[515]

8.4 Economic Participation via Diversification of the economy

One of the causes of poverty and underdevelopment in the Niger Delta region is
government's over concentration on the oil and gas sector thereby neglecting
other branches of the economy. This situation has led to economic deprivation
and exclusion of the generality of the people. In the light of Sen's commodity
entitlement and economic facility as well as CST on distributive justice, solidarity
and subsidiarity, government must improve and diversify the economy. We believe
that "using existing assets, including oil and other natural resources, a diversified
economy would reduce the heavy focus on oil and gas – a non-renewable resource – while providing a basis for growth clusters within the region."[516] In this
regard, skill acquisition and capacity building programmes for the people could
be promoted by the government. This would enable people to initiate and participate in productive economic activities. In other words, the state must challenge
and promote people's initiatives to actively and productively participate in the
economy. People should be accessible to favorable credit facilities or grants to
enable those who can and are willing to establish small and or medium scale
industries. Micro-credit should be made available to poor people willing to engage in gainful economic activities after acquiring the necessary skills to do so.

There is the need to promote agriculture and other agro allied industries or
businesses. This is because the region is noted for being conducive for the production of rice, sugar, cocoa, roots and tubers, citrus fruits, plantains, rubber and
rubber products and is blessed with many resources for aquaculture and forestry.
Moreover, the generality of the people is engaged in agriculture, though on a
subsistent level.

Promoting agriculture implies that the polluted environment needed for it
must be cleaned up and a process of soil regeneration must begin. Effective environmental laws need to be put in place to protect the environment. Not only to
ensure sustainable development but also to uphold intergenerational justice.

---

515 NDHDR, p. 6.
516 NDHDR, p. 5.

There must also be land reform that would guarantee or rather restore the ownership of land to communities or families. That means that the 1978 Land Use Act
that is now ingrained in the constitution (3.5) must be reformed or abrogated.
This would in turn reduce the tensions or conflicts between the state and the
communities.

Diversifying the economy would include the deregulation of the downstream
sub-sector of the oil industry. That would enable more people to participate in
the oil and gas business. That means the petroleum and mineral act must either be
abrogated or reformed so that private individuals and group especially Nigerians,
particularly indigenes of Niger Delta could obtain licenses to establish refineries
thus creating job opportunities for more people. The deregulation should not stop
with the removal fuel subsidy by the government; it must be carried out to its logical
end. Savings from the fuel subsidy must be used to promote other branches of
the economy, provide social security and infrastructure for the people.

8.5 Transparency and Eradication of Corruption

We have noted that the enclave nature of the oil economy makes most of the
transactions and negotiations by oil multis and government agents to be shrouded
in secrecy, and thus making accountability and transparency to be shady. This
situation has given rise to oil bunkering, theft, round trips or sharp practices
among oil marketers, and sabotage in the country's oil refineries etc. The corruption in the oil industry can also be attributed to the lack of accountability and
transparency there. Therefore in other to bring about integral and authentic and
thus sustainable development in the region, the Nigerian state must enforce
transparency and accountability first in the extractive industry. Concurrently, the
state must wage war against corruption until it is eradicated or at least reduced to
its barest minimum in all the structures of the society. Corruption must be fought
in all the levels of governments; federal, state and local as well as in all ministries
and departments, agencies and commissions. The activities of the Ministry of
Niger Delta, the NDDC, the oil multis as well as NNPC must constantly be on
the watch by anti-corruption agencies.

Part IV
Assessment of and Suggestions for Agents of Development

9. Transnational Contributions to Development

9.1 Introduction

The previous part emphasized Sen's capability approach which considers development as freedom in its dimensions as substantive (6.4.6.1) and instrumental freedoms (6.4.6.2). Similarly the Catholic social teaching offers impulses in the forms of the guiding principles of reflection like personality (7.1.1), solidarity (7.1.2), subsidiarity (7.1.3), the common good (7.2), social justice (7.3) and human rights (7.4). As the criteria for judging development, the social teaching of the Church offers the model of integral human development (7.5.1) and authentic human development (7.5.2). This fourth and last part of the work will examine current efforts of institutions and organizations that have direct and indirect impact on the development of the Niger Delta, and in the light of our ethical orientation make suggestions as to what can be done better or initiated to bring improvement to the situation of development in Niger Delta region.

To begin with, we shall examine in this chapter the transnational contributions to development and suggest ways that ethically motivated contributions could improve the lot of the Niger Delta region. In chapter two we shall consider the contributions of Nigerian stakeholders and also suggest ethically guided approaches to the development of the Niger Delta. Last, but not the least, we shall consider the role of the Church in the development of the region. Our central argument is that Christian development ethics (ethical orientation) can make significant contribution to development of the Niger Delta by providing guidance to all development efforts there.

9.2 Contributions of Multilateral Institutions

There are several contributions of multilateral institutions to development. These are easily noticeable in the areas of environmental protection, human rights and good governance, human development, gender consciousness, anti-corruption efforts, and health.[517] Contributions of multilateral institutions include the work

---

517 Langhorst, Peter, Kirche und Entwicklungsproblematik, Paderborn: Ferdinand Schöningh 1996, pp. 246-248.

of the United Nations in the aspect of its development program (UNDP), the Debt Cancellation Campaigns, the Poverty Reduction Strategy Paper of the World Bank and IMF, the development-oriented reforms of the World Trade Organization and the initiatives for transparency and against corruption. Actors of these contributions are people of the world from all nationalities, the governments of countries in the northern and southern hemispheres. The positive actions of these international bodies do influence the national structures of the different countries that are beneficiaries of their contributions.

9.2.1 United Nations Development Program

In our discussion on the normative concept of development, we presented the UNDP understanding of development as focusing on human development as it is being promoted and reported in its annual human development report since 1990. UNDP did not just give a definition or description of what human development (2.5.4) should be, but it is also making conscious efforts to promote human development everywhere, particularly in the developing countries. Its annual reports present the various aspects or dimensions of human development. Since the MDGs were proclaimed in 2000, UNDP has been stressing on how best to realize the set goals in all countries, particularly in the Third World. UNDP produces the annual national as well as regional human development reports. In the process, it highlights areas of human development in need of urgent attention in each country and region.

The UNDP Niger Delta Human Development Report 2006 is the first comprehensive report on the situation of human development in the Niger Delta.[518] The UNDP Human Development Report on the Niger Delta has not only given credence to the claims of the Niger Delta people, it has since become a model for other development plan of action, for example the Master Plan of the NDDC. By its activities and reporting UNDP draws the attention of powerful, influential and wealthy stakeholders to the plight of the poor, who on their own are, in most cases, not able to articulate and present their predicament to the world. As a multilateral institution, effects of its activities cut across different nations.

From the point of view of the principle of solidarity (7.1.2), we consider the work of UNDP directed at overcoming poverty and ensuring worthwhile living conditions for all as a contribution to promoting the dignity of the human person (7.1.1). However, it is not enough to report on the development situation of a developing country, more concrete actions need to be done. In the light of peoples'

---

518   UNDP Nigeria, Niger Delta Human Development Report 2006.

right to development (third generation human right), the UNDP must intensify its partnership with developing nations like Nigeria by insisting that governments commit themselves to the human development of their people particularly those in the rural areas as in the Niger Delta.

9.2.2 Millennium Development Goals as Condition for Debt Cancellation

At the Millennium summit of the United Nations in September 2000 at its headquarters in New York, the heads of state and governments of member states made the so-called Millennium declaration. Both rich and poor countries pledged to do everything possible to eradicate poverty, to promote human dignity and equality, to realize peace, democracy and ecological sustainability. The Secretary General of the United Nations was mandated to formulate on the basis of the Millennium declaration, urgent goals and concrete plans for implementation until 2015. The outcomes of the mandate are the Millennium Development Goals:

1. Eradicate extreme poverty and hunger
2. Achieve universal primary education
3. Promote gender equality and women empowerment
4. Reduce infant mortality
5. Improve maternal health
6. Combat HIV/AIDS, Malaria and other deceases
7. Ensure environmental sustainability
8. Develop a global partnership for development[519]

These development goals appear to express a comprehensive or an all-embracing understanding of development in the semblance of the Church's model of integral human development (7.6.1), but they are not comprehensive enough, for example, the aspect of transcendence is not considered. However, it is a commendable attempt by the international community to set goals of common interests to international politics. The goals are the minimum conditions for a worthwhile human life.[520] The MDGs present a collective, binding framework for international development politics and entail a catalogue of goals with measurable indicators. It is expected that comparing the data between 1990 and 2015, measurable progress should have been achieved. Each of the goals has its respective indicators

519 The World Bank, World Development Indicators, World Bank, Washington DC: 2005, p. 20.
520 Nuscheler, Franz & Roth, Michele (Hg.), Die Millennium Entwicklungsziele – Entwicklungspolitischer Königsweg oder ein Irrweg?, Bonn: Dietz 2006, p. 39.

for monitoring progress. For example, by 2015 the number of hungry people, that is, people living on less $1 a day should be reduced to half. The number of boys and girls obtaining primary education should be optimal and the infant mortality rate of children under the age of five should have been be reduced by two-thirds. What makes MDGs transnational contribution to development is the fact that the international community, particularly with the developing countries, is presented with a set of goals to be attained within a time limit.

To assist highly indebted poor countries (HIPC) to reach the goals, the cancellation of their debt by creditor countries and institutions was attached with the condition that savings from such relief should be spent to pursue the MDGs.[521] According to the Debt Management Office in Abuja, Nigeria, the debt relief is being used to finance the MDGS and National Economic Empowerment Development Strategy which is Nigeria's version of the PRSP. According to the special adviser to the Nigerian President on the MDGs Hajia Amina Az-Zubair, the Nigerian government has been receiving over $1 billion annually since 2006 from the Paris Club's debt relief package that should be spent to execute the MDGs.[522] This amount is being shared between the federal and state governments as follows: Federal Government $750 million (N112.50 billion) and State Governments $250 million (N37.5 billion). In addition, the Federal government is said to have budgeted N110 billion for the MDGs in the 2010 budget. As at July 12, 2010 Nigerian Government has spent a total of N1.04 trillion on the MDGs so far.

Progress reports from the various regions of the world on the MDGs show on the one hand that generally there has been considerable improvement in primary education, portable water, immunization and reduction of infant mortality. On the other hand, the situations of infectious deceases, sanitation, and the protection of the environment have not improved.[523]

We have pointed out in part one that among the problems hindering development in Niger Delta are lack of access to educational and health facilities as well as lack of social infrastructure (3.2). Others are environmental degradation (3.3), HIV/AIDs (3.4) violent conflicts (3.6) and so on. We have also said that each of these problems constitutes a condition of unfreedom (1.3 of part three chapter

---

521 Homi, Kharas, Debt relief and sustainable financing to meet the MDGS. *In*: Primo Braga, Carlos A. & Dömeland, Dörte (eds.), Debt relief and Beyond, Washington DC: The World Bank 2009, pp. 117-140.

522 Az-Zubair, Amina, "Government spends N1 trillion on MDGs" in The Nigerian Guardian, http://www2.guardiannewsngr.com/index.php?option=com_content&v. Visited on 13.7.2010. See also http://www.nigeriannews.com. Visited on 13.7.2010. Az-Zubair gave this report at the public hearing on the MDGs of the House of Presentatives on the 12 July 2010.

523 Nuscheler & Roth (Hg.), Die Millennium Entwicklungsziele, 45.

one) and poverty (7.6), and that removing them is the goal of development. It is also noted in part three, chapter three (situation of Niger Delta in the light of Sen's capability and the Catholic tradition of Social Thought) that those who suffer these problems are human persons endowed with dignity and therefore subjects of all human rights (7.1.1). It follows that countries which have received debt relief package and have failed to pursue the MDGs to a logical end with the fund have not only abused the rights of their people, they have also breached the contract with the international community. Social justice (7.3) demands that governments keep to their promises by ensuring that the gains of debt relief packages are actually spent on attaining the MDGs. We suggest that the UN and the group of creditors as well as the civil society should monitor and insist on regular reports on the use of such funds from debt relief by recipient countries. Such reports must contain empirical evidences of progress in the living standard of the people. State and local governments in the Niger Delta region should be held accountable for the use of their share of the fund from debt relief.

9.2.3 The Poverty Reduction Strategy Program

As a follow up on the post-Washington Consensus (2.4.2.1) and perhaps the Jubilee debt relief campaign 2000, the World Bank and the International Monetary Fund (IMF) have, since 2000, proposed the Poverty Reduction Strategy Papers (PRSP) to Highly Indebted Poor Countries (HIPC) and countries of the Third World as condition for debt relief and further loans. The Poverty Reduction Strategy Papers (PRSP) are supposed to be prepared by member countries in broad consultation with stakeholders and development partners, including the staffs of the World Bank and the IMF (2.4.3 of part one chapter two). This seems to be a reform from the world finance institutions. If the proposals as envisaged by IMF and World Bank could be carried out accordingly, it could contribute greatly to the development of the Third World countries and thus the eradication of poverty.

However, a report from VENRO (*Verband Entwicklungspolitik deutscher Nicht-tregierungsorganisationen e. V.*) has shown that most countries that have prepared their PRSP have not taken enough pain to include the voices of the poor people who are supposed to be the beneficiaries of the arrangement[524] (2.4.3). Since participation is an aspect of social justice (7.3) and a guarantee of part-taking in the common good (7.2), it is necessary that the concerned countries ensure that

---

524 VENRO/GKKE, Fighting Poverty without Empowering the Poor? Cf. http://www.venro.org/fileadmin/publikationen/E. Visited on 7.1.2010.

PRSP is people-centred, by not only making the poor contribute to the preparation of the document but also actually seeing them benefiting from debt relief
and soft loans that they may receive from world finance institutions. Müller has
rightly argued that people's participation is an essential element of development.[525] Similarly, we have pointed out under the magic pentagon of development (2.5.3) in part one that participation is part and parcel of development
(2.5.3.4). It is in this way that the poor can benefit from the world financial reforms which PRSP seems to represent. PRSP should not be a cunning development plan put together by the government. Poor people must participate in the
formulation and actual execution of PRSP otherwise it would not serve their
purpose. PRSP should offer the opportunity for people to actively and productively participate in their own development.

9.2.4 Development oriented Reform of World Trade

The World Trade Organization is the umbrella institution for three main world
trade management mechanisms namely the *General Agreement on Trade and
Tariff* (GATT) founded in 1947 to regulate trading in goods, the *General Agreement
on Trade and Services* (GRATS) and the *Trade Related Aspects of Intellectual
Property Rights* (TRIPS). WTO was established in 1995 with headquarters in
Geneva, Switzerland.[526] A study carried out by the group of expert on world
economy and social ethics of the German Bishops' Conference on the world
trade *"Welthandel im Dienst der Armen"* reveals that though the primary goal of
GATT at the beginning was the liberalization of trans-border trade, the industrialized countries are taking the greatest advantage of the organization to trade
among themselves while the most important exports of developing countries
(agriculture and textile) continue to meet high import barriers set by industrialized countries.[527] Through the so-called market protectionism, many industrialized countries still block off their markets to agricultural products from developing
countries.

An example is the practice of agricultural subsidy by European Union as well as
export subventions. The consequences of this development politic from developed
countries are that farmers in industrialized countries are able to embark on mass
production and sell at prices below the cost of production. With trade liberalization

525   Müller, Johannes, Entwicklungspolitik als globale Herausforderung, Stuttgart: Kohlhammer
       1997, pp. 159-165.
526   Nuscheler, Lern- und Arbeitsbuch Entwicklungspolitik, 330-335.
527   Die Deutschen Bischofskonferenz, Welthandel im Dienst der Armen, Bonn: Deutschen Bischofs-
       konferenz 2006, pp. 7-8.

they are able to flood many developing countries' markets with their products at prices cheaper than what the local farmers could sell their own products. In the process majority of local farmers in the developing countries are put out of business. This is because their products are not able to compete favourably with the subsidized imported products from the industrialized countries. As it were, despite the development-oriented reform of the world trade, many least developed countries are not benefiting from WTO and thus their people who are mostly farmers are excluded from world trade.

Nuscheler has also observed that despite the UN principle of "one country – one vote", there is an imbalance in power and influence between the advanced and the developing countries. Three main reasons are responsible for this situation: firstly, preparation for important decisions often takes place in an informal setting, the so called "*Green Room Discussions*" where delegates from G7 countries and strategically important developing countries like Brazil, India and South Africa meet to work out the technicalities. Secondly, many developing countries do not have permanent delegates at the WTO. And thirdly, many of the developing countries' delegates do not possess the necessary expertise that would enable them take active part in the discussions or negotiations on complicated issues that could have far-reaching effects on their own economies and societies.[528]

At this juncture, we want to point out that the development reform of WTO has brought benefits to some people while others are still not able to overcome their poverty and underdevelopment. Our presentation of the development problems in the Niger Delta (3.1) lends credence to this point.

In the light of principle of human dignity (7.1.1 of part three) which is the basis of all human rights (7.4.) including civil and political rights of civil contract as well as economic, social and cultural rights of social contract (see third generation human rights 7.4.2), the challenge is to make a preferential option for those whose rights are being excluded in the workings of world trade. In the light of authentic development (7.5.2), it is either all participate in development or it is not true development. We have pointed out in the principle of personality that all societal institutions or structures are made by man to serve the human purpose and that they can also be changed by man. We fully agree with the group of experts when they noted in the study, *Welthandel im Dienst der Armen* that:

> The World Trade is not an end in itself, rather it is to be judged above all, whether and in which form it is contributing to guarantee the human rights in all its various dimensions and to eradicate poverty and underdevelopment. The political measures for the formation of world trade on national as well as international levels are therefore to be considered from the point of view of what they can contribute to poverty reduction or what use they have for the poor[529].

---

528 Nuscheler, Lern- und Arbeitsbuch Entwicklungspolitik, 332.
529 Die Deutschen Bischofskonferenz, Welthandel im Dienst der Armen, 19.

On the strength of the principle of personality, we insist that the human being should be the beginning, bearer and goal of all development. Therefore, the world trade must also consider the dignity of the people in the developing countries who are suffering poverty and underdevelopment resulting from its operations whether willingly or unwillingly. A just world trade politics must fulfill commutative justice (7.3). This is because weaker market participants are expected to share according to their ability in the entire welfare effects of the economy. The world economic frameworks should guarantee a just economic exchange. The current practice of world trade exhibits a considerable institutional deficit, that is, structural disadvantages. In order that the world trade may serve the interest and thus improve the trade perspective of the economically least developed countries,[530] the current world trade system and trading options must be reformed. Such reforms should be inspired by solidarity that would lead industrialized countries to assist the developing countries to produce goods and services to meet their own needs and also permit the importation of products from developing countries into their markets. This point is very important because should a Third World country like Nigeria decide to diversify its economy to include agriculture and other sectors apart from petroleum, the next question would be where is the market for such products outside of Nigeria? Opening up the market of industrialized countries to the Third World means that goods and services towards the developing world would not just be a one-way traffic as it is now. Already such programs as "Fair Trade" and "Eine-Welt-Laden" are examples of how globalization could bring about development in the Third World. But these are still too small to make noticeable global impact. Development assistance to the Third World would become meaningful when it empowers the people to participate actively and productively in the world economy.

9.2.5 Initiatives for Transparency and Anti-Corruption

In treating the socio-economic analysis of the development problems in part two chapter one, we have pointed out that corruption is one of the hindrances of development and that corruption is global phenomenal (4.4). We have also indicated that corruption thrives in the petroleum industry involving multinational oil companies as well (4.4.1). It follows that if corruption is to be tackled on the local or national level, there must a global framework of action that should give the direction. Two global efforts in this regard readily come to mind: the Extractive Industry Transparency Initiative and the United Nations Convention Against Corruption.

---

530   Die Deutschen Bischofskonferenz, Welthandel im Dienst der Armen, 23.

9.2.5.1 Extractive Industry Transparency Initiative

In October 2002, the former British Prime Minister Tony Blair launched the EITI at the World Summit for Sustainable Development in Johannesburg. The aim of EITI is to strengthen governance by improving transparency and accountability in the extractive sector thus making natural resources to benefit all. Stakeholders of this initiative are governments, companies, civil society and NGOs. The method adopted is the Publish What You Pay (PWYP)[531] and the governments are to disclose what they receive. It has been endorsed by the G8 since June 2004 at its summit in Sea Island.[532]

Principally, the EITI is based on the principle that: All funds inflow and distribution must be recorded and reported. Distributions of funds must pass through the due process of legislation and approval. Funds released and received funds must be published.[533] Since its endorsement, EITI has been internationalized and has become a directive by which all countries with which the industrialized countries of the North and the Bretton Wood institutions would have to do business must transparently live by. But whether all industrialized countries are following this directive is another question.

The overall benefit of the EITI is poverty reduction, and thus development of resources of oil rich-countries that are implementing the initiative. The EITI is set to provide a clear signal to investors and IFIs that the government is committed to greater transparency, accountability and good governance. This leads to political stability which in turn contributes to the prevention of conflicts arising from the oil, gas and mining sectors. This again offers the conducive climate for investment, job creation that further leads to reduction in unemployment. The EITI also gives information to the civil society and NGOs with which to hold the governments accountable for the revenues collected on behalf of the citizenry. Nigeria is among the countries that have signed into the initiative.[534]

The EITI has the potentiality of contributing to development of oil-producing regions like the Niger Delta. This is because it is directed at fighting corruption in the extractive industry. As we have noted corruption is one of the causes of

---

531 To demystify the secrecy surrounding the enclave nature of the oil industry, the George Soro's Open Society Foundation, in coalition with about 200 NGOs launched the Publish What You Pay – PWYP campaign in 2002. It was adopted by PM Tony Blair government and sold to the G8. The campaign was to get oil company operators and their sovereign owners to disclose all financial transactions in the oil industry as a way of fighting corruption and financial crimes world-wide Cf. CSN, Nigeria – The Travesty of Oil and Gas Wealth, pp. 153-155.

532 EITI, http://eitransparency.org/eiti/. Visited on 31.1.2010.

533 CSN, Nigeria – The Travesty of Oil and Gas Wealth, p. 146.

534 CSN, Nigeria – The Travesty of Oil and Gas Wealth, p. 156.

poverty. And poverty amounts to the denial of people's right to development (7.4.2) and exclusion of some people from it cannot be said to be an authentic development (7.5.2). In order that EITI may contribute more effectively to development, we suggest that the international community make it compulsory for all stakeholders in the extractive industry to sign into it and make this a condition of transacting business.

9.2.5.2 United Nations Convention Against Corruption

Over the years the United Nations or rather the international community has come to the realization that one of the greatest obstacles against development is corruption. This made the general assembly of the UN to adopt the convention against corruption by resolution 58/4 of 31 October 2003. The goals of the convention are:

- To promote and strengthen measures to prevent and combat corruption more efficiently and effectively.
- To promote, facilitate and support international cooperation and technical assistance in the prevention of and fight against corruption, including asset recovery.
- To promote integrity, accountability and proper management of public affairs and public property.[535]

The convention came into force on 14 December 2005. It provides a unique opportunity for tackling global corruption. This is because it is the first ever global agreement on how to prevent and fight corruption. In the meantime, 140 countries have signed and 104 have ratified it. That means that interstate conditions for its implementation in national law have been established.[536] Nigeria signed and ratified it in 2004. The practical demonstration of Nigeria's official commitment was the establishment of the anti-corruption agency Economic and Financial Crime Commission (EFCC).

---

535 UN Convention against Corruption, http://www.unodc.org/pdf/corruption/publication visited on 26/2/2010.
536 GTZ, Beitrag zur Umsetzung der UN-Konvention gegen Korruption, http://www.gtz.de/de/themen/politische-reformen/korruption/19075.hmt.Visited on 26.2.2010.

9.3 International Stakeholders in the Oil Industry

9.3.1 International Policy Report

In our political analysis of interest groups we pointed that international stakeholders' interests have not always included the concerns of the local people of the governments with whom they transact business (2.1 of part II, chapter 2).

The fact that the governments of the U.S.A, Western Europe, China and India have not considered the real needs of Nigerians, particularly the people in the Niger Delta in the pursuit of their energy interest in the region is confirmed by the International Policy Report of February 2007.[537] This is partly responsible for the situation of poverty and underdevelopment in the Niger Delta which has snowballed into violent conflicts, disrupting energy security from the region since the end of 2005. The report points out that Nigerian governments have not been paying sufficient attention and funding to the resolution of the conflicts and human rights abuses in the Niger Delta, a condition traceable to the deficiencies in democratic institutions in the country as well as the "hard line" security approach to solving the problems of violence and insurgencies in the region by both Nigerian and the U.S governments. The report therefore suggests the need to strengthen democracy and all that it entails that would secure good quality of life for Nigerians in place of military strategies or other strategies that would further escalate the situation in the region. For instance, the reports says: "democratic governance and conflict resolution are the only routes to securing the Delta and that multilateral institutions, the United States, and Nigeria must increase funding and support for democratization programs in the Delta and in Nigeria more generally."[538] We consider this suggestion not only tenable for the Nigerian and U.S governments, but it holds as well for all those who are interested in the oil and allied industries in Nigeria in general and in the Niger Delta in particular.

9.3.1.1 Military assistance and Offshore Strategy

We have pointed out in part one that one of the problems facing the development of Niger Delta is violent conflicts (3.6). The continued violence and insurgences, which often result to major attacks on oil facilities by armed youth militias in the Niger Delta region pose a great deal of challenge to the stability and security of

---

537 Lübeck, Paul et al., Convergent Interests: U.S. Energy security and the securing of Nigerian Democracy, International Policy Report. http://www.ciponline.org/NIGERIA_FINAL.pdf. Visited on 1.3.2008.

538 Lübeck et al., Convergent Interests, p. 5.

energy supply to the economies of the U.S., Western Europe, China and India. Unlike the UNDP Niger Delta Human Development Report published in August 2006 attributing the major cause of the problems in the region to the failure of the state and concluding that "vast revenues have barely touched the Niger Delta's own pervasive poverty",[539] a report prepared for Royal Dutch Shell in 2004 describes the situation in the region as follows: "The recent history of the Niger Delta has been associated with communal disputes and conflict, accentuated by the oil factor in criminal actions of youth against oil and gas companies, violent confrontations between the security forces and emerging militias, hostage taking, piracy and seizure or destruction of oil platforms and installations, pipeline vandalism and crude oil theft or illegal bunkering."[540] The latter report seems to link the problems only to that of instability and insecurity of energy supply. This may have informed the decision of the U.S and its European allies to renew or intensify military options and offshore strategy in trying to ensure stability and security of energy supply from Niger Delta.

According to a report on the history of the U.S in the Niger Delta prepared by Michael Watts and others, the United States has dramatically increased its military involvement in Nigeria over the past decade, as a direct result of America's growing dependence on oil imports from the Niger Delta. The United States has provided arms, military training, and other security assistance to the Nigerian government in the hope that the Nigerian military will be able to maintain "stability and security" in the Delta and keep the oil flowing. But the Pentagon is also preparing for the day when American troops may be ordered to intervene directly in the Delta.[541]

There seems to be a blurred line between energy security and terrorist concerns. The attacks of September 11, 2001 provided added opportunity for U.S to intensify its search for stability and security of sources of uninterrupted energy supply. Citing energy security and terrorist concerns, the U.S. military radically revised its strategic vision for the West African region; strategy shifted primarily from training for peacekeeping mission in Africa to training for counterterrorism and energy security. Nigeria has been particularly a target of this shift in energy security policy, not only as a strategic ally in the region but also as a "front line" state in the Global War on Terrorism (GWOT).[542]

---

539 Niger Delta Human Development Report, UNDP, Abuja, 2006, p. 14.
540 Lübeck et al., Convergent Interests, 8. Cf. also NNPC, "Report of the Niger Delta Youths Stakeholder Workship", Port Harcourt, Nigeria April 15-17, 2004, p. 4 I am of the opinion that this report only presents the symptoms and not the real problem. I think the question should have been, "What led to all these?".
541 Watt, Michael et al., History of the U.S in the Niger Delta, http://www.nigerdeltarising.org/history-us-niger-delta. Visited on 29.9.2009.
542 Lübeck et al., Convergent Interests, 1.

It has been reported that the United States delivered four surpluses U.S. Coast Guard Balsam-class coastal patrol ships in 2003 through the Excess Defense Articles program of the U.S. Defense Security Assistance Agency. These ships had a total value of more than $4.1 million at the time they were delivered to Nigeria. Military assistance in form of bomber jets and military hardware were being supplied from China and India. The governments of Britain and France are also offering their readiness to give military assistance to Nigeria to ensure stability and security of the Niger Delta. These strategies and assistance are certainly not the basic needs and concerns of the Niger Delta people who have the right to development (2.4.2).

Though one must add to it that the European Commission and EU member states have not only reduced reckless lending to ill-governed countries such as Nigeria (where the borrowed money has more often than not been stolen), they have also increasingly stressed governance as key to development, both in Africa in general and in Nigeria in particular. It is on record that the European Commission and EU governments have been funding a number of governance-related projects in Nigeria. For example, the EU provides substantial funds to the EFCC. Not only that the EU supported elections in Nigeria, the EU election-monitoring teams have been highly critical of the manipulations used to distort Nigeria's election results.[543] On a general note however, the EU countries' aid profile in Nigeria is weak. Only the United Kingdom and Germany have bilateral aid programs of any substance in the country.

Another strategy being adopted is investment in offshore exploration. The oil in West Africa or the Gulf of Guinea is attractive to international interest groups because most of the oil reserves are located at countries' coasts, i.e. offshore area. Not all oil-producing companies can afford the needed technology to explore the oil because it is technically complicated and capital-intensive. From the point of view of the TNOCs, this is advantageous because it is certain that it would not have direct contact with the local population unlike with the onshore-production. Exploration and production can be carried out successfully at a great distance and independent of the political situation of a host country. The TNOCs can carry on with their work extensively undisturbed by possible instability in host countries, by violent conflicts or civil wars.[544] In other words, the bulk of new discoveries are found offshore, reducing, in the eyes of the companies, potentially explosive interactions with local population and possible social turmoil onshore. This lowers political risk.[545]

---

543   Khankee, Anna, Energy and Development: Lessons from Nigeria, http://www.edc2020.eu/fileadmin/Text dat. Visited on 21.10.2010.

544   Müller & Strohscheidt, Misereor Themen, Erdöl Reichtum, der arm macht, 15.

545   Gary & Karl, Bottom of the Barrel, p. 13. The reports on the activities of the youth militants have reveal that even offshore oil facilities are not save from attacks, if the major cause of the attacks is not addressed.

From the two strategies of military assistance to the Nigerian government to suppress all kinds of violence and insurgences that may disturb stability and security of energy supply and the continued investment in offshore exploration, it is obvious that the welfare and quality of life of the Nigerians, and thus the Niger Delta people are not on the priority list of this group of international stakeholders. This is despite the fact that human rights are constantly being violated by government security forces and that the government has not been paying sufficient attention to the state of poverty and underdevelopment in the region. We suggest therefore that democracy and the rule of law should be promoted by the international community. This would help to guarantee good quality of life for Nigerians, Niger Deltans inclusive.

9.3.1.2 Democracy: Quality of Life for Nigerians

The report mentioned above confirms the fact that oil has brought neither prosperity nor tranquility to the Niger Delta or the country as a whole. It further confirms that the politics and management of the oil revenues have given rise to the oil complex which in turn has produced the socially unjust and inequitable functioning of all political economies in Nigeria. The political economies operate freely without effective democratic institutions through structural institutions and incentives produced by oil complex as follows:

> First, vast revenues have accumulated in the hands of political elites whose practices lack any social discipline normally associated with production for a competitive market. This frees the state from the need to rely on taxation which would, in turn, induce taxpayers to make demands on the state authorities for transparency, performance standards and meaningful political representation...second, opportunities to skim or appropriate revenues are legion in the absence of an institutionalized private or public agency committed to transparency and fiscal discipline...third, the environmental and social cost of resource extraction are imposed on groups that are underrepresented or even excluded from power while the resource flows are captured by a political oligarchy skilled at spreading the petro-rents among a network of cronies[546]

The report acknowledged the fact that once corruption is institutionalized, as is the case with the Niger Delta, democratic reform and fiscal accountability are extremely difficult to implement. All the same, it argues that unless democracy is consolidated in the Niger Delta, American energy security (like other stakeholders) will be at risk as supplies will continue to be threatened by chaos. It is effective democracy that can guarantee development in the region, for as the report argues: "the only way to secure the Delta is to raise health, education and living standards, ensure free and fair elections, ameliorate conflicts over resources and

---

546   Lübeck et al., Convergent Interests, p. 6.

broadly transform residents of the region into bona fide stakeholders who will benefit from oil revenues."[547] In the light of peoples' right to participation in their natural resources (Third Generation human right), and the principle of personality (2.1.1), we suggest that the concern of the people should be priority of all stakeholders. In pursuing their interest in the oil industry, international governments must pay attention to the quality of life of the people in the oil-producing communities by working to ensure effective democracy in their partner countries like Nigeria.

9.3.2 Corporate Social Responsibility of Multinational Oil Companies

In the light of integral and authentic human development (2.5. of part three), there is the need for corporate social responsibility (CSR) of companies operating the oil and gas industry in the Niger Delta. There are various definitions of CSR but the general understanding is that "corporate social responsibility is about how businesses align their values and behaviors with the expectations and needs of stakeholders, not just customers and investors, but also employees, suppliers, communities, regulators, special interest groups and society as a whole."[548] The concept of CSR itself emanated from the growing concern that companies must necessarily and increasingly become good corporate citizens with people and community-friendly outlook in their dispositions and actions vis-à-vis host communities and host countries. Basically, the focus is that companies must integrate social and environmental concerns in management and operational practices, and voluntarily and from time to time interact with other stakeholders, especially the host communities. According to the World Business Council for Sustainable Development, corporate social responsibility is the continuing commitment by businesses to behave ethically and contribute to economic development while improving the quality of life of the workforce and their families as well as of the local community and the society at large.[549]

We discussed the involvement of the MNOCs in the development problems in the Niger Delta particularly in the area of environmental degradation (3.3), legal and regulatory framework (3.5) and violent conflicts (3.6). This places on them a moral or ethical responsibility to contribute to the development of the

---

547 Lübeck et al., Convergent Interests, p. 5.
548 CORPORATE social responsibility, http://www.csrnetwork.com/csr.asp. Visited on 4.01.2010.
549 Hopkins, Michael, Corporate Social Responsibility & International Development – Is Business the Solution? London: Earthscan 2007, p. 25. See also CSN, Nigeria – Travesty of Oil and Gas, p. 142.

region in all the areas that should promote integral and authentic human development. This can be done by adopting the corporate social responsibility approaches. This responsibility of the MNOCs could be in the form of more involvement in area of community development projects like the provision of agricultural extension services, educational facilities, and portable water in some communities in the region.

Following the tragic judicial killing of the human rights activist and environmentalist Ken Saro Wiwa and his eight compatriots by the military government of late General Sani Abacha in November 1995, the involvement of *Shell-BP* in the process incurred it international condemnation, including those from its shareholders. Consequently, *Shell* seems to be playing a leading role in CSR in the Niger Delta region since 1996 as a way of laundering its image in the international community as well as securing the region for energy supply to the international markets. Indeed, scholars on the Niger Delta like Ikelegbe, Okonta and Omeje et al. have corroborated the *Shell*'s several annual reports showing their expenditure on CSR in the various community projects that they have been involved in in the region since 1996. *Shell*'s CSR activities are evident in its community development programs in some local communities. This takes, for instance, the form of supporting education by giving scholarships (primary, post-primary and university) to local people, building of classrooms, providing equipment and sometimes paying the allowances of post-primary school teachers. The Membe community of Bayelsa state is one of the beneficiary communities.[550] A concise study on CSR in the region carried out by Adam Groves (2009) reveals that *Shell* has taken a leading role in promoting CSR by shifting its paradigm from repression to responsibility for some oil-producing communities in the region in partnership with some selected civil society and governments. *Shell* is investing, on the average, an annual budget of $60 million in community development projects as well as making contributions to relevant government development commissions like the NDDC.[551] What is said about *Shell* holds too for other MNOCs working in the region though to various degrees.

This annual investment in CSR notwithstanding, hostility from host communities and militias towards *Shell* and its installations as well as other MNOCs remain unabated. As it were, the desire to secure uninterrupted energy supply from the region to the international markets remains unfulfilled. According to Groves,

---

550 Tuodolo, Felix, Corporate Social Responsibility: Between Civil Society and the Oil Industry in the Developing World, *ACME, An International E-Journal for Critical Geographies* 8,3 (2009) 530-541.

551 Groves, Adam, Shell and Society: Securing the Niger Delta? (Un)civil Society and Corporate Security Strategies in the Niger Delta, Oxford: University Press 2009, Cf. also http://www.e-ir.info. Visited on 6.10.2009.

Shell fails to ensure uninterrupted energy supply because of its own style of CSR which is characterized by divide-and-rule tactics in selecting which host community to engage in and which civil society organization to form partnership with. Thereby, it ends up creating unhealthy rivalry among communities (inter-communal conflicts – 3.6.2 of part one) and competition for superiority between civil society groups. Rather than contributing to development and peace in the region, *Shell's* CSR has unfortunately further aggravated conflicts, violence and insecurity.

Certainly, the MNOCs would argue that they are already engaging in community development programs costing millions of dollars in their annual budget, but as we pointed out with the case of *Shell* and under inter-communal conflicts, their approach of involvement in community development programs has been contributing to conflicts. This is because projects are awarded to certain communities as a reward for their loyalty and support while other communities are denied similar projects as punishment for their protests and agitations against the MNOCs and the state. Similarly Groves has pointed out that in selecting which civil societies to work with, MNOCs have opted for civil societies they considered to be capable of protecting their installations and securing them the access to their flow stations even if they are 'uncivil' in intent and outfit. This situation has brought about bitter rivalry between different militia groups.

As a matter of fact, the Niger Delta Regional Development Master Plan has indicated six reasons why the previous CSR approach of MNOCs (perceived as community assistance) failed to make impact in the development of the oil-producing communities[552] and the need to adopt a new approach tagged "Sustainable Community Development" (SCD).

The SCD aims to ensure that MNOCs community interventions are sustainable and deliver real and measurable benefits to intended beneficiaries right across communities, and not just concentrated in the hands of a few influential individuals. To ensure sustainability, benefiting communities need to take the lead in the decisions and planning for their own development, and ownership of the resulting projects and programmes. To provide them the skill and confidence to do so, SCD places emphasis on capacity building – helping communities (other

---

552 NDRDMP, p. 110. Reasons for the failure include: A) an excessively community-pressure driven or crisis management approach, which reduced development efforts to meeting a set of demands expressed in Memoranda of Understanding (MOUs) with the communities. B) A high rate of default on the MOUs, which have usually been explained as due to budgetary constraints. C) A high cash-payment and placatory tendency to dealing with community agitations. D) The absence of any long-term or integrated view of development challenges. E) The limited arrangements if any for maintenance of infrastructure provided, leading to a very short-lived benefits from the rapid collapse of structures erected. F) The poor networking and synergy with other agencies and governments, leading to duplication of infrastructure and poor resource use.

development partners) to build their capacity. The SCD strategy also recognizes the 'symbiotic relationship' between development and peace.[553] This new approach is not only in conformity with the principle of subsidiarity (7.1.3 of part three); it is also a practical recognition that people have the right to participate in their own development.

We therefore suggest that MNOCs should embrace corporate social responsibility with the goal addressed in SCD, in that way, they could contribute greatly to bring about authentic development in the Niger Delta region. As long as it is being informed by merely engaging in cheap, short-term community projects for the sake of image-making (that is, media propaganda), doing what international shareholders want to see in their glossy annual reports, promoting human capital of their staff in order to enhance better chance of profits in the competitive markets – CSR as it is been traded by the MNOCs presently –, it is doubtful whether energy security, peace and development in the Niger Delta region will be guaranteed.

9.3.3 Chances and Limits of Global Compact

During the January 31 1999 World economic forum in Davos, Switzerland, the former Secretary General of United Nations Kofi Annan, proposed the establishment of a Global Compact. In July 2000 the United Nations launched the Global Compact as an initiative to encourage business to contribute to human development. The UN Global Compact is both a policy platform and a practical framework for companies that are committed to sustainability and responsible business practices. It is to strengthen the cooperation between the UN and business enterprises. It serves as a voluntary alignment of the goals of international community and those of the business world. It seeks to achieve two complementary objectives namely:

- Mainstream the ten principles in business activities around the world.
- Catalyze actions in support of broader UN goals, including the Millennium Development Goals (MDGs).

In the light of the disadvantaged position of the Third World countries in the globalization process (2.4.1 of part one chapter two), there are chances that Global Compact could contribute to development of the Third World countries. This is because in pursuing the objectives of Global Compact, business as the primary agent driving globalization can help ensure that markets, commerce, technology and finance advance in ways that benefit economies and societies

---

553 NDRDMP, p. 109.

everywhere and contribute to a more sustainable and inclusive economy.[554] Proponents of Global Compact have argued that it serves as a value-oriented platform to showcase good practices in order to encourage enterprises to engage in the ten principles of Global Compact. It is on record that some MNOCs working in the Niger Delta are members of Global Compact, e.g *Shell* and *Chevron*.[555] The UN Global Compact has the potentiality of contributing to development. But that depends on whether the MNOCs and businesses in the Niger Delta would adopt and implement the ten principles that are reflected in over four thematic areas.

Human rights

- Business should support and respect the protection of internationally proclaimed human rights.
- They are to make sure that they are not complicit in human rights abuses.

Labour Standards

- Business should uphold the freedom of association and the effective recognition of the right to collective bargaining.
- The elimination of all forms of forced and compulsory labour.
- The effective abolition of child labour.
- The elimination of discrimination in respect of employment and occupation

Environment

- Business should support a precautionary approach to environmental challenges.
- Undertake initiatives to promote greater environmental responsibility.
- Encourage the development and diffusion of environmentally friendly technologies.

Anti-Corruption

- Business should work against corruption in all its forms, including extortion and bribery.[556]

The ample chances that the practice of Global Compact by MNOCs and businesses could promote development in the Niger Delta can be viewed from the

554 UN Global Compact, http://www.unglobalcompact.org. Visited on 26.2.2010.
555 Kebede, Rebekah, Shell Nigeria case may temper Big Oil policies, http://globalcompactcritics. blogspot.com/2009/06/shell-nigeria-cas. Visited on 9.11.2010.
556 UN Global Compact, http://www.unglobalcompact.org. Visited on 26.2.2010.

four main areas of focuses namely: human rights, labour standard, environment and anti-corruption. In the first instance, we have pointed out the complicit role that the MNOCs are playing in the violent conflicts (3.6), particularly the repressions and intimidations by the state (3.6.1) as one of the development problems in Niger Delta. We have also said that such actions all amount to abuse of fundamental rights of the people (3.5 in chapter three of part three) and that people have the right to development (2.4.2 of part three chapter two). It follows that the adherence to the above Global Compact principle of human rights by MNOCs and businesses in Niger Delta could solve one of the development problems. In the same way, the failure of the MNOCs to offer gainful employment to the indigenes, particularly the youth, provides one of the fertile grounds for youth restiveness and violent conflicts in the region (3.6.2). This is because majority of the people are excluded from the economy of the oil industry (1.2.2 of part two chapter one). If the MNOCs could be committed to the elimination of discrimination in respect of employment and occupation of management positions, they would be contributing immensely to the solving one of the development problems in the region. One of the problems hindering development in the Niger Delta is environmental degradation resulting from the activities of MNOCs (3.2). We have pointed out in our treatment of third generation human rights (2.4.2) that people have the right live in clean and healthy environment. We have also argued that sustainable development should guarantee the use of the environment in such a way that the future generations would be able to meet their needs (2.5.1 part one chapter two). The commitment of MNOCs to the Global Compact principle of environment as stated above could provide the chance of overcoming the problem of environmental degradation. Lastly, corruption in the oil industry involving both the Nigerian state and MNOCs is one of the causes of poverty and underdevelopment of the Niger Delta (1.3.1 of part two chapter one). It is therefore desirable that MNOCs enlist and abide by the Global Compact principle of anti-corruption as stated above and adopt the extractive industry transparency initiative. Thereby, they would be contributing to the development of the Niger Delta.

However, despite these chances of contributing to development, there are limitations to Global Compact. Barbara Unmüßig[557] of the *Heinrich Böll Stiftung* has rightly pointed out some of these limitations. Because Global Compact is a voluntary alignment between the UN and business enterprises, there are neither regulations nor legally binding obligations like independent and regular supervision or sanctions against member enterprises that are not keeping to the ten principles.

---

557   Unmüßig, Barbara, Freiwilligkeit und ihre Grenzen, http://www.boell.de/stiftung/struktur/struktur-2456.html. Visited on 10.11.2010.

Some member enterprises are taking the advantage of UN Global Compact logo as market strategy to launder their image even when they are not keeping to the principles. As it were, it is being used as public relation tools by enterprises. For instance, *Shell* is a member of the Global Compact and yet its involvement with environmental pollution via oil spillage and gas flaring in the Niger Delta is still a regular occurrence. Critics are of the view that there are a lot of stakeholders in Global Compact but none of them is directly accountable to the public about their performance. Since most members are from developed countries, critics are sceptical about the positive effect for the developing world.[558] There is no doubt that the goals of Global Compact are desirable, but in order that it may contribute to poverty eradication and thus development, it requires an independent monitoring and complaints mechanism with the possibility of imposing sanctions on erring members. Global Compact cannot serve as alternative to the existing national laws and regulations concerning activities of business and enterprises.

9.4 The Contributions of the Church in Industrialized Countries and other Active Transnational NGOs

The improvement of the condition of worldwide poverty and underdevelopment poses a challenge to the Church. Indeed it is part of the duty of the church to address the problem of poverty because the poor whose interests and rights are being neglected are included in a special way in the Christian commandment of love of neighbor.[559] The Church as the body of Christ cannot afford not to take up the manifesto of Jesus her head, as He states *"The spirit of the Lord is on me, for he has anointed me to bring the good news to the afflicted. He has sent me to proclaim liberty to captives, sight to the blind, to let the oppressed go free, to proclaim a year of favour from the Lord"* (Lk 4, 18-19). The commitment of the Church to solidarity with all men particularly those who are at the verge of the minimum existence is what has been motivating her social doctrine from where we have drawn impulses for ethical orientation in part three. The Church in Europe and North America where the home countries of the MNOCs as well as the powerful IMF and World Bank are headquartered has been actively contributing

---

558 Bandi, Nina, United Nations Global Compact: Impact and its Critics, Universite de Genève (Switzerland), intern analyst, Covalence SA, Geneva, 13.9.2007.

559 Die deutschen Bischofkonferenz, Soziale Sicherungssysteme als Elemente der Armutsbekämpfung in Entwicklungsländern, Bonn: Die Bischofskonferenz 1997, p. 10.

to fighting poverty thus development. Our focus in this study is the Niger Delta region. But because of the fact that the MNOCs' policies and the IMF and World Bank as well as WTO regulations provide the international framework under which oil producing countries operate makes the contribution of Church in the Northern hemisphere more imperative. Examples of this contribution are discussed below.

9.4.1 Debt Cancellation Campaigns

One of the hindrances and causes of poverty and underdevelopment is the debt burden of many poor developing countries in the Third World, Nigeria inclusive. This fact informed the formation of the Jubilee Debt Relief campaigns in 1996. The Church in Europe and America together with several international NGOs and civil societies like Green Peace, Friends of Earth, Pax Christi and ActionAid International etc. made up the campaigns. Aimed at celebrating the jubilee year 2000, the worldwide campaign was focused on seeking debt relief for poor countries all over the world that were suffering under the burden of their debt services and able to make any progress owing to their debts services. Several individuals and groups of people in Europe and America as well as in all countries in the world joined this campaigns demonstrating before the G8 summits wherever they were held. In Germany the campaign was tagged Jubilee 2000 *Erlassjahr* with the motto: „*Entwicklung Braucht Entschuldung*"[560] – development needs debt cancellation.

Campaigners formed human chains and put on chains to symbolize the enslaving nature of the debt burden which undermines the development, dignity and sovereignty of people of debtor countries. Debt forgiveness was meant to release people from their bondage of debt. Many people showed their commitment to debt relief for poor countries by demonstrating and travelling from one country to the other at personal costs. We consider these as responses to the clarion call to universal solidarity that is based on the equality of people in the world.[561] Many of the demonstrators and campaigners may never have visited any highly indebted Third World country in their lives whose ordinary people are suffering under the debt burden, but because they were motivated by a sense of solidarity (7.1.2 of part three), that is, "not a feeling of vague compassion or a shallow distress" but "a firm and persevering determination to commit oneself to

---

560   http://www.erlassjahr.de/dev2/cms/front_content.php. Visited on 2.12.2010.
561   Langhorst, Kirche und Entwicklungsproblematik, 275. Cf. also SRS, 39,4.

the common good; that is to say to the good of all and of each individual, because we are all really responsible for all".[562]

In the meantime, the actions of the Church in the industrialized countries, individuals and groups of people have yielded fruit. Many countries have been granted debt relief by their creditors from the rich and industrialized countries, the Paris Club or from the World Bank / IMF. Nigeria is one of the beneficiaries of the campaigns. The responsibility now lies on the leaders of countries that have benefited from the debt relief to translate such funds saved from the relief to the poverty eradication, or at least its reduction and thus development in their respective countries. We consider the debt cancellation campaign as a transnational contribution to development because it is not just informed by the principle of solidarity which entails an option for the poor, it has also contributed to liberating debtor countries from their debt burdens thus making funds saved from the cancellation available for recipient countries for development.

As we have discussed under PRSP above, one of the conditions for granting debt relief was that the recipient countries would spend the fund on the attainment of the MDGs. Now that many highly indebted Third World countries are receiving savings from their debt, the campaigners of Jubilee 2000 still have the assignment to ensure that recipient countries actually use funds to pursue the MDGs in such ways that the interests and rights of poor people are fulfilled. This can be done by building the capacity of partner Churches, NGOs and civil societies in the respective countries to monitor or collaborate with their home governments towards the fulfillment of the MDGs.

9.4.2 The Church's Development Assistance

In addition to being actively involved in the debt cancellation campaigns, the Church in industrialized countries also engages in practical development assistance to developing countries through her development agencies that form the *"Cooperation Internationale pour le Developpement et la Solidarite"* – CISDSE. It is an international alliance of Catholic development agencies working together for global justice. It is made up of 16 organizations from Europe and North America. With shared Christian values the CIDSE seeks to promote global justice and solidarity. CIDSE is working with local partner organizations in Africa, Asia and Latin America. According to its statement: "Contributing to the fight against poverty and inequality, as well as bringing about sustainable development and well-being by challenging global structural injustices are key elements of CIDSE's mission,

---

562 SRS, 38.

which we attempt to achieve through joint advocacy, campaigning and development cooperation work"[563]. Its priority issues are global governance; resources for development, food, agriculture and sustainable trade, climate justice and business and human rights.

Moreover, the CIDSE, Pax Christi International and Caritas Europa Peace and Conflict Coalition presented a position paper in September 2003 expressing the importance of transparency and accountability in the extractive industries. In addition to participating in the "Publish What You Pay" campaigns, Christians need to be active in defending the right of the poor to benefit from the sustainable exploitation of natural resources, which are part of their national patrimony. The actions and statements made, based firmly in social teaching of the church, challenge all Christians, but particularly those with the power and influence to effect change, to assume the moral responsibilities inherent in their faith, and to act in accordance with principles of good governance, transparency and accountability, so that the benefits accruing to resource-rich countries can best be employed to alleviate poverty and human suffering.[564]

The development activities of these Church agencies working in the Third World are contributing in no small measure to the reduction of poverty and underdevelopment. Not only that such international development agencies provide technical and financial support for their partners, they also help to articulate the real problems of poverty and underdevelopment in the respective countries, identify the causes objectively and bring such reports to the awareness of their own home governments and the attention of multinational companies and entrepreneurs that are engaged in the concerned countries as well as to the international arena. More so, the reports of international development agencies often highlight areas that are relevant and beneficial to the poor, which are often neglected by official government reports. Among Church's development agencies working in oil-exporting countries like Nigeria are Misereor, Trocaire, Justice and Peace Canada and Catholic Relief Service. In the present work we shall take the example of Misereor.

Misereor

Misereor is the Episcopal Development Aid agency of the Church in Germany. Through the agency, the people of Germany engage in the work of justice and solidarity with the poor and the oppressed in Africa, Asia and Latin America.

---

563   Http://www.cidse.org/aboutus/?id=31. Visited on 21.11.2009.
564   CIDSE et al., Transparency: A Christian Concern: Catholic Social Teaching and the Case for Transparent and Accountable Practices in Extractive Industries. A Position Paper of CIDSE, Pax Christi International and Caritas Europa September 2003, cf. http://www.caritas-europa.org/module/FileLib/TransparencyAChristianConcernENG.pdf. Visited on 7.12.2010 .

Since its establishment, Misereor has been supporting several development projects in different countries in the Third World. More important in the work of Misereor is its competence in presenting expertise for development cooperation in different areas such as in education, health, governance, economy, environmental issues and agriculture. These thematic areas of development by Misereor serve as basis of dialogue with its partner organizations wherever they work as well as engage in the development politics of education and lobby work in Germany.[565]

An important contribution of Misereor to the issue of making the wealth of oil and gas beneficial to tackling the problem of poverty and underdevelopment in oil-producing countries in Africa South of the Saharan is a publication it made in 2007 titled *"ERDÖL: Reichtum, der arm macht"*. It makes a big difference in the international community when a reputable agency like Misereor presents the real situation or human condition in the oil-producing countries of Sub-Saharan Africa. It gives credibility to the claims of the local inhabitants that they are not benefitting much from the wealth of oil under their feet. Their agitations and protests for self-realization are only understandable when it is noted that the framework for self-fulfillment is not being provided by the state.

With concrete projects in each of the countries studied, Misereor is demonstrating its optimism in the possibility of using the income from the extractive industry to transform the countries and regions of origin from poverty into prosperity if the appropriate and needed framework is provided by the state and multinationals or entrepreneurs. Misereor's work is in the form of providing technical and financial support for their local partners. Currently Misereor supports the work of a local NGO – Centre for Social and Corporate Responsibility (CSCR) being led by Fr. Kevin O'hara. The work of CSCR entails mediating between rivaling communities, e.g between Ijaws and Itsekiris, urging MNOCs to fulfill their corporate social responsibilities in the host communities, MNOCs to clean up the polluted environment, serving as mediator between local oil producing communities, the MNOCs and the state to ensure a fair share of the local people in the oil revenue etc.[566] In addition, Misereor is supporting the development efforts of the Justice Development Commissions of the various Dioceses situated in the Niger Delta region. In the light of the principles of solidarity and subsidiarity, we suggest that more international Church development agencies should emulate Misereor by making their presence more felt in the Niger Delta by way of building the capacity of and supporting local NGOs particularly the Diocesan JDP commissions in the Niger Delta to be pro-actively involved in the socio-economic and political issues in the region.

---

565 Müller &Strohscheidt (Hg.), Misereor Themen, Erdöl Reichtum, der arm macht, p. 1.
566 Müller &Strohscheidt (Hg.), Misereor Themen, Erdöl Reichtum, der arm macht, pp. 32-33.

9.5 Conclusion

Apart from military assistance, most of the other contributions from the international community have the potentiality of poverty reduction, thus contributing development. It is disappointing to note that neither the international interest groups nor the international efforts are geared towards compelling the Nigerian government and MNOCs to clean up the degraded environment through pollutions caused by their explorations and oil production. Since oil production began over 50 years ago in the region, the environment is constantly being polluted and the international community has not shown much concern about it. Unlike the oil spillage that was caused by the accident in Gulf of Mexico that occupied the attention of global media for months, one of the few times the global community turned attention towards Niger Delta environmental problems was November 10, 1995 when the environmental activist Ken Saro Wiwa and his eight compatriots were judicially hanged by the government of Late General San Abacha[567]. Another was during the Dezember 2010 Alternative Nobel Prize (Right Livelihood Award) in Stockholm to Nimmo Bassey from Nigeria "for revealing the full ecological and human horrors of oil production and for his inspired work to strengthen the environmental movement in Nigeria and globally"[568].

In the light of the universal destination of earth's goods and ecological question, we suggest that the international community should compel the MNOCs and the Nigerian government to clean up the environment. The Niger Delta people have a right to live in clean and healthy environment. The dignity of the human beings in the Niger Delta region is not lesser than those of the Gulf of Mexico. All the world summits and conferences on environment and sustainable development may appear to be sheer hypocrisy if Shell, Agip, Chevron, Mobil, Total and all other oil companies operating in region are not made to find lasting solution to the problem of environmental degradation.

Furthermore, such practices of international organizations that are still disadvantageous to poor developing countries would need to be reformed. For the example the World Trade Organization and the development politics of industrialized countries. The realization of international contributions in the life of the poor people depends very much on the responsible actions of all and the readiness of the policy makers and major stakeholders in the respective countries, particularly in Nigeria, to be committed to the development process.

---

567 Perras, Arne, Alarmstufe Delta, Süddeutsche Zeitung 280 (Freitag, 3. Dezember 2010) 3.

568 Http://rightlivelihood.org/laureates.html?&no_cache=1. Visited on 8.12.2010. Nnimmo Bassey is the executive director of Environmental Rights Action – ERA and Chair Friends of the Earth International.

The Church has been and should remain an important agent of this process, or even take a leading role in it. In this connection we would like to suggest that the Church in the industrialized countries should focus on the building the capacity of the local Churches in the developing countries like Nigeria to respond more pro-actively to the problem of poverty. In other words, the local Church should be empowered to engage constructively in policy debates that would lead to changing or at least transforming the structures that are inducing poverty and underdevelopment. For example, the JDPCs of local Churches can be empowered through the programs of good governance, advocacy campaigns, budget analysis, leadership training, democracy and the rule of law. This would enable them further engage in the work of structural transformation of the society.

10. Contributions of Nigerian Stakeholders

10.1 Introduction

The problems besetting the Nigerian state as an oil-exporting country have been highlighted in the socio-economic (4.0)) as well as political (5.0) analysis. Our analysis reveal the weakness of governance structures and institutions has provided the fertile ground for corruption, mismanagement of oil revenues and non-accountability of political office holders to the electorate. All these explain the state of poverty and underdevelopment in the Niger Delta. Even when government attempted to resolve the Niger Delta development problems with commissions in the past, the above named characteristics would always play themselves out.

In order to change the above scenario for better, Sen's capability approach to development and the impulses from the Catholic social thought present an ethical orientation that could guide stakeholders, particularly the structures operating on the international, national and local levels, in the dealings with the development problems in the Niger Delta region. The first chapter of this part has treated the contributions of international community and how further transnational contributions to development could be accompanied by ethical considerations. In this second chapter we shall point out how the ethical orientation should address the development problems in the region on all levels of government, national, state and local. To begin with, we shall revisit how the Nigerian state has been responding to the development of the region and suggest how further engagement in the development of the region should be ethically guided in order to ensure authentic development. Last but not the least; we shall address the role of the local Church in the development of the region. Thereby we shall present the Church's role model of commitment to development by highlighting what Church is doing notwithstanding her limited resources. We shall also suggest what she can do better.

10.2 Responses of the Federal Government

In part one chapter three, we have pointed out that the federal government has in past responded to the Niger Delta development issues by enacting legal and regulatory measures to secure the control of oil and mineral resources (3.5). It has resorted to repressions and intimidation of the people (3.6.1) and at the same time established development commissions (3.7). None of these measures has brought about the desired development; instead they have also constituted hindrances to development. Our socio-economic analysis in part two has showed that the failure of the state to judiciously use income from oil is peculiar to most oil-exporting countries in the Third World (1.1-1.2.2). This syndrome is tagged the resource curse. Most importantly is the mismanagement of the revenue from oil by the state through corruption. Our political analysis of Nigerian stakeholders has also revealed that the interests of the state and policy makers are not always in consonance with the interests and concerns of the people (2.2). Success stories are told in instances where people's interests are considered and their active participation is sought after (3.7.3).

Perhaps pressures from the international community in the form of the work of UNDP, debt cancellation, MDGs, PRSP, initiatives for transparency and anti-corruption and, of course, the activities of NGOs (5.2.5), youth militias (5.2.6) and unions and civil society (5.2.7) may have compelled the state, particularly the federal government to consider new approaches to the solving the development problems in Nigeria generally and in the Niger Delta region in particular. The four current responses of the federal government tend to point in this direction: National Economic Empowerment and Development Strategy (NEEDS), the anti-corruption agencies, the Niger Delta Regional Development Master Plan and the Ministry of Niger Delta Affairs.

10.2.1 National Economic Empowerment and Development Strategy

Under PRSP (2.4.3) we discussed that the IMF/World Bank have adopted a new condition which countries seeking debt relief and loans must fulfill. This new approach is that each country must prepare a poverty reduction strategy paper which should reflect the needs according to priority for a specific period of time. In 2004 Nigerian government produced its own version of PRSP in the form of national economic empowerment and development strategy (NEEDS). The strategy was to cover the period from 2004 to 2007. It is Nigeria's plan for prosperity.[569] The NEEDS document has the overall goal of promoting the welfare, health, employment, education, political power, physical security and empowerment of

---

569 National Planning Commission, Nigeria: National Economic Empowerment and Development Strategy (NEEDS), Central Bank of Nigeria, 2004, p. viii.

all Nigerians. It provides a model for all the 36 state governments in the country. Each state is expected to design its strategy according its priority and tag it State Economic Empowerment Development Strategy. Critiques of NEEDS are of the view that it is more a product of Harvard-trained technocrats and staff of World Bank[570] as the language and content tend to suggest. However, on reading the document one tends to agree with Harneit-Sievers (of Heinrich Boell Foundation Nigeria) that:

> Civil society actors should be aware that proponents of NEEDS ... share a common enemy: the structures, institutions, and (in many cases) personnel of the corrupt and inefficient rentier state that has wasted Nigeria and the lives of Nigerian for decades, that is responsible for mass poverty, and that has resisted most reform attempts so far. NEEDS appears to be the first serious attempt at structural reform of the rentier state. Given the popular frustration about the economic outcome of democracy so far, it may as well be the last chance for reform.[571]

The NEEDS document has the chances or opportunities of contributing to the development of the Niger Delta region because it provides the national blueprint, a road map of actions to be followed to achieve the development for the whole country, Niger Delta inclusive. For instance, it seeks to address the problem of poverty and underdevelopment (3.2) by proposing to invest in the Nigerian people, their health, education, employment, happiness, sense of fulfillment, and general well-being. It is adopting the human rights approach (rights based approach – RBA) to development planning that places people at the center of development efforts.[572] The problem of HIV/AIDs (3.4) is acknowledged in the NEEDS document as having a disastrous impact on social and economic development. NEEDS therefore seeks to create an environment in which all Nigerians can live socially and economically productive lives free of the disease and its effects.[573] To address the problem of violent conflicts (3.6), NEEDS plants to adopt the strategy of conflict prevention. It would be a program that would offer the opportunity for public officers as well as civil society members to be trained in the prevention, management, and resolution of conflicts.[574] The document

---

570   Amadi, Sam, Contextualizing NEEDS: Politics and Economic Development. *In*: Amadi, Sam & Ogwo, Frances (eds.), Contextualizing NEEDS Economic/Political Reform in Nigeria, Report of Civil Society Policy Dialogue on the National Economic Empowerment and Development Strategy (NEEDS), Lagos: HURILAWS & CPPR 2004, pp. 18-19.

571   Harneit-Sievers, Axel, Reforming the Rentier State: Some Thoughts on NEEDS. *In*: Amadi & Ogwo (eds.), Contextualizing NEEDS Economic/Political Reform in Nigeria, Report of Civil Society Policy Dialogue on the National Economic Empowerment and Development Strategy (NEEDS), p. xviii.

572   NEEDS, p. 28.

573   NEEDS, p. 42.

574   NEEDS, p. 49.

admits that the government had neglected other sectors of the economy in the past; it then plans to diversify the economy by promoting agriculture, where majority of Nigerians are still actively engaged, strengthening the private sector, small and medium entrepreneur and encourage private investors in the economy.

The adoption of the rights based-approach[575] to development by the NEEDS is commendable. It means that the government admits that it has not been respecting the fundamental rights of people in the past. Governments' commitment to this approach could guarantee the success of the opportunities for development laid out in the NEEDS document. The opportunities notwithstanding, there are some weakness or limitations also in the NEEDS document. For instance, it recognizes the problem of environmental degradation but only offers to assess the environmental health impact on communities in oil-producing and mining areas,[576] without any mention of how to clean up the polluted environment and stopping or minimizing pollution of the environment.

The 2007 progress report on NEEDS indicates that success has been recorded in the area of stable macroeconomic environment, civil service reforms, due process, the banking sector, privatization and liberalization. It admits to the failure of NEEDS in the area of poverty reduction, employment generation and power supply, etc. This failure is attributed to the weakness in monitoring and evaluation and effective coordination.[577] We suggest that government should give priority to implementing the aspect of NEEDS that would bring about rapid poverty reduction and employment generation as these would be of greater benefit to the poor people whose human dignity (7.1.1) are trampled by the state of poverty. It would afford the poor people the chances of participation in the common good (7.2) of the society. Social Justice demands that the state should enable people to participate actively and productively in the life of the society. As Heimbach-Steins noted, "social justice means that people are obliged to participate actively and productively in the life of the society, and that the society is duty bound to create for them the opportunity for such participation."[578] It is not enough for progress to be recorded in the banking, privatization and liberalization aspects of NEEDS while the aspects that benefit the poor – poverty reduction, employment generation and power-supply are neglected. In the light of authentic development, it cannot be a true development that some people are

---

575   A rights based approach uses human rights as framework to guide the development process. It starts from the assumption that people have a human right to achieve economic, social and cultural development.

576   NEEDS, 33, 40.

577   IMF Country Report No. 07/270, Nigeria: Poverty Reduction Strategy Paper – Progress Report, 2007, p. 3.

578   Heimbach-Steins, Marianne, Beteiligungsgerechtigkeit, Stimmen der Zeit, 217 (1999) 149.

progressing through the banking, privatization and liberation sectors while others are not, because of government's failure in poverty reduction, employment generation and power supply.

10.2.2 Anti-corruption Agencies

Corruption has been identified as one of the causes of poverty in Nigeria (4.3) as indeed elsewhere in the world. We have identified the oil industry as one of the main sources of corruption in Nigeria, and that it reduces the Nigerian oil industry's earning potential by misallocating funds and contracts, rewarding inefficiency, and permitting the theft of oil. In other words, corrupt practices in the oil sector deprive the state of enormous revenues that could be available for development work. This means that there is shortage of funds available to the state to provide adequate social infrastructure in the society – roads to ease transportation, electricity, drinkable water, schools, and health facilities and to promote other sectors of the economy that could provide employment opportunities for the unemployed. The inadequacy of these infrastructures is contributing to the shortage of life expectancy (untimely death) of so many people, maternal mortality, undernourishment and infant mortality and illiteracy of so many, morbidity, and the spread of HIV/AIDs, that is, state of underdevelopment (3.2). From the point of view of Christian social ethics, all deprivations of life, health, development, literacy and etc., that are caused by corruption amount to violations of fundamental human rights (7.4) of the victims.[579] In the light of the common good (7.2), those who suffer the effects of corruption are denied the opportunity of their participation in the common good. The revenue from oil, as in the case of the Niger Delta, is one of the sum totals of what are required by the people to live a life of self fulfillment in the society. The situation created by the effect of corruption is a condition of unfreedom (4.3). It is a condition less than human that must be overcome through development (7.5).

We have pointed out that responsible for the corruptions in the oil industry are the operational structures or institutions that are managing the affairs of the sector. Consequently, any solution to the problem of corruption must begin with reforming the defective structures that are generating or inducing people to corruption.

The fact that the federal government has admitted that corrupt practices are found within the rank and file of the government and the society at large is a sign

---

579   For more details on this, see „Corruption and Human Rights: Making the Connection. 2009. International Council on Human Rights Policy, Versoix, Switzerland. http://www.ichrp.org. Visited on 19.9.2009.

of hope that there could be solution in sight. In his inaugural speech in May 29, 1999 the ex-President Obasanjo openly admitted that state apparatus was ridden with corruption. In the course of his presidency, a number of novelties were introduced to stem the wave of corruption, for example, the ICPC, the EFCC, the Publish What You Pay (PWYP) as part of the Nigerian Extractive Industries Transparency Initiative (NEITI), Due Process and the Rule of Law etc. In fact, President Obasanjo became one of the supporters of Transparency Initiative (TI).[580] These efforts of his government to put some anti-corruption structures in place are obviously commendable. For want of time we shall limit our discussion to three of the anti-corruption agencies namely: The Independent Corrupt Practices and Other Related Offences Commission (ICPC) 2000, the Nigerian Extractive Industry Transparency Initiative (NEITI) 2003 and the Economic and Financial Crimes Commission (EFFC) 2004.

10.2.2.1 Independent Corrupt Practices and Other Related Offences Commission

In his inaugural speech on 29 May 1999, the ex-President Olusegun Obasanjo admitted that Nigeria was ridden with corruption and promised to fight it structurally. The ICPC bill turned out to be the first to be sent to the National Assembly for passage. It was passed and signed into law on the 13th June 2000 and the commission was inaugurated on the 29th September 2000. The Act establishing the commission saddles it with the responsibility of fighting corruption and other related offences. Section 3 (14) of the Act provides for the independence of the Commission and gives the Chairman authority to issue orders for the control and general administration of the commission. The ICPC has three basic responsibilities namely: to receive, investigate reports of corruption and when need be prosecute offender(s), to enforce the correction of corruption prone-systems and procedures of public bodies, and to educate and enlighten the public on and against corruption.[581] Since its inception, ICPC has made some progress in its fight against corruption. For instance, it has instituted investigative activities into allegations of bribery against principal officers of National Assembly. A recent report from the commission indicates that so far the ICPC has filed 232 cases with 447 persons

---

580   In Berlin in November 2003, TI brought together Nigerian President Olusegun Obasanjo and executives from oil companies, successfully drawing out commitment from Obasanjo to maximize transparency in the oil sector, and for Nigeria's oil sector to become part of the Extractive Industries Transparency Initiative, where foreign oil companies should disclose the payments they make to the host government and state oil companies.

581   ICPC, Nigeria, http://www.icac.org.hk/newsl/issue17eng/button2.htm. Visited on 17.11.2010.

being prosecuted for corruption charges.[582] There is no doubt that this is a positive trend in a country where not a single person had been charged to court for corruption before the commission was created. In addition, as part of its public education and enlightenment program the ICPC is working with the National Educational Research Development Council with the aim of integrating the values of patriotism, integrity, honesty, loyalty, etc into the curriculum of Nigerian educational institutions. The commission has staff strength of 300 workers. The efforts of this commission at fighting corruption are commendable, but critiques are of the view that this success is little when compared with enormity of problem of corruption in Nigeria. The main complaint of the commission is that it faces the problem of shortage of fund from the government to carry out its responsibilities effectively. To demonstrate its commitment to fighting corruption in the society, we suggest that the government give all that the commission requires to perform its assignment effectively.

10.2.2.2 Nigerian Extractive Industry Transparency Initiative

NEITI is the Nigerian version of the EITI. Following the endorsement of EITI by the countries of G8 in 2004, Nigeria has not only signed into it, she is a pilot country for a G8 partnership to promote transparency and combat corruption. NEITI was launched with the mandate to monitor, audit and report on the payment of all revenues by the oil, gas and mining companies to the government and its agencies as well as report on the receipts of such payments. Composed of NEITI are representatives of government, companies, civil society and NGOs.

The enabling act backing NEITI was formally passed into law by the National Assembly in 2007. One of the functions of NEITI is to ensure that all fiscal allocations and statutory disbursement due from the Federal government to statutory recipients are duly made.[583] For instance, since its formal inauguration in 2003, all monthly allocations to states and local government from the Federal accounts are being regularly published in national newspapers. This practice enables the general public to have an idea of how much money goes to each state and local government every month and therefore ask political office holders questions on what they are doing with the money.

According to the press release of NEITI based on the audit reports of 2005 on the extractive sector, there are a lot of discrepancies and irregularities in the claims and counter claims by oil companies (particularly NNPC) of amounts

---

582   Sowe Mike, The Icpc and the quest for a corruption-free Nigeria, http://sunday.dailytrust.com/index.php?option=com_content&view=a. Visited on 17.11.2010.
583   NEITI Press release, 2009, http://www.neiti.org.ng. Visited on 30.12010.

remitted to the Federal government. Their findings have provided cases yet to be resolved by Federal Inland Revenues Service (FIRS).[584] The physical audit issues of the same report reveal that there are lapses in the infrastructure of the department of petroleum resources (DPR). For instance, it says that "the amount of oil produced (at the well head) is not reliably known" and that in 2005, the DPR had no system for measuring production other than monitoring terminal receipts.[585] In order to ensure accurate remittance of revenue to the government by the oil companies NEITI should be auditing the activities and accounts of oil companies regularly and insist that all memoranda of understanding between the federal government and the oil companies are adhered to strictly. The lapses in the infrastructure of the department of petroleum resources (DPR) must be rectified. The infrastructure must be up to date to meet global standards.

An assessment of the performance of NEITI shows that it is gradually impacting a sense of accountability among those who handle government revenues. However, critiques of NEITI have rightly pointed out that it is not enough to publish what governments earn, it should also be made known to the public how governments spend what they receive.[586] This is because people have the right to know whether resources collected on their behalf are being used to promote the common good or not. It is important to know whether or not the government is using the revenue to promote the welfare of all, especially the weakest in the society.

It is worth noting that though NEITI may not have stopped corruption and financial crimes in the extractive industry, its activities have signaled to the company operators of the oil industry and the government officials that business in the industry could not continue as usual. Information received from NEITI could serve as tools in the hands of the civil society and NGOs to hold companies and governments accountable for the revenues generated from oil industry on behalf of the citizens in the country, particularly in the Niger Delta. If such revenues are not invested in the development of the people, then the government has a case to answer. The three transparency initiatives and anti-corruption agencies provide government's framework or structure to combat corruption.

10.2.2.3 Economic and Financial Crimes Commission

Following Nigeria's membership and ratification of the United Nations Convention Against Corruption (1.2.5.2) in 2004, EFCC was established in 2004 to demonstrate the federal government's commitment to fighting corruption. The

---

584 FIRS is one of the arms of Federal Ministries, Departments and Agencies in charge of all Tax collections and distributions to fund governance in Nigeria.

585 NEITI Press release, 2009, http://www.neiti.org.ng. Visited on 30.1.2010.

586 HRW, Nigeria: Chop fine, 103.

Act of the national assembly establishing the commission states: "... [It] is the designated Financial Intelligence Unit (FIU) in Nigeria, which is charged with the responsibility of co-coordinating the various institutions, involved in the fight against money laundering and enforcement of all laws dealing with economic and financial crimes in Nigeria."[587] Unlike its counterpart ICPC, the Chairman and members of the Commission other than ex-officio members shall be appointed by the President and the appointment shall be subject to confirmation of the Senate.

Reports from commission reveal that since its establishment in 2004, many cases of corrupt practices are being tackled and several billions of Dollars and Naira amounts of money have been recovered into the treasury of the government. Such cases of corruption involving high profile politicians like serving and ex-governors and prominent individuals like the former head of the police in the country and bankers have been handled. A recent report of the commission tabulating on-going high profile cases 2007 – 2010 shows that 55 cases relating to such amounts ranging between 10 million and 277.2 billion Naira are still pending.[588] In this connection, one may add that banks in industrialized countries are being accused of keeping accounts for corrupt politicians and individuals from Nigeria as elsewhere, thereby encouraging corruption. We suggest that banks both in Nigeria as well as in industrialized countries should be thorough in determining the sources of their customers' wealth and be ready to repatriate to country of origin such corruptly acquired money traceable to their banks.

The activities of the anti-corruption agencies are commendable. Through their work the government is demonstrating that funds meant for the common good (2.2) must be used for that purpose and not to be pocketed unaccounted for by the public officers. It is indicating that corruption is a form of denying some people their rights to development (2.4.2). However, critics are of the view that most of the activities of these anti-corruption agencies are directed at perceived opponents of the serving government whether from within or outside of the same political party. The fact that members of the EFCC are being appointed by the President and confirmed by Senate does not give it free hand to operate without bias. We suggest that it becomes autonomous of the Presidency and be seen to be fair to all persons accused of corruption.

Much as these anti-corruption agencies have exposed corrupt persons and their practices, the structures that are generating corruption in the oil industry

---

587   Economic and Financial Crimes Commission (Establishment) Act 2004, 1: (2) c.
588   ECONOMIC &FINANCIAL CRIMES COMMISSION, EFCC ON-GOING HIGH PROFILE CASES – 2007-2010. http://efccnigeria.org/index.php?option=com_doc_view&gid. Visited on 17.11.2010.

have not been addressed. The weaknesses in the operational structures that are characterized by the injustices operating within the system provide the opportunities and excuses for the operators to be corrupt. This is however not to deny the tendency to human greed and selfishness that often propel some people to corruption.

In the light of the principle of personality (2.1), we insist that the human person is the subject of all societal structures and formulations. As *Gaudium et Spes* of the Vatican II puts it, "The social order and its development must constantly yield to the good of the person, since the order of things must be subordinate to the order of persons and not the other way round ... the social order must be founded in truth, built on justice, and enlivened by love" (GS. 26). That is to say, all societal structures are formed by human persons to serve the dignity of all human persons and therefore they can always be changed by the human person as well, when such structures become detrimental to upholding and protecting the dignity of the human persons. The corruption-inducing operational structures in the oil industry have become detrimental to the majority of Nigerians. The structures have permitted corruption to percolate into virtually all other aspects and sectors of the Nigerian society. It is not enough to arrest prosecute and jail corrupt persons, the structures that are inducing or encouraging corruption must be reformed in such a way as to minimize the temptation to corruption. Such structural reforms must begin with oil industry particularly the NNPC and all the ministries related to the oil industry.

In 4.3.2 of part two (socio-economic analysis) we noted that ex-President Olusegun Obasanjo himself confirmed that at the root of the corruption quagmire in Nigeria is the failure and virtual collapse of governance, the contamination of democratic values, the erosion of accountability procedures, and the prevalence of bad leadership.[589] This implies that the Federal government cannot fight corruption successfully without the practice of good governance that would guarantee the values of democracy and the rule to law. For instance, the practice of petroleum subsidy by government has encouraged dealers in petroleum products to be engaged in sharp practices including oil bunkering. Though the intention of the government is to make petroleum products affordable to the generality of Nigerians, those who actually profit from it more are the dealers who engage in import and export of petroleum products. We suggest that petroleum subsidy should stop and money saved there from should be invested into promoting local entrepreneur-

---

589   Olusegun Obasanjo, Nigeria: From Pond of Corruption to Island of Integrity: Lecture delivered by His Excellency; Chief Olusegun Obasanjo, GCFR, President, Commander-in-Chief of the Armed Forces of the Federal Republic of Nigeria at the 10th Anniversary Celebration of Transparency International, Berlin, 07 November 2003 Cf. http:// www.dawudo.com/obas35.htm. Visited on 14.08.2009.

ship and to subsidize agriculture. Commendable as the works of the anti-corruption agencies are, it is important that money recovered from corrupt persons is spent by the government to provide social infrastructures and services to the generality of the people such that Nigerian people, particularly those in the Niger Delta could live a life of self fulfillment.

10.2.3 Niger Delta Regional Development Master Plan

Lack of direction and planning has been identified as one the problems militating against the performance of the commissions charged with development of Niger Delta in the past (3.7). To address this problem, one of the assignments of the Niger Delta Development Commission was to draw up a road map of actions that would lead to the overall development of the region. The Master Plan produced in 2007 serves as the blueprint to achieving the desired sustainable development for the region. This was the outcome of the expert consultancy of *Gesellschaft für technische Zusammenarbeit* (GTZ) of Germany and Wilbahi Engineering Consortium of Nigeria. It is the first integrated development plan in Nigeria that is solely based on a comprehensive analysis of life, development imperatives, challenges and opportunities in the Delta.[590] It is the outcome of stakeholders' participatory inputs and experts' assessment on 26 sectors including health, education, transportation, and agriculture. Its objectives embrace economic growth, infrastructural development, communities' peculiar needs and environmental preservation. The plan addresses all the thematic areas of development problems of the region including violent conflicts, poverty reduction, community development and governance, HIV/AIDS and youth unemployment. According to the document, "the vision running through all aspects of the Master Plan is to improve the quality of life of the Niger Delta people, with particular attention to those with the greatest need, and for this region to flourish by making good use of its rich natural resources."[591] The Master Plan is structured in three 5-year phases, namely: the foundation phase (2006-2010); the expansion phase (2011-2015); and the consolidation phase (2016-2020). Since its publication, the Master Plan has gained acceptance with all stakeholders. This is attributable to two main factors: firstly, representatives of all stakeholders were involved in the preparation and secondly, it was anchored by internationally and nationally reputable consortiums, GTZ of Germany and Wilbahi Engineering Consortium of Nigeria.

---

590 Niger Delta Regional Development Master Plan, p. 14.
591 Niger Delta Regional Development Master Plan, pp. 18 & 125.

An assessment of the Master Plan reveals that it seeks to tackle the development problems that we pointed out in chapter three of part one of this work. For instance, the Master Plan seeks to address the problem of poverty and underdevelopment (3.2) caused partly by lack of people's access to the oil income (1.2.6 of part two), by focusing on poverty reduction and diversification and growth of the regional economy[592]. Reading through the Master Plan, it would appear that the federal government has good intentions towards the development of the Niger Delta region. There are ample chances that the Master Plan could bring about the development of the region. However, like every other government-induced plans, there is the danger that the Master Plan may be plagued by the usual disease of corruption, mismanagement and outright embezzlement of funds by the implementing officials and contractors of NDDC. Already it has been observed that "if the Master Plan is to be implemented successfully, lessons must be learnt from the failures and mistakes of past programmes in the region and incorporated into the current or planned initiatives."[593] In order to ensure its success, we suggest that the communities, civil society, anti-corruption agencies, and the international consortium GTZ and its Nigerian counterpart Wilbahi Engineering Consortium of Nigeria that helped to draw up the Plan should be involved in its execution and monitoring. In this connection, the new Ministry of Niger Delta Affairs could be able to checkmate NDDC officials and contractors.

10.2.4 Ministry of Niger Delta Affairs

Lack of coordination and supervision of government development efforts in the past has been pinpointed as a hindrance to the realization of development in the Niger Delta (3.7). As a response to the problem, the late President Yar'Adua announced the creation of the Ministry of Niger Delta Affairs on September 10, 2008, as part of the federal government's responses to address the Niger Delta's development problems. He said that the new ministry would have a Minister in charge of development of Niger Delta area, and a Minister of State in charge of youth empowerment. The existing Niger Delta Development Commission (NDDC) was to become a parastatal under the ministry. It was further explained that the new ministry would coordinate efforts to tackle the challenges of infrastructural development, environment protection and youth empowerment in the Niger Delta region. The ministry has N61 billion allocations approved for the 2010 budget.

---

592   Niger Delta Regional Development Master Plan, p. 15.
593   Niger Delta Regional Development Master Plan, p. 18.

Despite the state of poverty and underdevelopment in the region, mega projects seem to be receiving priority over human development. For example, the Minister Obong Ufot Ekaette is considering such big projects like the 700-kilometre Calabar-Ondo coastal road, the East-West Railway and new towns development.[594] These are no doubt laudable projects that would open up the region for free movement of goods and people, thus improving the economy of the region. In view of the principle of personality (2.1.1), we state that the Niger Delta people are the subjects and bearers of development, and therefore suggest that the Ministry should begin its work primarily with the people. Priority should be given to improving the living conditions of the people. Over 20.000 ex-militants are yet to be provided with gainful employment. Many communities are yet to enjoy functional health facilities like clinics and hospitals, educational facilities – primary and secondary schools, etc. In fact, the editorial of the Nigerian Guardian Newspaper of January 19, 2010 captures the sentiments of the people towards the new Ministry as follows:

> The minister has been more than one year in office, but it is arguable whether any change has occurred in the Niger Delta as a result of the creation of the ministry. Whatever the reason, the high hopes created at the inception of this dedicated ministry for the Niger Delta appear not to have been realized. The region is still in a state of gross neglect, gas is still being flared, and there are few schools and even fewer hospitals. The cost of living is unacceptably high. Unemployment is rife and the youths are still restive ... We call on the minister to justify the confidence reposed in him by transforming his ministry into a change agent in the Niger Delta ... With improved funding in 2010, the people of the Niger Delta and indeed all Nigerians expect him to deliver without any more excuses.[595]

It seems that the government is now showing serious concern for the development of the region. However, while these critiques are understandable considering the situation in the Niger Delta region, we must know that the development is a gradual process and what has been left undone for over 50 years cannot be achieved within a few years. But that is not to excuse the slow pace of work in the region. In the light of integral human development (2.5.1) we suggest that people's immediate needs for a better living condition should be addressed first, or at best, be attended to simultaneously along other long-term mega projects. In the past such federal government efforts in the forms of commissions have failed the people of the region because of politics, shortage of funds, corruption and mismanagement but above all lack of participation by the local people in the

---

594 Ekaette, Ufot J., "The Challenges and potential of the Niger Delta"; being a keynote address by the Honorable Minister of Niger Delta Affairs at the Commonwealth Business Council workshop for the generation of the Niger Delta at Marriot Hotel, Grosvenor Square, London on 7 July 2009.

595 The Nigerian Guardian, Niger Delta Ministry: One year later, in http://www.ngrguardiannews. com/editorial_opinion/article01/indexn2_html?pdate=1. Visited on 19.1.2010.

decision-making and execution of development programs (3.7). We have argued that in the light of the principles of subsidiarity (2.1.3), participatory justice (2.3) and capability approach (1.4) that people must participate in their own development. We suggest that the new Ministry should involve the local people and the civil society, in the execution of its projects in order to avoid past mistakes. The Ministry must be guided by accountability and transparency.

10.3 State Governments

We have noted above under NEEDS that each state of the federation is expected to produce its own SEEDS to reflect the development peculiarity and priority of each state. We have also said that the 9 states in Niger Delta receive additional 13% of oil revenue from the federation account together with the statutory allocation to all the states in the country (1.3.1.2). The funds so received are supposed to be used to finance secondary and tertiary education, functional hospitals, social infrastructure like tarred roads, pipe borne water, electricity and so on. Reasons why these allocations have not translated to the development of the people are that most of the state governors and public office holders are not accountable to the people and therefore they mismanage or embezzle the funds through corruption (2.2.1.2). The basic concerns of the poor people are not the priority of most state governors.

Social justice (7.4) demands that the state should provide the basic means required by its citizens to live a decent worthwhile life in dignity. In the light of capability approach, it is the duty of state to provide the situation of instrumental freedom (6.4.6.2), that is the social arrangement, facilities and enabling environment which the individuals need to exercise their substantive freedom (6.4.6.1), to choose to being and doing what they have reason to value. The failure of the state governments to meet the basic needs of the people amounts to injustice. We suggest therefore that the states be accountable to the people to justify the funds they are receiving on their behalf by using such funds to provide enabling environment for the people to live a life of dignity. The federal government has given the blueprint of NEEDS, Niger Delta Regional Development Master Plan, and the Ministry of Niger Delta affairs. We suggest that the states should replicate these in their respective states. We suggest too that the anti-corruption agencies should monitor the activities of the state governments. The civil society and NGOs should be involved in the development of the people. Ondo State has taken the lead by preparing its State Economic Empowerment Development Strategy (SEEDS). It has also set up a separate commission (OSOPADEC) to manage its share of 13% for the development of oil producing communities. As far as we know, Delta State too has set up the Delta State Oil Producing Development Commission to perform similar functions like its Ondo state counterpart. It is desirable that other states in the region follow suit.

10.4 Local Governments

We have noted that the local governments have the duty to provide primary health care, primary education, basic social infrastructure in the rural areas being the closest arm of government to the people. To carry out these responsibilities, they receive their share of 20% from the federation account monthly. We have also said that in allocation of money to budget items, recurrent expenditure on staff salary, transport and allowances for chairmen, councilors and officials of the local governments as well as capital projects (as means of corruption) take priority over financing of primary education health care and agriculture. Again in the light of capability approach, local governments are obliged to provide the situation of instrumental freedom, that is, the social arrangement, facilities and enabling environment which the individuals need to exercise their substantive freedom, to choose to being and doing what they have reason to value. In the light of the social teaching of the Church, the people in the rural areas have the right to share in the common good, which in this case, are the resources meant for them from the federal government. Social justice demands that the local government give to the people what are due to them. We suggest therefore that in its budgets, the local government should give priority to the basic needs of the people by investing into primary education, health care delivery and agricultural development. There must be budget discipline on the part of the local government officials. We suggest that the attention of anti-corruption agencies should also be focused on the local government officials. Civil society and NGOs should insist on monitoring the budgets and activities at the local government level; in doing so the mass media should be carried along to report their findings to the public.

10.5 Minority Elites

Under political analysis, we have shown that the political and economic influences of the elites easily pave the way for them to either occupy political offices or determine who occupy such positions as soon as states and local governments are created in the region (2.2.4). Even when the elites claim to be fighting for the interests of their oil-producing minority communities, they usually end up being the main beneficiaries of such agitations and not the local communities. In many cases, the votes of the electorate are not respected during elections. In other words, the much of the people are politically excluded. As we earlier pointed out while discussing the intra-communal conflicts (3.6), the practices of the elites who try to short-change the communities have been a major cause of conflicts and violence that have also been a hindrance to development. The approach of the elites and elders has given rise to the emergence of youth militias.

The role of the elites in helping to articulate and represent the voices and concerns of the local people is inevitable. However, in the light of principle of personality (7.1.1) people are endowed with dignity, they are subjects and therefore cannot be used as means to an end. It is wrong for the elites to simply occupy political positions and determine what to do with people's resources without recourse to the concerns and needs of the people. It amounts to instrumentalization of the people by the elites for their selfish ends. In the light of participatory justice (7.3), people have the rights to share in the common good (7.2) and elites who claim to be working for the people must work in the spirit of solidarity (7.1.2) with the people. We suggest that the electoral system should ensure that people decide who their political leaders are through their votes. For that to happen, people must be educated in the values of democracy.

10.6 The Local Church and the Development of the Niger Delta

In chapter 1 of this part we discussed the contributions of the Church in industrialized countries to the development of developing countries like Nigeria. The Church in Nigeria is also making contributions to the development of the country in general and in the Niger Delta in particular. Besides proclaiming the truth about man and society, in the light of her rich tradition of social thought, the Church also makes contributions by offering social services through schools, hospitals and charity homes. As a formidable structure of the society the Church in Nigeria is duly represented by the Justice Development and Peace Commissions that are active in most of the 52 Dioceses in the country. Development efforts are being made too on the national level by the Catholic Bishops' Conference of Nigeria through Catholic Secretariat of Nigeria. Some Dioceses are engaged as well in one project or the other that could on the long run contribute to the development of the region. Generally, efforts directed at the development of Niger Delta are still at their infancy.

10.6.1 Justice Development and Peace Commission

Since the Second Vatican Council (1963-1965), the Church has rediscovered herself as "a sign and safeguard of the transcendence of the human person" (GS 76). Aware of the world-wide dimension of the social question, "the council, considering the immensity of the hardships which still afflict the greater part of mankind today, regards it as most opportune that an organism of the universal Church be set up in order that both the justice and love of Christ towards the poor might be developed everywhere. The role of such an organism would be to stimulate the Catholic community to promote progress in needy regions and international social justice" (GS 90,2). This call for the establishment of a structure found response from Pope Paul VI, when in 1967 he formed the Pontifical commission *Iustitia et Pax*.[596] The commission, in turn, encouraged Episcopal conferences to establish similar commissions. The Justice, Development and Peace Commission (JDPC) of the Catholic Bishops' Conference of Nigeria is a replication of this development of the universal Church.

As an organ of the Church in Nigeria the JDPC is saddled with the task of contributing to the realization of integral and authentic human development for all in the Nigerian society. Its programmatic activities are to be guided by the following objectives:

- Promote the quality life for all people
- Promote human rights (e.g. U.N. Charter on Human Rights 1948)
- Enhance peace building and conflict resolution processes
- Form and animate groups to participate in their own development
- Make a preferential option for the poor and marginalized and to act as the voice of the voiceless
- Identify unjust structures and to take corrective action for the integral development and social welfare of people
- Promote the Catholic Social Teaching
- Intervene in emergencies to help victims of natural disasters, violent conflicts, and other situations, which deserve immediate response
- Research, document and publish information on social issues
- Cooperate with International Agencies, Government and NGOs for integral development
- Build channels of dialogue at local, national and international level[597]

---

596 Powers, Gerard, Peace and Justice Commissions. *In*: Dwyer, Judith (ed.) The New Dictionary of Catholic Social Thought, 722-724. Cf. also Keenan, Marjorie, Pontifical Council for Justice and Peace. Ibid, pp. 754-755.

597 Catholic Secretariat of Nigeria, Operational Guidelines and Handbook for Justice, Development and Peace/Caritas Work in Nigeria, p. 10.

These objectives reflect the principles of the social teaching of the Church as well as the Church's model of development. All the Dioceses and Vicariates are to replicate the JDPC. There is no doubt that these objectives have the chances or potentials of contributing to the development Nigerian society at large and the Niger Delta in particular. Indeed, the JDPC has recorded success stories in some of its objectives, particularly in the areas human rights, democracy work like election monitoring and reporting, agriculture and rural development, etc.[598] These efforts are commendable but, most of these success stories are on projects being executed and not necessarily tailored towards transforming unjust structures in the Nigerian society. At it were, the JDPC's impacts are only felt in places where it has on-going projects. According to the JDP/Caritas national report 2008, not all the Dioceses in the Niger Delta region have on-going projects directed at solving the development problems in the region. In other words, the impact of JDPC needs to be more felt in the development of the region. We have shown in our analysis that the causes of the development problems in the region are structural and policy-related. It is not enough to concentrate on projects executions and running time-bounded and target groups-related programs. There is the need to also address the causes of the development problems. Limiting one's efforts to project executions alone would amount to treating the symptoms rather than the causes of the problems.

In order that the objectives and thus the contributions of JDPC to development may be effective everywhere in Nigeria, particularly in the Niger Delta, we suggest that JDPC should engage in policy-related public debates on development strategies and efforts concerning the Niger Delta region. As a formidable structure of the Church that has credibility in the society, JDPC stands the chances of making impact on policy issues and strategies relating to the Niger Delta. But that depends on the competence of JDPC on such matters and there remains the challenge. Perhaps other efforts of the Church on the national level could complement the work of JDPC and vice versa

10.6.2 Efforts on the National Level

Other efforts at the Catholic Bishops' Conference of Nigeria are the Catholic Legislative Liaison Office, communiqués or press releases and the new Catholic Caritas foundation of Nigeria. We shall examine each briefly to see what they hold for the Niger Delta region.

---

598   Catholic Secretariat of Nigeria, JDPC/Caritas Nigeria, Annual Report 2008.

10.6.2.1 Catholic Legislative Liaison Office

As part of the efforts of the Nigerian Catholic Church to bring the social teachings on integral and authentic development to bear on the social structures of Nigerian society, especially in the area of promoting democracy and good governance, the CSN through the JDPC/Caritas applied for and was accorded a Catholic Legislative Liaison Office in the National Assembly in 2008.[599] The rationale for the liaison office is that the Church needs to engage the structures and institutions that are formulating laws and policies that are governing the people and giving directions of development. The Church in Nigeria is convinced that: "it is when the Church is involved with these institutions that it can influence the laws right from the moment of their articulation and thus make them respond to the needs of the people. It is only in this way the Church can bring the Social Teaching to life in Nigeria."[600] Some of the objectives of the legislative liaison office are stated as follows:

(i) To participate actively in coordinating and promoting initiatives, in the National Assembly, that bear concrete relationship with life situations of the Nigerian people.

(ii) To participate in the promotion of programmes and policies which enhance integral human development, ideals of democracy, justice, reconciliation and peace.

(iii) To promote appropriate and effective legislative advocacy that would foster pro-poor legislation in the national assembly.

(iv) To promote initiatives that would facilitate popular participation especially with regard constituency campaigns of the members of the National Assembly.[601]

The CLLO is a step in the right direction. Like the JDPC, the CLLO would serve as the bridge between the Church and the state and constitute an enhanced means of communication between both. It is hoped that through the activities of the CLLO, the Church would be bringing her concerns for the human condition to reflect on the social, political and economic structures of the Nigerian society in general and in the Niger Delta region in particular. In this way, she would be contributing to eradicate poverty and underdevelopment and thus bring about integral and authentic development. In order that its effect may be felt everywhere in Nigeria, we suggest that CLLO should be replicated on state level,

599   JDPC/Caritas Nigeria, Catholic Secretariat of Nigeria, Annual Report, 2008, 35.
600   JDPC/Caritas Nigeria, Catholic Secretariat of Nigeria, Annual Report, 2008, 37.
601   JDPC/Caritas Nigeria, Catholic Secretariat of Nigeria, Annual Report, 2008, 38.

whereby Diocesan JDPC/Caritas could also seek the same office at State Houses of Assembly. Where there are more Dioceses in a state, it could be a joint effort of all the JDPC/Caritas in that particular state. Though not specifically directed to the development of Niger Delta, the objectives of the CLLO appear plausible and have the chances of contributing to the overall development of Nigeria in general and the Niger Delta in particular. Again, the success of CLLO depends on the competence and the technical know-how of the Church's personnel in that regard.

10.6.2.2 Communiqués and Public Statements

On the national level particular focus is being given to the extractive industry. In 2006, the Justice Development and Peace Commission issued a statement titled "Nigeria – The Travesty of Oil and Gas Wealth".[602] The document highlights all the nuances involved in the extractive industry in the Niger Delta. In some details, the document educates the reader on the relationship between the government, the multinational oil companies and the host oil communities. Attention is given to the laws and regulations relating to the oil and gas industry, the environmental impact of oil and gas activities in the Niger Delta, the corporate social responsibility of the multinational oil companies, as well as the issues of transparency and accountability in the use of the oil revenue by the state and finally presents the position of the Church by stating that:

> The [C]hurch now calls for a zero-tolerance transparency culture (ZTTC) as an obligatory mandate for all people, in and out of government, nationals and non-nationals alike because it promotes justice and peace, delivers God's endowments equitably to all the co-inheritors of the earthly good. In the case of oil when it is inside the earth below their feed, it belongs to all equally. When it is lifted up and exchanged for money, it must still belong to all, not appropriated or mismanaged, even partly by individuals, corporate bodies and governments. All stakeholders commit a social sin if it is not ZTTC. Nigeria must sustain the eagerness to operationalise EITI guidelines and progress to installing a Zero-Tolerance Transparency Culture.[603]

Similarly, in its communiqué titled "Keeping Hope Alive" issued at the end of the meeting in Abuja, March 6-11th 2006, the CBCN stated that "the worsening crises in the Niger Delta came principally from the long-standing social injustice against that region which contributes immensely to our national economy is regrettable. We call on government to exercise utmost prudence in responding to the intermittent violence there, as well as launch a more innovative and decisive

602 Catholic Secretariat of Nigeria, Nigeria – The Travesty of Oil and Gas Wealth, Statement of the Justice Development and Peace Commission of the Catholic Bishops' Conference of Nigeria, Lagos: Gazub Prints 2006.
603 CSN, Nigeria – Travesty of Oil and Gas Wealth, p. 157.

infrastructural development programmes for the region than we have seen the past"[604] In 2008, a follow-up pastoral letter of the Catholic Bishops' Conference of Nigeria was issued titled "That Our Oil and Gas Wealth May Serve the Common Good – The moral challenges of oil and gas wealth in Nigeria" with the central message that "Oil and gas wealth belongs to all Nigerians and should be so equitably and justly distributed such that all must benefit there from since the destination of all created earthly goods is for the care and common good of everyone."[605]

In his capacity as the Chairman of CBCN, Archbishop Alaba Job of the metropolitan See of Ibadan Archdiocese reacted to the violent clashes between militant groups and the Joint Military Taskforce (JTF) in the Niger Delta especially in the areas of south-west Warri in May 2009 by issuing a statement titled "Violence is not the answer in the Niger Delta". The Archbishop expressed the concern of the Church about the sufferings, displacements and deaths of innocent citizens in the Niger Delta region which resulted from military operation there. He condemned in no unmistakable terms the military bombardment of the communities of Oporoza, Kunukunuma, Kurutie and Okerenkoko where altogether over 20,000 people had become vulnerable to diseases, hunger and starvation and over 65 people had lost their lives. He called for a total and unconditional ceasefire on both sides. While calling on the Federal government to urgently halt all air bombardment in order to arrest further destruction of lives and properties of innocent people, he appealed that all aid workers, including the Red Cross, the National Emergency Management Agency, Justice Development and Peace/Caritas Nigeria should be urgently granted access to the region in order to take care of the displaced persons and the injured. Among several vexed issues in the region, he addressed two: the need for the Federal government to increase revenue allocation from 13 to at least 17percent as recommended by the National Political Reform Conference of 2006 and the issue of corporate social responsibility of oil companies in the host communities, particularly on the environment.[606]

At the end of its September 2009 meeting in Kafanchan, the CBCN issue a communiqué on "Conversion for Justice and Reconciliation". Addressing the issue of Niger Delta, the Bishops stated that:

We commend the federal government for the general amnesty it has granted to militants in the Niger Delta. We ask that this programme of amnesty be implemented with sincerity, and with sensitivity to justice and reconciliation. We advise that the government continue on the

---

604   CBCN, "Keeping Hope Alive"; being a communiqué issued in Abuja on 11 March 2006.

605   Catholic Secretariat of Nigeria, That Our Oil and Gas Wealth May Serve the Common – The Moral Challenges of Oil & Gas Wealth in Nigeria, (a Joint Pastoral Letter of the Catholic Bishops' Conference of Nigeria), Abuja: Mac-Pama Press Ltd 2008, p. 8.

606   Archbishop Alaba Job, Violence is not the answer in the Niger Delta, in: http:/blog.caritas.org/2009/05/29/violence –is-not-the-answer-in-the-niger-delta/. Visited on 5.3.2010.

path of drastically improving the quality of life of the people of the Niger Delta. It is not enough to wave an olive branch. The situation in the Niger Delta is deeply rooted in injustice. It is simply unjust to impoverish the people who live on the land that produces the bulk of Nigeria's wealth. We urge government to fulfill its promise on the development of the people of the Niger Delta. We equally appeal to the militants to accept the amnesty.[607]

The Bishops attributed the cause of all the ills in the society to sin which is the absence of right relationship between us and God, and the absence of right relationship amongst us, and therefore called for conversion, a change of heart that must both be personal and collective.

The communiqués and statements from the CBCN on the Niger Delta problems are laudable. However, it is worth noting that attributing the crises in the Niger Delta to sin appears to be an individual ethics approach rather than social ethics-structure related approach. The fact that the CBCN published the first seemingly systematic publication on oil and gas in 2006 fifty years after the discovery and exploitation of crude oil began in 1956 shows that the local Church lacked the competence to make any categorical statement on the technical issues of oil and gas and the socio-ethical implications for a long time. As a matter of fact, Archbishop Onaiyekan raised this point during the sensitization visit to him by the implementing team of the project "Making oil and gas wealth serve the common good" in CSN led by Fr. Babangida, when he said: "Dioceses in the Niger Delta who are at the heart of the devastation have been surprisingly quiet. What are they doing? How can the Bishops of the Church in the region be mobilized to be seen in the spotlight as advocating for the promotion of human dignity in the Niger Delta?" Furthermore, he said: "Given the Church's structure and respect for ecclesiastical/local jurisdiction, it will be out of place to have only Bishops from other places making statements on the Niger Delta. If Bishops in the area make active efforts in advocacy, then it will be easy to have the support of the larger Church in the project."[608]

We therefore suggest that the Bishops, priests, religious and laity in Nigeria particularly in the Dioceses with oil-producing communities must be duly educated or sensitized on the nuances involved in the development problems of the Niger Delta region and the socio-ethical implications. This is because oil and gas may be found elsewhere in Nigeria in the future. Whatever lessons learnt in the Niger Delta case could be applied somewhere else. We suggest also that social ethics should be a course of study on the curriculum of all major seminaries, novitiates or religious formation houses, catechist training centers as well as in

---

607   CBCN, "Conversion for Justice and Reconciliation"; being a communiqué at the end of the Second Plenary Meeting of the Catholic Bishops' Conference of Nigeria (CBCN) at the Centre of Transfiguration Kafanchen, Kaduna State, 2009, p. 8.

608   JDPC/Caritas Nigeria, Catholic Secretariat of Nigeria, Annual Report, 2008, p. 10.

the syllabus of catechesis for first communion and confirmation candidates in all parishes where it has not been. In fact, Archbishop Onaiyekan, who was a former rector of S.S Peter and Paul Major Seminary, Ibadan, recognizes the need for the social teaching of the Church to be on the curriculum of major seminaries and houses of formation when he says: "even at the seminary level, the social teachings of the Church are to be taught in such a way that the young priest is well equipped to face the political and social realities around him."[609]

10.6.2.3 Catholic Caritas Foundation of Nigeria

The Catholic Caritas Foundation of Nigeria is a recent establishment of the Catholic Bishops' Conference of Nigeria. It is dedicated specifically to promoting human development. As an arm of the Church in Nigeria, it is empowered to fight against hunger, disease and ignorance – a role previously played by the Department of Church and Society of the Catholic Secretariat of Nigeria. It has the vision of a harmonious environment where every man, woman and child in Nigeria enjoys fullness of wellbeing as a child of God. Strategically, it seeks to advance the wellbeing of people through participatory intervention measures from all sectors of the Catholic social ministry in Nigeria.[610] As it is still a recent outfit which only began recruitment of its staff in October 2010, CCFN cannot be evaluated yet. However, we need to point out that because its activities are directed primarily at the about 30 million Catholics in Nigeria, it may be difficult for it to focus attention specifically at the development of the Niger Delta region. For this reason there may be a need for another establishment from the CBCN that is specifically dedicated to the development of the Niger Delta region.

10.6.2.4 Catholic Education

Another area of Nigerian Church's contribution to development is through education of the citizenry. The history of education in Nigeria cannot be told completely without mentioning the role of the Catholic Church. The local Church in the various dioceses runs several educational institutions beginning with nursery/ primary, secondary and post secondary schools. Others are the vocational or skill acquisition centers. In recent times, some Dioceses and religious congregations have started universities and institutions of higher learning. On the national level, the CBCN in collaboration with the Association of Episcopal Conferences of Anglophone West Africa (AECAWA) established the Catholic Institute of West

---

609   Onaiyekan John, Thy Kingdom Come: Democracy and Politics in Nigeria Today, a Catholic Perspective, Ibadan: Daily Graphics 2003, p. 22.
610   Catholic caritas foundation of Nigeria, http://www.ccfn.org. Visited 24.11.2010.

Africa (CIWA) Port Harcourt in 1981.[611] Similarly the CBCN has started the Veritas University, Abuja (VUNA) as a Catholic university in Nigeria. Though the provisional license to operate the university was granted by the Nigerian National University Commission in May 2007, it commenced activities with the 2008/2009 academic session at its take-off campus in Obehie, Abia State.[612] To streamline the quality and identity of Catholic education in the country the CBCN through its education committee issued a guideline in 2005.[613] These institutions serve as instruments of evangelization and at the same time, through her educational services the Church is helping to reduce the rate of illiteracy and thus contributing to improving quality of life of the beneficiaries and the society at large. That is to say, through her "social facilities" she is promoting the "capability" of the people and thus integral human development.

However, there is the need to ask how far the poor and disadvantaged in the society particularly those in the rural creeks of the Niger Delta region are benefiting from her services. This question is pertinent because the educational services of the Church are not completely free of charge. The CBCN answers the question by affirming the fact that "in many part of the world today (Niger Delta region inclusive), material poverty prevents many youths and children from having access to formal education and adequate human and Christian formation" and therefore recommends that "every diocese should endeavour to establish an Education Endowment Fund that will cater for the poor. This endowment could also be established at the school level."[614] These efforts are noble and laudable. They are expressions of the Church's solidarity with the citizenry. But then, how many poor and disadvantaged are being served with such Education Endowment Funds, where they exist? In order to demonstrate the Church's preferential option for the poor more concretely for the majority of the poor, we suggest that the Church as advocate of the poor should engage the government by insisting that the state provides free compulsory and qualitative education for all citizens at least from primary to secondary school levels. In this way, the poor and disadvantaged who cannot afford to pay for Catholic educational services would still have the alternative to attain formal education. Parents would be at liberty to choose where their children should be educated. The Church's advocacy on behalf of the poor and disadvantaged in this regard, would make Church's claim to preferential option for the poor more credible.

---

611 Http://Www.Ciwa.Org.Ng/En/Home/6-About-Ciwa. Visited on 4.12.2010.

612 Http://Www.Veritas.Edu.Ng/Content/History. Visited on 4.12.2010.

613 Catholic Bishops Conference of Nigeria, The Catholic Church Policy on Education in Nigeria, Catholic Secretariat, Lagos, 2005.

614 Catholic Bishops Conference of Nigeria, The Catholic Church Policy on Education in Nigeria, p. 44.

10.6.2.5 Need for a Directorate of Niger Delta Affairs

We have mentioned that JDPC is making efforts to contribute to the development of the country, but that such efforts are yet to make significant impact in the Niger Delta (2.6.1). Since the Catholic Liaison Office came on board, its activities have been centered on the National Assembly (2.6.2.1), though with vision of influencing policies and laws governing the whole country, Niger Delta inclusive. We have commended the communiqués and statements from the CBCN and pointed out the need for such official positions of the Church to be approached from a social ethical perspective (2.6.2.2). Even the new organ of the CBCN, Catholic Caritas Foundation of Nigeria is not directed at the Niger Delta region specifically (2.6.2.3).

In the light of the enormity of the development problems in the Niger Delta region, affecting the majority of a population of about 30 million people, the Federal government has set up the NDDC to produce the Master Plan (2.2.3). It has also established a Ministry of Niger Delta Affairs to coordinate all development efforts in the region. As a further demonstration of the seriousness of the Church's concerns for the poor and disadvantaged people in the Niger Delta region, we suggest that a complementary structure be set up name it, for example, a directorate of Niger Delta Affairs at the CBCN level. The following responsibilities could be entrusted to the proposed directorate:

- To study continuously the socio-economic and political situations in the region vis a vis national and international interest groups, propose a social ethical position and advice the Church accordingly
- To work hand in hand with Catholic Legislative Liaison Office, NDDC, the Ministry of Niger Delta and all relevant agencies and NGOs or CSOs on behalf of the Church.
- To collaborate with all the Diocesan JDPCs in the region.
- To engage in public debates on policies and issues affecting the development of the region.
- To initiate and anchor ongoing projects on making the oil and gas serve the common good.
- To adopt and seek to implement the Niger Delta Development Agenda proposed in chapter 8.

We propose further that it could serve as a "step-down" of the CLLO on the state level. As it is a technical assignment, those to be charged with such as a responsibility must be knowledgeable and competent personnel in development problems associated with the extractive industry as well as in the social teaching of the Church.

10.6.3 Efforts of Dioceses in the Niger Delta

10.6.3.1 Making Oil and Gas Wealth Serve the Common Good

As a follow up on the international conference on "Making Oil and Gas Wealth Serve the Common Good" that took place in Enugu 2006, the Nigerian Church through the Catholic Secretariat of Nigeria started an advocacy program involving 4 Dioceses in the Niger Delta region (Bomadi, Ondo, Port Harcourt, and Uyo) in 16 pilot communities. The aim of the project is to train the host communities by "raising their abilities to critically examine their needs and conditions and to come up with problem solving skills by organizing themselves, getting united and into negotiations with all stakeholder parties involved in the conflict around resources."[615] The project is being supported by the Catholic Relief Services (CRS) and Trocaire. In Ondo Diocese, the JDPC has identified 4 communities in Ilaje Local Government Area as pilot communities. They are: Obenla, Molutehin, Awoye and Obere-Woye. With a trained animator to support the advocacy efforts of the host communities and raise problem-solving skills, the identified host communities are expected to be empowered and equipped with the necessary skills to speak with one voice and to successfully claim their rights for compensation and infrastructural development.

10.6.3.2 The Example of Ondo Diocese

Ondo is one of the Dioceses that have oil-producing communities in their territories. There are 250 oil-producing communities along the coast of Ondo State, thus making the state the longest coastal region in Nigeria. The pastoral care and the social services being given to the faithful and the society by the Dioceses in the Niger Delta can be considered as part of the Church's contribution to the development of the region. One can say that like in the rest of the country that the Church is contributing to the development of the region by promoting education in the various schools established by the church, healthcare through the hospitals and clinics as well as other social services being provided by the religious congregations and lay apostolates particularly the Justice Development and Peace Commission/Caritas.

Currently the JDPC/Caritas is involved in a number of projects and programs ranging from trainings for conflict resolution, peace-building and community development projects in partnership with other NGOs and Civil society as well as promoting good governance through its involvement in democratic process

---

615   Catholic Secretariat of Nigeria, JDPC/Caritas, Lenten Campaign 2008, p. 28.

and the rule of law. Other activities include budget analysis and budget monitoring of the state with the view to educate the public on how the revenue from oil and gas is being expended by the government.

Some diocesan JDPCs are working in partnership with other NGOs and CSOs in some development programs and projects in the Niger Delta. For example, the JDPC of Ondo Diocese is collaborating with Ondo State Action Committee on Aids (ODSACA) to sensitize and educate the public on the HIV/AIDS pandemic. It is also involved as partner in the implementation of the EU project MPP6 now MPP9 in providing social infrastructure in some rural communities in Ondo State. As lead CSO, the Ondo Diocesan JDPC is working with Action Aid International Nigeria (AAIN) on the program called Partnership Against Poverty (PAP 6) in Ondo State. It is a program aimed at eradicating poverty through empowerment of the people using the Rights Based Approach (RBA) to development. Other programs include supporting the traditional cooperative savings and credit societies and groups with micro-credit.

The various activities of the JDPC in Ondo Diocese are expressions of the local Church's solidarity with poor and disadvantaged in the society. The beneficiaries of the activities appreciate the efforts of the Church. However, in the light of this study, it is clear to me that generally the JDPC seems to be associated mainly with sourcing for funds and executing projects for the people.[616] In line with the principles of subsidiarity and participatory justice, we suggest that the JDPC in Ondo Diocese should engage more in empowering through training the people in the parishes and outstations along with their parish priests and catechists to respond to local problems while the JDPC concentrates its energy and focus on engaging the structures that are precipitating the development problems in the society. This suggestion holds too for all other JDPCs in the country.

In addition to the work of the JDPC, the Diocese of Ondo also offers other social services that are contributing to the development of the society. It provides health care services through hospitals. Through the educational institutions like nursery/primary and secondary schools as well as vocational training centres the Diocese provides literacy and education, and thus quality of life for the people. In the area of agricultural development it runs a demonstration farm project where interested youth and local farmers could learn about modern farming techniques and different forms of farming like fishery, bee-keeping, piggery, oil-palm production and vegetable cultivation.

---

616   JDPC/Caritas Nigeria, Annual Report, 2008, p. 84.

General Conclusions

In first part of this study we set out to present the development problems in the Niger Delta region. We began in chapter one by taking a bird view of Nigerian political history from Independence in 1960 to date and concluded that the political scenario of Nigeria is characterized by instability and inconsistency in policy. The theoretical framework on development in chapter two revealed the evolution of development theories and concepts from modernization to dependency, from the Washington Consensus as expressed in the Structural Adjustment Program to the Post Washington Consensus, driven by the wave of globalization along the era of PRSP of the World Bank and IMF with MDGs as the global package for development of the third world countries. The chapter treated the situation of poverty and underdevelopment, thus presenting the development problems in the Niger Delta.

The socio-economic and political analysis in part two indicated that the dependency of Nigeria as a petroleum exporting country has made her to run a rentier economy focusing mainly on income from the sale of petroleum to the neglect of agriculture and other sectors of the economy. In the process, the oil income does not percolate to the generality of the people. Corruption and mismanagement of the oil income have made it more difficult for the generality of the people to benefit from it through provision of social amenities. International stakeholders and the political class in Nigeria appear to be pursuing their own selfish interests with little concern for the plight of the poor and the disadvantaged in the Niger Delta.

The ethical orientation in part three, chapter one offered the position of Amartya Sen on development with the capability approach as a way of overcoming the condition of unfreedom, all forms of poverty, and thereby attaining development. Chapter two presented the impulses from the Catholic Social thought in the principles of personality, solidarity and subsidiary as well as the common good, social justice and human rights. In addition, the model of integral human development in line with *Populorum Progressio* and authentic human development according to *Sollicitudo rei Socialis* were also presented. A comparison between Sen's Capability approach and the Church's teaching on development revealed that the concern for the improvement of the human condition is central to both. This fact serves as a reason for collaboration or cooperation of Church

275

with development efforts based on the Capability approach. Bringing the ethical orientation to bear on the development problems in the Niger Delta, chapter three concluded that the state of poverty and underdevelopment in the region is a condition of unfreedom and a condition less than human which development must overcome.

Part four, which is the assessment of and suggestions for development agents, took a critical look at the efforts of the international community directed at tackling poverty and thus promoting development globally particularly in the third world countries. It was seen in chapter one that apart from military assistance, most of the other contributions from the international community have the potentiality of poverty reduction, thus contributing to development. However, such practices of international organizations that are still disadvantageous to poor developing countries would need to be reformed. We concluded that the roles of the Church in the industrialized countries are inevitable. The second and last chapter of part four treated the contributions of national stakeholders, the various governments, the minority elites, and last but not the least, the local Church.

While we admit that the governments are putting structures and programs in place to solve the development problems in the Niger Delta region, such efforts have not yielded the desired goal because they are often top-down arrangement by the government. The local people have to be involved and be empowered to participate positively and productively in their development. The socio-economic and political structures operating in Nigeria are still prone to corruption and inefficiency, and therefore they need to be reformed. Arresting and prosecuting corrupt persons amount to treating the symptoms rather the causes of corruption.

The local Church is fulfilling her mission of evangelization and providing social services to the people and thus contributing to integral human development. However, as advocate of the poor and disadvantaged, her commitment to preferential option for the poor would be more effective if she would engage more in public debates on policy issues that could lead to the transformation of structures that are responsible for poverty and underdevelopment in the society. In that way, the poor and the disadvantaged in the region would experience truly that their "joy and hope, grief and anguish" are also that of the Church. She has all it requires in the rich tradition of her social thought. All her personnel and the laity must be grounded in the knowledge of the social teachings of the Church through the teaching of social ethics in all her educational institutions.

List of Abbreviations

AAS	Acta apostolicae sedis
AIDS	Acquired Immune Deficiency Syndrome
ANEEJ	African Network for Environment and Economic Justice
CA	Capability Approach
CBN	Central Bank of Nigeria
CCC	Catechism of the Catholic Church
CD	Campaign for Democracy
CDHR	Committee for the Defence of Human Rights
CFD	Comprehensive Framework for Development
CLO	Civil Liberty Organization
CPI	Corruption Perception Index
CSO	Civil Society Organizations
CSR	Corporate Social Responsibility
DFFRI	Directorate for Food Road and Rural Infrastructure
DPR	Department of Petroleum Resources
ECLA	Economic Commission for Latin America
EFCC)	Economic and Financial Crimes Commission
EITI	Extractive Industry Transparency Initiative
EJA	Economic Justice for All
EU	European Union
FCT	Federal Capital Territory
FDI	Foreign Direct Investment
FEC	Federal Executive Council
FEPA	Federal Environmental Protection Agency
FIRS	Federal Inland Revenue Service
GATT	General Agreement on Trade and Tariff
GDI	Gender-related Development Index
GDP	Gross Domestic Product
GGESS	Gulf of Guinea Energy Security Strategy
GKKE	Gemeinsame Konferenz Kirche und Entwicklung
GNP	Gross National Product
GRATS	General Agreement on Trade and Services
GWOT	Global War on Terrorism

HDI	Human Development Index
HDR	Human Development Report
HIPC	Highly Indebted Poor Countries
HIV	Human Immunodeficiency Virus
HPI	Human Poverty Index
IFIs	International Finance Institutions
IMF	International Monetary Fund
ISI	Import Substitution Industrialization
JDPC	Justice Development and Peace Commission
LEEDS	Local Economic Empowerment and Development Strategy
LGAs	Local Governments Areas
MAMSER	Mass Mobilization for Social and Economic Recovery
MEND	Movement for the Emancipation of the Niger Delta
MOSOP	Movement for the Survival of Ogoni People
NADECO	National Democratic Coalition
NAPEP	National Poverty Eradication Programme
NCS	Nigeria Customs Services
NDDC	Niger Delta Development Commission
NDHDR	Niger Delta Human Development Report
NDVF	Niger Delta Volunteer Forc
NEEDS	National Economic Empowerment Development Strategy
NEITI	Nigerian Extractive Industry Transparency Initiative
NNPC	Nigerian National Petroleum Corporation
NRC	National Republican Convention
OECD	Organization for Economic Cooperation and Development
OMPADEC	Oil Mineral Producing Areas Development Commission
OPC	Odua People's Congress
OPEC	Organization of Petroleum Exporting Countries
OSOPADEC	Ondo State Oil-Producing Areas Development Commission
PAP	Poverty Alleviation Programme
PRSP	Poverty Reduction Strategy Paper
SAP	Structural Adjustment Program
SDP	Social Democratic Party
SEEDS	State Economic Empowerment and Development Strategies
TI	Transparency International
TNOCs	Transnational Oil Companies
TRIPS	Trade Related Aspects of Intellectual Property Rights
UNDP	United Nations Development Program
VENRO	Verband Entwicklungspolitik deutscher Nichtregierungsorganisationen

WAI	War Against Indiscipline
WB	World Bank
WCED	World Commission on Environment and Development
WTO	World Trade Organization

Bibliography

1. Church and Papal Documents

BENEDICT XVI, Caritas in Veritate, AAS 186 (2009)

JOHN PAUL II, Apostolic Exhortation, *Christi fideles Laici.* The Vocation of the Lay Faithful in the Church and in the World, AAS 81 (1989) 396-431.

–, Apostolic Exhortation, *Ecclesia in Africa,* AAS 88 (1996) 12-72.

–, Encyclical, *Redemptor Hominis,* AAS 71 (1979) 274-286.

–, Encyclical, *Solicitudo Rei Socialis,* AAS 80 (1988) 547-286.

–, Encyclical, *Centessimus Annus,* AAS 88 (1991) 833-858.

–, Encyclical, *Laborem Exercens,* AAS 73 (1981) 580-583.

–, The Church in Africa. Post-Synodal Apostolic Exhortation Ecclesia in Africa, Nairobi: Paulines Publications Africa 1995.

PAUL VI, Encyclical, *Populorum Progressio,* AAS 59 (1967) 257-296.

–, Apostolic Exortation, *Evangelii Nuntiandi,* AAS 68 (1976) 9-26.

JOHN XXIII, Encyclical, *Mater et Magistra,* AAS 53 (1961) 405-447.

–, Encyclical, *Pacem in Terris,* AAS 55 (1963) 257-301.

LEO XIII, Encyclical, *Rerum Novarum,* 15 May 1891.

PIUS XI, Encyclical, *Quadragessimo Anno,* AAS 6 (1931) 177-228.

Pastoral Constitution on the Church in the Modern World, *Gaudium et Spes,* AAS 58 (1966) 1025-1120.

SYNOD OF BISHOPS, Justice in the World, *Iustistia in Mundo,* AAS 63 (1971) 923-942.

CONGREGATION FOR THE DOCTRINE OF THE FAITH, Instruction on Certain Aspects of the „Theology of Liberation" *Libertatis Nuntius* AAS 76 (1984) 876-909.

–, Instruction on Christian Freedom and Liberation, *Libertatis Conscientia,* AAS 79 (1986).

CATECHISM OF THE OF CATHOLIC CHURCH, Liguori, Liguori Publications 1994

GERMAN BISHOPS' CONFERENCE, Many faces of Globalization. Perspectives for a Humane World Order, Bonn: Zentralstelle Weltkirche der Deutschen Bischofskonferenz 2000.

PONTIFICAL COUNCIL FOR JUSTICE AND PEACE, Compendium of the Social Doctrine of the Church, Vatican City: Libreria Editrice 2004.

–, The Social Agenda of the Catholic Church – The Magisterial Texts, London: Burns & Oates 2000.

CATHOLIC SECRETARIAT OF NIGERIA (CSN), That Our Oil and Gas Wealth May Serve the Common Good – The Moral Challenges of Oil & Gas Wealth in Nigeria, Joint Pastoral Letter of the Catholic Bishops' Conference of Nigeria, Lagos: Mac-Pama Press 2008.

–, Nigeria, The Travesty of Oil and Gas Wealth, Lagos: GAZUB Prints Ltd 2006.

–, JDPC/Caritas, Annual Report 2008.

2. Books and Articles

–, Solidarität, Frankfurt am Main: Suhrkamp 1998.

–, Using Capability Approach: Prospective and evaluative analysis, www.capa bilityapproach.com/pubs/Alkire%.

ADEBANWI, Wale, Nigeria: Shell of a State, *Dollar and Sense* (July/August 2001), www.thirdworldtraveler.com/Africa/Nigeria_Shell_State.html.

ADOLFI, Albert, Das lange Ringen der Katholischen Soziallehre um den Begriff Solidarität. *In*: PALAVER, Wolfgang (Hg.), Centesimus Annus – 100 Jahre Katholischen Soziallehre, Thaur: Kultur Verlag 1991.

AFRICAN NETWORK FOR ENVIRONMENT AND ECONOMIC JUSTICE (ANEEJ), Oil of Poverty in Niger Delta, Benin City: 2004.

AKANI, Christian (ed.), Corruption in Nigeria – The Niger Delta Experience, Enugu: Fourth Dimension 2002.

AKE, Claude, Democracy and Development in Africa, Washington, D.C: The Brookings Institution, 1996.

ALABA, Job, Violence is not the answer in the Niger Delta. Statement on the Current Military/Militant Clashes in the Niger Delta in Nigeria, Abuja: 29 May 2009, http://blog.caritas.org/2009/05/29/violence-is-not-the-answer-in-the-niger-delta/.

ALDEN, Chris, China in Africa, London: Zed Books 2008.

ALKIRE, Sabina, Valuing Freedoms. Sen's Capability Approach and Poverty Reduction, Oxford: University Press 2002.

ALVIN, Y. So, Social Change and Development, Modernization, Dependency and World-System Theories, Newburyport: Sage Publications 1990.

AMADI, S. and OGWO, F. (eds.), Contextualizing NEEDS, Economic/Political Reforms in Nigeria, Lagos: HURILAWS & CPPR 2004.

AMIN, S., Capitalism in the Age of Globalization, London: Zed Press 1997.

ANZENBACHER Arno, Christliche Sozialethik, Paderborn: Schöningh 1997.

ARMIN, Barthel, Die Menschenrechte der dritten Generation, Aachen: Alano Edition Herodot 1991.

AUTY, Richard M. Sustainable Development in Mineral Economies: The Resource Curse Thesis, London, Routledge, 1993.

BAMBU, Boniface M., Gerechtigkeit kann nur für alle geben, Münster, ITP-Kompass 2009

BARNET, Tony, Sociology and Development, London: Hutchinson 1988.

BAUM, G., Logic of Solidarity. Commentary on Pope John Paul II's Encyclical on Social Concern, Maryknoll – New York: Orbis Books 1989.

BAUMGARTNER, Alois und KORFF, Wilhelm, Das Prinzip Solidarität – Strukturgesetz einer verantworteten Welt, StdZ 208 (1990) 237-250.

BAUMGARTNER, Alois, Personalität. In: HEIMBACH-STEINS, Marianne (Hg.), Christliche Sozialethik – Ein Lehrbuch, Band1, Regensburg: Verlag Friedrich Pustet 2004, 265-269.

BAYERTZ, Kurz (ed.), Solidarity, Dordrecht: Kluwer Academic Publishers 1999.

BILGRIEN, Marie Vianney, Solidarity – A Principle, an Attitude, a Duty? Or Virtue for an interdependent World? New York: Peter Lang 1999.

BÖCKENFÖRDE, Ernst-Wolfgang, Das neue politische Engagement der Kirche. Zur „politischen Theologie" Johannes Pauls II, StdZ 198 (1980) 219-234.

BUNGARTEN, Pia und KOCZY, Ute, Handbuch der Menschenrechtsarbeit, Bonn: J.H.W. Dietz Nachfolger 1996.

CARTAGENAS Aloysius Lopez, Catholic Development Ethics: Forty Years Populorum Progressio: Cross-Cultural Revisions and the Prospects of Global Solidarity, Hapag 5, A Journal of Interdisciplinary Theological Research 1-2 (2008) 35-85.

CLARK, David A., The Capability Approach: Its Development, Critiques and Recent Advances, Global Poverty Research Group (GPRG) 2, www.gprg.org.

CLIFF, Jeremy, Beyond The Washington Consensus, Finance & Development, September 2003, www.imf.org/external/pubs/ft/fandd/2003/09/pdf/cliff.

COLEMAN, John A. and RYAN, William F. (eds.), Globalization and Catholic Social Thought – Present Crisis, Future Hope, Maryknoll – New York: Orbis Books 2005.

COLLIER, Paul, The Bottom Billion – Why the Poorest Countries are Failing and What can be Done about It, Oxford: University Press 2007.

CORRUPTION PERCEPTION INDEX: www.transparency.org/policy_results/ surveys_indices/CPI/2002.

COULTER, Michael L. et.al (eds.), Encyclopedia of Catholic Social Thought, Social Science, and Social Policy, vol. 2, Maryland – Toronto: The Scarecrow Press 2007, 1040.

CROCKER, David A., Development Ethics: Sources, Agreement, Controversies, 17 June 2004, www.wam.umd.edu.

CURRAN, Charles E., Catholic Social Teaching – A Historical Theological and Ethical Analysis, Washington, D.C.: Georgetown University Press 2002.

CURRAN, Charles E., et al., Commentary on Sollicitudo rei Socialis. In: HIMES, Kenneth R. et al. (eds.), Modern Catholic Social Teaching, Commentaries and Interpretations, Washington, D. C.: Georgetown University Press 2004, 415-435.

DeBERRI, Edward P. et al. (eds.), Catholic Social Teaching, Our Best Kept Secret, Maryknoll – New York: Orbis Books [4]2003.

DENEULIN, Severinè, Poverty: Amartya Sen Compared to Catholic Social Thinking, Hügel Institute, Cambridge. www.theology-centre.org/Leuven 28_04.

–, Amartya Sen's Capability Approach to Development and Gaudium et Spes: On Political Participation and Structural Solidarity, Hügel Institute, Cambridge.

–, Thinking about International Development: Insights from the Encyclical Populorum Progressio, 20 July 2008, http://exerceojournal.org/index.php? option=com_content&task.

DENEULIN, Severinè and SHAHANI, Lila (eds.), An Introduction to the Human Development and Capability Approach – Freedom and Agency, London: Earthscan 2009.

DIBIE, Robert, Public Management and Sustainable Development in Nigeria: Military Bureaucracy Relationship, England, Ashgate Publishing Ltd 2003.

DICKE, Klaus, et al. (Hg.), Menschenrechte und Entwicklung, Berlin: Duncker & Humblot 1997.

DIOCHI, Michael Ndubueze, The Quest for Integral Development in Nigeria – Its Social Ethical Requirements, Frankfurt, Peter Lang 2006.

DOORMAN, Frans, Global Development: Problems, Solutions, Strategy – A Proposal for Socially Just, Ecologically Sustainable Growth, Utrecht: International Books 1998.

DORAN, Kevin P., Solidarity – A synthesis of Personalism and communalism in the Thought of Karol Wojtyla /John Paul II, New York: Peter Lang 1996.

DORR, Donal, Option for the Poor, Catholic Social Teaching, Dublin 8: Gill and Macmillan 1992.

–, Solidarity and Integral Human Development. *In*: BAUM, G.,(ed.), Logic of Solidarity. Commentary on Pope John Paul II's encyclical on Social Concern, Maryknoll – New York: Orbis Books 1989, 143-154.

DREZE, J. and SEN, Amartya, India Development and Participation, Oxford: University Press 2002.

DURKHEIM, Emile, The Division of Labour in Society, New-York: Free Press 1997.

DUZE, Mustapha et al. (eds.), Poverty in Nigeria – Causes, Manifestations and Alleviation Strategies, London: Adonis & Abbey2008.

DWYER, John C., Person, Dignity of. *In*: DWYER, Judith A. (ed.), The New Dictionary of Catholic Social Thought, Minnesota: The Liturgical Press 1994, 724-737.

EASTERLY William, The White Man's Burden: Why the West's Efforts to Aid the Rest Have so Much Ill and So Little Good, New York: Penguin Books 2006.

EDER, Hans, Politische Dimensionen der Theologie der Befreiung – Impulse der Jesuiten und Indigenas für eine solidarische Gesellschaft der Anderen, Frankfurt am Main: Peter Lang 1993.

EDEVBARO, Daniel Osakponmwen, The Political Economy of Corruption and Underdevelopment in Nigeria, Helsinki: Yliopistopaino 1998.

EDMUND, Arens, Internationale, Ekklesiale und Universale Solidarität, *Orientierung* 53 (1989) 216-220.

EHUSANI George Omaku, A Prophetic Church, Ede: Provincial Pastoral Institute Publications 1996.

–, The Social Gospel – An Outline of the Church's Current Teaching on Human Development, Iperu: Ambassador Publications 1992.

ELAIGWU, Isawa The Politics of Federalism in Nigeria, London: Adonis & Abbey 2007.

EMMUNDS, Bernhard, The Integration of Developing Countries into International Financial Markets. Remarks from the Perspective of a Christian Economic Ethics, Paper presented at the Fourth International Symposium on Catholic Social Thought and Management Education, "Rethinking Wealth Creation and Distribution in the Jubilee", July 11-14, 2000, Universidad Iberoamericana, Puebla, Mexico.

ETZIONI, Amin and ETZIONI, Eva (eds.), Social Change, New-York: Basic Books 1960.

FERDOWSI, Mir A. (Hg.) Afrika zwischen Agonie und Aufbruch, München: Bayerische Landeszentrale für politische Bildungsarbeit 1998.

FISCHER Karin et al. (Hg.) Entwicklung und Unterentwicklung, Ein Einführung in Probleme, Theorie und Strategien, Wien: Mandelbaum Verlag 2006.

FREIRE, Paulo, Pedagogy of the Oppressed, England, Penguin Books 1972

FUKUDA-PARR, Sakiko and SHIVA KUMAR, A. K. (eds.), Readings in Human Development, Concepts, Measures and Policies for a Development Paradigm, New York: Oxford University Press 2003.

FURGER, Franz, Christliche Sozialethik: Grundlagen und Zielsetzung, Stuttgart: Kohlhammer 1991.

GABRIEL, Karl et al. (Hg.), Die gesellschaftliche Verantwortung der Kirche. Zur Enzyklika Sollicitudo rei Socialis, Düsseldorf: Patmos Verlag 1988.

GARY, Ian, et al., Bottom of the Barrel – Africa's Oil Boom and the Poor, Baltimore, Catholic Relief service 2003.

GASPER, Des, The Ethics of Development, Edinburgh: University Press 2005.

GHAZVINIAN, John, Untapped – The Scramble for Africa's Oil, London: Harvest Book 2007.

GIERS, Joachim, „Partizipation" und „Solidarität" als Strukturen der sozialen Gerechtigkeit. In: MERTENS, Gerhard (Hg.), Markierung der Humanität – Sozialethische Herausforderungen auf dem Weg in ein neues Jahrtausend, Paderborn: Ferdinand Schöningh 1992.

GILLIES, Alexandra, Reforming corruption out of Nigerian Oil?, Anti-Corruption Resource Centre 2 (February 2009), www.U4.no.

GIRE, James T., A Psychological analysis of Corruption in Nigeria, www.jsdafrica.com/Jsda/summer1999/articlespdf/ARC.

GORDON, David and SPICKER, Paul, The International Glossary of Poverty, London: Zed Books 1999.

GOULET, Denis, Development Ethics at Work, Explorations 1962 – 2002, London: Routledge 2006.

GOULET, Denis, The Search for Authentic Development. In: BAUM, G.,(ed.), Logic of Solidarity. Commentary on Pope John Paul II's encyclical on Social Concern, Maryknoll – New York: Orbis Books 1989, 127-142.

GREINACHER, Norbert (Hg.), Leidenschaft für Die Armen. Die Theologie der Befreiung, München: Piper Verlag 1990.

GUARDIAN NEWSPAPERS, Niger Delta Ministry. One year later, www.ngr guardiannews.com/editorial_opinion/article01/indexn2_html?pdate=1 v

GÜNDER, Franz Andre, Latin American Underdevelopment or Revolution, New-York: Monthly Press 1969.

HARNEIT-SIEVERS, Axel, Reforming the Rentier State: Some Thoughts on NEEDS. In: AMADI, Sam and OGWO, Frances (eds.), Contextualizing NEEDS. Economic/Political Reform in Nigeria, Lagos: HURILAWS & CPPR 2004, xi-xix.

HAYAMI, Yujino, From Washington Consensus to Post-Washington Consensus. Recent Changes in the Paradigm of International Development Assistance, www.fasid.org. jp/daigakuin/fa_gr/kyojyu/pdf/s.

HEIDENHEIMER, A.J. et al. (eds.), Political Corruption. A Handbook, New Brunswick: Transaction 1989.

HEIMBACH-STEIN, Marianne (Hg.), Christliche Sozialethik. Ein Lehrbuch, Bände 1&2, Regensburg: Verlag Friedrich Pustet 2004.

–, Beteiligungsgerechtigkeit, StdZ 217 (1999) 147-160.

HEIMBACH-STEINS, Marianne und LIENKAMP Andreas (Hg.), Für eine Zukunft in Solidarität und Gerechtigkeit, München: Bernward bei Don Bosco ¹1997.

HENGSBACH, F., Strukturentgiftung, Kirchliche Soziallehre im Kontext von Arbeit, Umwelt, Weltwirtschaft, Düsseldorf: Patmos 1991.

–, Reformen fallen nicht vom Himmel, Freiburg: Herder 1997.

–, Abschied von der Konkurrenzgesellschaft – Für eine neue Ethik in Politik, Wirtschaft und Gesellschaft, München: Knaur Verlag 1995.

–, et al. (Hrsg), Jenseits Katholischer Soziallehre – Neue Entwürfe christlicher Gesellschaftsethik, Düsseldorf: Patmos Verlag 1993.

–, Die andern im Blick, Christliche Gesellschaftsethik in den Zeiten der Globalisierung, Darmstadt: Wissenschaftliche Buchgesellschaft 2001.

–, Eure Armut kotzt uns an! Solidarität in der Krise, Frankfurt am Main: Fischer 1995.

–, Gegen Unmenschlichkeit in der Wirtschaft. Der Hirtenbrief der Katholischen Bischöfe der USA „Wirtschaftliche Gerechtigkeit für alle" Aus deutscher Sicht, Freiburg: Herder 1987.

HENGSBACH, F. und MÖHRING-HESSE, Matthias, Zwanzigjährig – Volljährig?, Orientierung 6,52Jg (31 März 1988) 62-65.

HENRIOT, Peter, What is Development? Promoting the Good of Every Person and of the Whole Person, www.cfj.ie/images/stories/56pdf/development.pdf.

HERR, Theodor, Katholische Soziallehre – Eine Einführung, Paderborn: Bonifatius Verlag 1987.

HIGH COMMISSION OF INDIA, Abuja. www.indianhcabuja.com and www.hicomindlagos.com/docs/Nigeria-Fact-Sheet.htm.

HILPERT, Konrad, Die Menschenrechte – Geschichte Theologie Aktualität, Düsseldorf: Patmos Verlag 1991.

–, Menschenrechte und Theologie – Forschungsbeiträge zur ethischen Dimension der Menschenrechte, Freiburg im Breisgau: Herder 2001.

HIMES, K.R. et al., Modern Catholic Social Teaching – Commentaries & Interpretations, Washington, D.C.: Georgetown University Press 2004.

HOFFMANN, Johannes (Hg.), Theologisch-Ethische Werkstatt: Kontext Frankfurt, Bd 5, Wer befreit ist, kann befreien, Frankfurt am Main: IKO – Verlag für Interkulturelle Kommunikation 1997.

HÖFFNER, Josef Kardinal, Christliche Gesellschaftslehre, Kevelaer: Butzon & Becker, [4]1983.

HOLLENBACH, David, Modern Catholic Teaching Concerning Justice. In: HAUGHEY, John C. (ed.), The Faith that Does Justice – Examining the Christian Sources for Social Change, New York: Paulist Press 1977.

–, The Common Good & Christian Ethics, Cambridge: University Press 2002.

HONDRICH, Karl Otto und KOCH-ARZBERGER, Claudia, Solidarität in der modernen Gesellschaft, Frankfurt am Main: Fischer Taschenbuch Verlag 1994.

HOPKINS, Michael, Corporate Social Responsibility & International Development. Is Business the Solution? London: Earthscan 2007.

HUMAN DEVELOPMENT AND CAPABILITY ASSOCIATION (HDCA), Briefing Note: Capability and Functionings: Definition and Justification, www.capabilityapproach.com/pubs/HDCA_Briefing_Concepts.pdf.

HUMAN RIGHTS WATCH, The Niger Delta. No Democratic Dividend, vol. 14, 7 (A) 2002.

–, The Price of Oil – Corporate Responsibility and Human Rights Violations in Nigeria's Oil Producing Communities, Human Rights Watch, New York – London, 1999.

–, Nigeria, Chop Fine, The Human Rights Impact of Local Government on Corruption and Mismanagement in Rivers State, Nigeria: January 2007 vol. 19, No. 2 (A)

IKELEGBE, A., The Economy of Conflict in the Oil rich Niger Delta Region of Nigeria, Nordic Journal of African Studies, 14,2 (2005) 208-234.

IKELEGBE A., Civil Society, Oil and Conflict in the Niger Delta Region of Nigeria: Ramifications of Civil Society for Regional Resource Struggle, The Journal of Modern African Studies 39,3 (September 2001) 437-469.

IMOBIGHE, T.A. et al., Conflict and Instability in the Niger Delta – The Warri Case, Ibadan: Spectrum Books 2002.

INTERNATIONAL JESUIT NETWORK FOR DEVELOPMENT, The Development of Peoples: Challenges for Today and Tomorrow, Essays to Mark the Fortieth Anniversary of Populorum Progressio, Dublin: The Columba Press 2007.

INTERNATIONAL MONETARY FUND, Country Report 2005: Nigeria. Poverty Reduction Strategy Paper – National Economic Empowerment and Development Strategy, No. 05/433, www.imf.org.

JEDRZEJ, Georg Frynas, Oil In Nigeria – Conflict and Litigation between Oil Companies and Village Communities, Münster: Lit Verlag 2000.

JILL, Shankleman, Oil, Profits, And Peace – Does Business Have a Role in Peacemaking? Washington: United States Institute of Peace Press 2006.

JOSEPH, Richard A, Democracy and Prebendal Politics in Nigeria: the Rise and Fall of the Second Republic, Cambridge: University Press 1987.

KARL, Terry Lynn, Paradox of Plenty – Oil Booms and Petro-States, Berkeley: University of California Press 1997.

KESSELRING, Thomas, Ethik der Entwicklungspolitik, Gerechtigkeit im Zeitalter der Globalisierung, München: C.H. Beck 2003.

KHAKEE, Anna, Energy and Development: Lessons from Nigeria, www.edc 2020.eu/fileadmin/Textdateien/EDC2020_PolicyBrief.

KÖSS, Hartmut (Hg.), Entwicklungsethische Konkretionen – Herausforderungen, Begründungen, Perspektiven, Münster: Lit Verlag 2002.

KORFF, Wilhelm und BAUMGARTNER, Alois, Solidarität – die Antwort auf das Elend in der heutigen Welt. Enzyklika Sollicitudo Rei Socialis, Freiburg im Breisgau: Herder 1988.

KUBIK, Jan, The Power of Symbols Against the Symbols of Power – The Rise of Solidarity and the Fall of State Socialism in Poland, Pennsylvania: State University Press 1994.

KUKAH, Hassan Matthew, Democracy and Civil Society in Nigeria, Ibadan: Spectrum Books Ltd. 1999.

KYMLICKA, Will, Contemporary Political Philosophy, Oxford: University Press 1990.

LAND, Philip and HENRIOT, Peter, Towards a New Methodology in Catholic Social Teaching. In: BAUM, G. (ed.), Logic of Solidarity. Commentary on Pope John Paul II's encyclical on Social Concern, Maryknoll – New York: Orbis Books 1989, 65-74.

LANGHORST, Peter, Kirche und Entwicklungsproblematik, Paderborn: Ferdinand Schöning 1996.

LUBECK, Paul M. et al., Convergent Interests: U.S. Energy security and the securing of Nigerian Democracy, International Policy Report, www.ciponline.org/NIGERIA_FINAL.pdf.

MAIER, Karl, This House Has Fallen – Nigeria in Crisis, Oxford: Westview Press 2002.

MARITAIN, Jacques, The Person and the Common Good, Indiana: University of Notre Dame Press 1946.

MARX, Reinhard und WULSDORF, Helge, Christliche Sozialethik – Konturen, Prinzipien, Handlungsfelder , Paderborn: Bonifatius 2002.

MAXWELL, Simon, The Washington Consensus is dead! Long live the meta-narrative. http://web.worldbank.org/WBSITE/EXTERNAL/EXTABOUTUS/ORGANIZATIONAL//o.

MCKENNA, Kevin E., A Concise Guide to Catholic Social Teaching, Indiana: Ave Maria Press 2002.

MERKLE Judith A., From the Heart of the Church, The Catholic Social Tradition, Minnesota: Liturgical Press 2004.

MERKE, Karl-Heinz, Das Gottespostulat unbedingter Solidarität und seine Erfüllung durch Christus, *Internationale Katholische Zeitschrift Communio* 21 (1992) 486-499.

MISEREOR, Solidarität – die Andere Globalisierung zur Zukunft der Eine Welt-Arbeit, Aachen: MVG Medienproduktion 1999.

–, Erdöl – Reichtum, der arm macht, Aachen: MVG Medienproduktion 2007.

MÜLLER, Johannes, Entwicklungspolitik als globale Herausforderung – Methodische und Ethische Grundlegung, Stuttgart: Kohlhammer 1997.

MUNONO, Bernard (ed.), The Challenge of Justice and Peace – The Response of the Church in Africa Today, Rome: Libreria Editrice Vaticana 1998.

NAIM, Moises, Fads and Fashions in Economic Reforms: Washington Consensus or Washington Confusion?, IMF, Washington, 1999, www.imf.org/external/pubs/ft/seminar/1999/reforms/naim.HTM.

NATIONAL PLANNING COMMISSION, Nigeria: National Economic Empowerment and Development Strategy (NEEDS), Central Bank of Nigeria, Abuja, 2004.

NATUFE, Igho, The Problematic of Sustainable Development and Corporate Social Responsibility: Policy Implication for the Niger Delta, A Conference Paper. www.urhobo.kinsfolk.com/Conferences/SecondAnnualConference/ConferenceM.

NEITI Press release, 2009, www.neiti.org.ng.

NELL-BREUNING,O. von, Unsere Verantwortung für eine Solidarische Gesellschaft, Freiburg: Herder 1987.

NEU, Elke M., An Analysis of Constellation of Interests Regarding the Conflict in the Niger Delta, Nigeria, M.A Abschlussarbeit, Johann Wolfgang Goethe-Universität, Frankfurt am Main, 2000.

Niger Delta Regional Development Master Plan 2007.

NNADOZIE, Emmanuel U., Oil and Socioeconomic crises in Nigeria: A Regional Perspective to the Nigerian Decease and the Rural Sector, Enugu: Edwin Mellen Press 1995.

NOHLEN, Dieter (Hg), Lexikon Dritte Welt, Rowohlt Verlag, 2002.

NOHLEN, Dieter und NUSCHELER, Franz, (Hg.), Handbuch der Dritten Welt, Band 1, J.H.W. Bonn: Dietz 1993.

NOTHELLE-WILDFEUER, Ursula, „Duplex ordo cognitionis", zur systematischen Grundlegung einer Katholischen Soziallehre in Anspruch von Philosophie und Theologie, Paderborn: Ferdinand Schöningh 1991.

–, Soziale Gerechtigkeit und Zivilgesellschaft, Paderborn: Ferdinand Schöningh 1999.

NUSCHELER, Franz, Lern- und Arbeitsbuch Entwicklungspolitik, Bonn: Dietz ⁶2005.

NUSCHELER Franz und ROTH, Michele (Hg.), Die Millennium-Entwicklungsziele – Entwicklungspolitischer Königsweg oder ein Irrweg?, Bonn: Dietz 2006.

NWANGBU, John (ed.), Niger Delta – Rich Region, Poor People, Enugu: Snaap Press Ltd 2005.

NWANKWO, Peter O., Social Development in Rural Communities in the South-Eastern Nigeria, Frankfurt am Main: Iko Verlag 2006.

OBASANJO, Olusegun, Nigeria: From Pond of Corruption to Island of Integrity: Lecture delivered at the 10th Anniversary Celebration of Transparency International, Berlin, 07 November 2003 Cfr. http://www.dawudo.com/obas35.htm visited on 14-08-2009.

OBI, Cyril, The Changing Forms of Identity Politics in Nigeria under Economic Adjustment – The Case of the Oil Minorities Movement of the Niger Delta, Nordiska Afrikanstitutet, Uppsala, 2001.

OBIORA, Chinedu Okafor, Legitimizing Human Rights NGOs – Lessons from Nigeria, Trenton: Africa World Press 2006.

OBODOECHINA, Uchechukwu, The Imperative of Self-Reliance for the Churches in Africa, Frankfurt am Main: Peter Lang 2006.

O'HARA, Kevin, Port Harcourt, Corporate Sustainability: Accountability in an African Context. Case study: Shell and Batan Oil Spill in the Niger Delta. Paper presented at the International Conference on Making Oil and Gas Wealth serve the Common Good, organized by CBCN from 2-4 November 2006, Enugu, Nigeria.

OJAKAMINOR, Efeturi, Catholic Social Doctrine. An Introductory Manual, Nairobi: Pauline Publications Africa 1996.

OJAMERUAYE, Emmanuel, Lessons from the Chadian Model For Distribution of Oil Wealth in Nigeria's Niger Delta, http://www.waado.org/Environment/ Remediation/Chadian_model_niger_delta.htm.

OKONJO-IWEALA, Ngozi, Managing Natural Resources Revenue: Lessons from Nigeria's Experience, hppt://web.worldbank.org/WEBSITE/EXTERNAL/ COUNTRIES/EA.

OKONTA, Ike and DOUGLAS, Oronto Where Vulture Feast; Shell, Human Rights and Oil, London: Verso 2003.

OLAYEMI, Akinwumi, Crises and Conflicts in Nigeria: A Political History since 1960, Münster: Lit Verlag 2005.

OLOJA, Martin, Accountant-General lists points of corruption in government, *Guardian* Newspaper, Monday, 14 July 2008.

OMEJE, Kenneth C., High stakes and stakeholders: Oil conflict and security in Nigeria, England, Ashgate Publishing Ltd 2006.

OMOLE, Wale (ed.), Corporate Social Responsibility Performance in Nigeria, Lagos: New Nigeria Foundation 2007.

OMOTOLA, J. Shola, From the OMPADEC to the NDDC: An Assessment of the State Responses to Environmental Insecurity in the Niger Delta, Nigeria, *Africa Today* 54,1 (2007) 73-90.

OMOWEH, Daniel A., Shell Petroleum Development Company, The State and Underdevelopment of Nigeria's Niger Delta – A Study in Environmental Degradation, Trennton N.J.: Africa World Press 2005.

ONAIYEKAN, John, Making Oil and Gas Wealth Serve the Common Good: Catholic Bishops' Conference of Nigeria, JDPC DRACC Enugu, 2 and 3 November 2006.

ONUOHA, Austin, From Conflict to Collaboration – Building Peace in Nigeria's Oil-Producing Communities, London: Adonis and Abbey 2005.

OROBATOR, A.E., The Church as Family – African Ecclesiology in Its Social Context, Nairobi: Paulines Publications Africa 2000.

ORONTO Douglas, et al., (FPIF Special Report): Alienation and Militancy in the Niger Delta: A Response to CSIS on Petroleum, Politics, and Democracy in Nigeria. www.fpif.org /papers/Nigeria 2003 html.

OSAGHAE, Eghosa et al., Youth Militias, Self-determination and Resource Control Struggles in the Niger-Delta Region of Nigeria, 2007, www.ascleiden.nl/ pdf/cdpnigeriaRevisedOsaghae%5B1%5D2.pdf.

OTIVIE, Igbuzor, Strategies for Winning the Anti-corruption war in Nigeria, Abuja, ActionAid 2008.

OVERSEAS DEVELOPMENT INSTITUTE (ODI), Briefing Paper November 2001, Economic Theory, Freedom and Human Rights: The work of Amartya Sen, 2 Cf. http://www.odi.org.uk.

OWEN, R. Jackson, Dignity and Solidarity – An Introduction to Peace and Justice Education, Chicago: Loyola University Press 1985.

PALAVER, Wolfgang (Hg.), Centesimo Anno – 100 Jahre Katholischen Soziallehre, Thaur: Kultur Verlag 1991.

PANAGARIY, A. Developing Countries at Doha: A Political Economy Analysis, in: *The World Economy* 25/9, Pp. 1205-1233.

PARKINS Colen, A Post Washington Consensus? www.cseweb.orguk/downloads/ parkins.pdf.

PERRAS, Arne, Alarmstufe Delta, In: Süddeutsche Zeitung Nr. 280/Seite 3 Freitag 3. Dezember 2010.

PIEPEL, Klaus, Lerngemeinschaft Weltkirche – Lernprozesse in Partnerschaften zwischen Christen der Ersten und der Dritten Welt, Aachen: Misereor 1992.

POGGE, Thomas (ed.), Global Justice, Oxford, Blackwell Publishing 2004.

POGGR, Thomas, World Poverty and Human Rights, Cambridge, Polity Press 2010

PÖNER, Ulrich und HABISCH André (Hrsg), Signale der Solidarität, Wege christlicher Nord-Süd-Ethik, Paderborn: Ferdinand Schöningh1994.

PONTIFICAL COUNCIL FOR JUSTICE AND PEACE, The Social Agenda of the Catholic Church – The Magisterial Texts, London: Burns & Oates 2000.

PRESTON, P.W., Theories of Development, London: Routledge and Kagen Paul 1982.

PRÜLLER-JAGENTEUFEL, Günther, Solidarität – eine Option für die Opfer, Frankfurt am Main: Peter Lang 1998.

RANDALL Jay Woodard, Common Good, In: COULTER Michael L. et.al (eds.), Encyclopedia of Catholic Social Thought, Social Science, and Social Policy, Vol. 1, Toronto, The Scarecrow Press Inc 2007, 213-214.

RAUSCHER, Anton, Kirche in der Welt 3Bd, Würzburg: Echter Verlag 1998.

ROBEYNS, Ingrid, The Capability approach and welfare policies, Paper presented at the conference on gender auditing and gender budgeting Bologna, Italy, 28 January 2005.

–, The Capability Approach: A Theoretical Survey, *The Journal of Human Development*, March 2005.

RODGER, Charles, Christian Social Witness and Teaching. The Catholic Tradition from Genesis to Centesimus Annus vols. 1 & 2, Herefordshire: Gracewing 1998.

ROTTER, Hans, Christliches Handeln – Seine Begründung und Eigenart, Graz: Styria Verlag 1977.

ROTTLAENDER, Peter, Vom Eigeninteresse zur Moral? Überlegung zur ethisch-normativen Grundlegung von Entwicklungspolitik. In: PÖNER, Ulrich und HABISCH, André (Hg.), Signale der Solidarität, Wege christlicher Nord-Süd-Ethik, Paderborn: Ferdinand Schöningh 1994, 153-180.

–, Ethische Rechtfertigung Weltweiter Solidarität. In: BRIESKORN, Norbert (Hg.), Globale Solidarität. Die verschiedenen Kulturen und die Eine Welt, Stuttgart: Kohlhammer 1997, 117-154.

SACHS, Jeffrey D., The End o f Poverty, Economic Possibilities for Our Time, London: Penguin Books 2005.

SALIU, Hassan A. (ed.), Issues in Contemporary Political Economy of Nigeria, Ilorin: Haytee Books 1999.

SAUTTER, Hermann, Weltwirtschaftsordnung, München: Vahlen Verlag 2004.

SCHASCHING, Johannes, In Sorge um Entwicklung und Frieden. Kommentar zur Enzyklika „Sollicitudo rei Socialis" von Papst Johannes Paul II., Düsseldorf, Soziale Brennpunkte 14 1988.

SCHMELTER, Jürgen, Solidarität: Die Entwicklungsgeschichte eines sozialethischen Schlüsselbegriffs, Dissertation, Ludwig-Maximilians-Universität München 1991

–, Solidarität: Entwicklungslinien eines sozialethischen Schlüsselbegriffs. *In*: MERTENS, Gerhard et al. (Hg.), Markierung der Humanität – Sozialethische Herausforderungen auf dem Weg in ein neues Jahrtausend, Paderborn: Ferdinand Schöningh 1992, 385-394.

SCHULDT, Jürgen und ACOSTA, Alberto, Ölrenten und Unterentwicklung: ein unauflösbarer Zusammenhang?, *Internationale Politik und Gesellschaft* 4 (2006) 63-79.

SEN, Amartya, Development as Freedom, Oxford: University Press 1999.

–, Commodities and Capabilities, Oxford: University Press 1999.

–, The Idea of Justice, London, Penguin Books 2010

–, Development as Capability Expansion. *In*: FUKUDA-PARR, Sakiko and SHIVA KUMAR, A.K., Readings in Human Development. Concepts, Measure and Policies for Development Paradigm, Oxford: University Press [3]2006, 3-16

–, Autobiography http://nobelprize.org/cgi-bin/. www.geocities.com/gfh_axds_ as/com/sen-autobio.html?200715.

–, What Difference Can Ethics Make?, www.iadb.org/etica/encuent/enc-wdc/ docs/dc sen queimp-i.htm.

–, Inequality Reexamined, New York: Russell Sage Foundation 1992.

–, Ökonomie für den Menschen – Wege zu Gerechtigkeit und Solidarität in der Wirtschaft, 4 Auflage, Deutscher Taschenbuch, München 2007.

Shell Petroleum Development Company (SPDC). *Shell Nigeria Annual Report 2006: People and the Environment, August 2007.* Shell Petroleum Development Company, Nigeria.

–, Shell Nigeria Annual Report 2005: People and the Environment, August 2006. Shell Petroleum Development Company, Nigeria.

–, *Sustainable Community Development in the Niger Delta,* presentations at the FMENV consultative forum Port Harcourt: April 11 – 12, 2005.

SHAHID, Yusuf et al., Development Economics through the Decades, Washington D.C.: World Bank 2009.

SIEBERT, Horst, The World Economy, London: Routledge [2]2002.

SIEVERNICH, Michael, Soziale Sünde und Soziale Bekehrung, *Theologie der Gegenwart* 36 (1993) 30-44.

SIX, Jean-Francois, Church and Human Rights, Maynooth, St. Paul Publications 1991.

SMITH, Daniel Jordan, A Culture of Corruption – Everyday Deception and Popular Discontent in Nigeria, Princeton: University Press 2007.

SMITH, I.O., The Constitution of the Federal Republic of Nigeria – Annotated, Lagos: Ecowatch Publications 1999.

SNYDER, Mary Hembrow, Development. *In*: DWYER, Judith A. (ed.), The New Dictionary of Catholic Social Thought, Minnesota: The Liturgical Press 1994, 278-282.

STIGLITZ, Joseph, Globalization and its Discontents, London: Penguin Books 2002.

STREETEN, Paul, Globalization. Threat or Opportunity? Copenhagen: Business School Press 2001.

TARCISIO, Agostoni, Every Citizen's Handbook – Building a Peaceful Society, Nairobi: Paulines Publications Africa 2000.

THE NEW JERUSALEM BIBLE – THE COMPLETE TEXT OF THE ANCIENT CANON OF THE SCRIPTURES, Standard Edition, New York, Doubleday 1999

THE SHELL SUSTAINABILITY REPORT 2007 Nigeria Cf. http://sustainability report.shell.com/2007 responsibleoperationstoday/nigeria.html.

THE WORLD BANK GROUP, Partners in Transforming Development: New Approaches to Developing Country-Owned Poverty Reduction Strategies, March 2000, www.imf.org/external/np/prsp/pdf/prspbroc.pdf.

THE WORLD BANK, Anticorruption in Transition: A Contribution to the Policy Debate, Washington D.C.: The World Bank 2000.

THE WORLD BANK, Helping Countries Combat Corruption: The role of the World Bank, Washington D.C.: The World Bank 2000.

TRANSPARENCY INTERNATIONAL, Frequently Asked Questions about the Corruption Perceptions Index: 2002, press release, 28 August 2002.

TROCAIRE: The 'Paradox of Plenty' in the Niger Delta, http://www.trocaire.org/print/597.

TSCHIERSCH, Joachim et al. (Hg.), Kirche und ländliche Entwicklung, Mainz: Matthias-Grünewald Verlag 1995.

TUODOLO, Felix, Corporate Social Responsibility: Between Civil Society and the Oil Industry in the Developing World, In: *ACME, An International E-Journal for Critical Geographies* 2009, 8 (3), 530-541.

UDO, Bassey, Niger Delta Master-Plan: Path to Sustainable Development, Daily Independent, July 3rd 2007 htt://www.independentngonline.com/?c=101&a=29733.

UKEJE, Charles Ugochukwu, Oil Capital, Ethnic Nationalism and Civil Conflicts in the Niger Delta of Nigeria, Thesis submitted for the award of the Degree of Doctor of Philosophy (Ph.D.) in International Relations, Faculty of Administration, Obafemi Awolowo University, Ile-Ife, Nigeria, 2004.

UL HAG, Mahbub, The Birth of the Human Development Index. *In*: FUKUDA-PARR, Sakiko and SHIVA KUMAR, A.K., Readings in Human Development, New-York: Oxford Press ³2006, 127-137.

UNDP Niger Delta Human Development Report, 2006, Abuja Nigeria.

UNITED NATIONS, Development Programme, Human Development Report, Oxford University Press, 1990 – 2003.

UNITED NATIONS, The Copenhagen Declaration and Programme of Action: World Summit for Social Development 6-12 March 1995, New York, United Nations Department of Publications 1995.

UNITED NATIONS' DECLARATIONS, http://www2.ohchr.org/english/issues/development/right/index.htm.

UNITED NATIONS, Declaration on the Right to Development, http://www.un.org/documents/ga/res/41/a41r128.htm.

VENRO/GKKE, Fighting Poverty without Empowering the Poor?, www.venro.org/fileadmin/publicationen/E.

WAEYENBERGE, Elisa Van, From Washington to Post-Washington Consensus, Illusions of Development. *In*: JOMO, K.S. and FINE, Ben (eds.), The New Development Economics After Washington Consensus, London: Zed Books 2006.

WALSCH, Michael and DAVIS, Brian (eds.), Proclaiming Justice and Peace. Documents from John XXIII to John Paul II, London: Collins Liturgical Publications 1984.

WATTS, Michael et al., History of the U.S in the Niger Delta, http://www.nigerdeltarising.org/history-us-niger-delta.

WATTS Michael, et al., FPIF Special Report: Alienation and Militancy in the Niger Delta: Response to CSIS on Petroleum, Politics, and Democracy in Nigeria. Foreign Policy in Focus (FPIF) www.fpif.org/papers/nigeria 2003.htmc.

WEBSTER'S THIRD NEW INTERNATIONAL DICTIONARY vol. 1, Chicago: Encyclopaedia Britannica Inc. 1986.

WEILER, Rudolf, Einführung in die Katholische Soziallehre – Ein systematischer Abriß, Graz: Verlag Styria 1991.

WESS, Paul, Strukturen der Liebe – Von der Kirchlichen Soziallehre zur Kirche als Sozialpraxis, *StdZ* 207 (1989) 110-12.

WETTSTIEN, Florian, Multinational Corporations and Global Justice – Human Rights Obligations of a Quasi-Governmental Institution, Stanford, California, Stanford University Press 2009

WILLIAMSON, James, A Short History of Washington Consensus, Paper Commissioned by Fundacion CIDB for a Conference. From Washington Consensus towards a new Global Governance, Barcelona, September 24-25, 2004, www.petersoninstitute.org/publications/papers/williamson.0904-2.pdf.

WILLIS, Katie, Theories and Practices of Development, London: Routledge 2008.

XUECHENG, Liu, China's energy security and its grand strategy, www.stanleyfoundation.org/publications/pup/pub06 Chinasenergy.pdf.

ZOLL, Rainer, Was ist Solidarität heute?, Frankfurt am Main: Suhrkamp Verlag 2000.

Peter Lang · Internationaler Verlag der Wissenschaften

Emmanuel Franklyne Onyemaechi Ogbunwezeh

Towards an Ethical-ecological Assessment of Companies in Nigeria

An Empirical Inquiry into the Relevance or Otherwise of the Frankfurt-Hohenheim Guidelines for the Ethical Assessment of Companies in the Nigerian Context
A Case of the Nigerian Microfinance Banking Sector

Frankfurt am Main, Berlin, Bern, Bruxelles, New York, Oxford, Wien, 2012.
335 pp., 100 graphs
European University Studies. Series 5: Economics and Management. Vol. 3384
ISBN 978-3-631-61696-3 · pb. € 57,80*

Multilateral evidence has continued to show that the conspicuous absence of reputable ethical-ecological criteria for evaluating companies and businesses in Nigeria is not only a lamentable disservice to the Nigerian people; but does not augur well for the Nigerian economy in particular and society at large. The Corporate Social Responsibility (CSR) concept and practice has been notoriously inadequate in meeting this challenge. The CSR, which came to Nigeria via the pressures and ire drawn by the rogue activities of multi-national oil concerns in the Nigeria Delta, quickly dissipated its reputational capital and fossilized on its pretensions by assuming a paternalistic character of a philanthropic nature in the policy philosophies of many companies in Nigeria. The results of this absence have been catastrophic. The Niger Delta became an ecological wasteland thanks to unethical and unsupervised rapacity convoked there by the oil companies. Many Nigerian families have been chaperoned into poverty thanks to the perennial failure of many Nigerian banks and financial institutions, which is predicated on massive fraud and other sharp practices of bank officials. Need we talk about the costs in lives and limbs of the unethical practices of many companies in almost all sectors of the Nigerian economy, whose activities have been destroying the ecological integrity of our environment; constantly degrading the dignity and human rights of their employees, and endangering the lives and wellbeing of consumers across the country?

*The e-price includes German tax rate. Prices are subject to change without notice

Frankfurt am Main · Berlin · Bern · Bruxelles · New York · Oxford · Wien
Distribution: Verlag Peter Lang AG
Moosstr. 1, CH-2542 Pieterlen
Telefax 0041 (0)32/376 17 27
E-Mail info@peterlang.com

40 Years of Academic Publishing
Homepage http://www.peterlang.com